Sir George Mackenzie, King's Advocate, of
Rosehaugh; His Life and Times 1636(?)-1691

SIR GEORGE MACKENZIE

Walter S.Bell. Ph. Sc.

Sir George Mackenzie of Rosehaugh.

Painted in 1665.

The property of the Earl of Wharncliffe.

SIR GEORGE MACKENZIE

KING'S ADVOCATE, OF ROSEHAUGH

HIS LIFE AND TIMES

1636 (?)–1691

BY

ANDREW LANG

WITH FOUR ILLUSTRATIONS

LONGMANS, GREEN AND CO.

39 PATERNOSTER ROW, LONDON

NEW YORK, BOMBAY, AND CALCUTTA

1909

Sir George Mackenzie
The property of the

SIR GEORGE MACKENZIE

KING'S ADVOCATE, OF ROSEHAUGH

HIS LIFE AND TIMES

1636 (?)–1691

BY

ANDREW LANG

WITH FOUR ILLUSTRATIONS

LONGMANS, GREEN AND CO.
39 PATERNOSTER ROW, LONDON
NEW YORK, BOMBAY, AND CALCUTTA
1909

PREFACE

IN the education of Scotland the Restoration was a bitter but necessary moment. The century of war between State and Kirk, arising from the intolerable claims which the Crown on one side, and the preachers on the other, asserted, must come to an end in one way or another, if Scotland was ever to be reasonably tranquil.

Between 1660 and 1689, the two contending powers wore each other down: the Government of William of Orange then entered perforce on constitutional paths; the pretensions of the preachers were henceforth maintained, but mainly in a platonic, not a practical fashion.

It is impossible to imagine what would have occurred had the ministers of Charles II. and James II. been less unscrupulous. "The good old cause" of the Covenant—that unhappy anachronism—might not have ceased to trouble, had Lauderdale, Rothes, and the other rulers been men of temperate character, well-meaning, large-minded Liberals. How the pretensions of the preachers could have been reduced, save by the ferocities of repression, I am unable to imagine. "Scotsmen are only governable by such usage," wrote Lauder of Fountainhall in notes intended only for his own eye, and Fountainhall was no persecutor, but a man of Liberal ideas.

In the long strife, almost all the virtues were in the camp of the Covenanters; almost all the vices haunted the council chamber, in which men were cruelly tortured. It is impossible to sympathise with Lauderdale, Sharp, Rothes, and the rest of the rulers; but I find it equally impossible to doubt that the work they did,—the separating of the vast body of Presbyterians from the irreconcilable

Remnant,—was a necessary process, with salutary results. Good men could scarcely have done the work; while good men suffered in the doing of it. The thing was certain to be done, sooner or later. The nature of things and of man could not for ever endure the claims of ministers to be prophets and judges, to threaten even the Head of the State with "ecclesiastical censures," practically equivalent to outlawry. But the rulers of the Restoration hastened the change; breaking down in a generation the pretensions of the pulpiteers, by secular tyranny.

Charles II. used to say that, "in his reign all tragedies must have happy endings." The Restoration, as far as Scotland is concerned, was itself a tragedy, with a happy ending, "as mortals reckon happiness." After the Restoration was past, the Union was at hand, the Union which destroyed the legal absolutism asserted for the Crown, north of the Tweed. Persecution, henceforward, was exercised by the Presbyterian majority over the Episcopalian and Catholic minorities; thus the greatest happiness of the greatest number was, so far, secured. Previously the minority had persecuted the majority.

In the great national drama, the tragedy of Sir George Mackenzie of Rosehaugh, (called "The Bloody,") was one scene. Few men were less naturally disposed to be persecutors. Mackenzie regarded right reason as his "one talent," and reason assured him, or so he persuaded himself, that the Government must choose between persecution and civil war. I am not sure that he was mistaken. Like Claverhouse he stands apart from his companions; he had no taste for riotous revel and licentious lusts. Both men, capable in different ways of infinitely higher things, served the Crown; and held that "a soldier only has his orders." Each man was true to his salt.

Mackenzie, like Claverhouse, did not take service under our Dutch deliverer, who was ready to use all available talents. These two had fallen on evil days, and each was too ambitious to stand apart from the strife. Their memories bear the consequences.

A biographer wholly destitute of sympathy for his hero makes dull work; but I trust that my sympathy with the Dr. Jekyll in Mackenzie has not blinded me to the Mr. Hyde in his composition. I have tried to be fair, and if I have omitted any of the offences charged to his account, it is rather through lack of knowledge than through partisanship. I owe much thanks to Dr. J. W. Barty, author of the *Mackenzie-Wharncliffe Deeds*, who has read the proof sheets and enlightened me on points of law. Dr. Hay-Fleming and the Rev. John Sturrock have kindly lent me rare books which I could not otherwise procure. Miss E. M. Thompson made researches, and transcripts of papers, in the British Museum and the Record Office, and verified the references. If ever my negligence has been unworthy of her careful aid, I must take all the blame to myself. To the Rev. John Anderson, of the Register House; and to Mr. Paton,—for making transcripts of documents; to Mr. Dickson, the learned and courteous Librarian of the Advocates' Library; to Professor Hume-Brown, and to Mr. Maclean, Secretary of the Clan Society of Maclean, I have to express my gratitude for many kindnesses.

The Earl of Wharncliffe is good enough to permit the reproduction of his portrait of his ancestor, Sir George Mackenzie, and the Earl of Strathmore is equally generous as regards his beautiful portrait of Bonny Dundee, at Glamis Castle. Mr. Caw, of the National Gallery in Edinburgh, enabled me to trace the likenesses of Dundee from the almost girlish beauty of the Melville portrait, to the proud manliness of the painting possessed by Lord Strathmore.

The *expertise* of Mr. Caw entirely rejects the miniature of a round-headed, red-haired Scot, which has lately been published as the true effigy of one who rivalled Marlborough in beauty, and, born under a more fortunate star, might have been equalled with him in renown.

CONTENTS

LIST OF ILLUSTRATIONS

PHOTOGRAVURE PLATES

ERRATA

Page 19, last line, *for* "1676," *read* "1677." Mackenzie was appointed as an *aide* to the King's Advocate in 1676, and promoted to his post in 1677.

Page 39, line 11, *for* "Alexander Blair" *read* "Alexander Colville of Blair."

Page 41, line 25, "Dowart." This place-name also appears as "Douart" and "Duart."

Page 88, line 17, *for* "could be," *read* "could not be."

Page 143, line 18, *for* "December 8, 1677" *read* "January 10, 1677–78"

Page 209, fourth line from foot, *for* "1654" *read* "1653."

Page 222, line 24, *for* "Duke" *read* "Earl"

Page 279, line 11, *for* "B C." *read* "A.D"

Page 310, line 5, *for* he "lies in that last home," we should probably *read* "was laid in that last home" It is not thought that Mackenzie's body was allowed by religious hatred or by idle ruffianism to rest in its sepulchre.

SIR GEORGE MACKENZIE

CHAPTER I

INTRODUCTORY

The Grey Friars Churchyard—Martyrs and the Persecutor—" Come out
if ye daur ' "—Mackenzie's versatility in Letters—Scott on "the Excommunicate Advocate "—*Heart of Midlothian—Redgauntlet—Dictionary of National Biography* on Mackenzie—Only " one redeeming
feature "—Tradition in Scottish History—Mackenzie and Maitland
of Lethington—Contrasted qualities in his character—To be described
by antitheses—Tenderness, ferocity, a Jacobite, a Socialist, a friend
of the Quakers, scrupulous, unscrupulous—The professional bias—The
Legist, the Lawyer, and the Man—Legend of his Repentance—Did
not play a wholly losing game—Nature of the contest.

UNDER the walls of Edinburgh Castle, and not far from
the Grassmarket of Edinburgh, where so many Saints of
the Covenant were "justified," is the ancient kirkyard of
the church of the Grey Friars, or rather here is the site
of the gardens of the monastery. Granted by Queen Mary
to the citizens as a place of burial, the yard is as rich in
memories and matter of moralising as Westminster Abbey.
Here, or in the church, the Covenant was subscribed by
enthusiastic multitudes, in 1638; here, in 1679, were penned
up hundreds of prisoners, who had fought at Bothwell
Bridge in belated adherence to that treaty with the Almighty.
Here the monument of the Covenanters declares, in rude
contemporary verse, that—

> " they were found
> Constant and steadfast, zealous, witnessing
> For the prerogative of Christ, their King,"

and here the foe of the Covenanters sleeps beside them,

A

Sir George Mackenzie of Rosehaugh, he who was zealous unto slaying—

"For the prerogatives of *Charles*, his King."

His tomb, built by himself, (ever mindful of death, which no man dreaded less) is in the form of a Grecian shrine: the eight columns are covered by a heavy cupola, crowned with an urn, and at the tall door of this sepulchre, the most daring street boys of Edinburgh used to shout—

> " *Bluidy Mackenzie, come oot if ye daur,*
> *Lift the sneck and draw the bar!* "

It is as " Bluidy Mackenzie" that a scholar, "the flower of the wits of Scotland," an erudite and eloquent pleader, a writer who touched on many themes,—morals, religion, heraldry, history, jurisprudence,—the author of perhaps the first novel written on Scottish soil,—is known, or used to be known, in popular tradition.

Sir Walter Scott, who first made the dry bones of Scottish history live, has touched but seldom on the memory of Mackenzie. In *The Tales of a Grandfather* he quotes a passage from his works in illustration of the great Advocate's pity for the most pitiable class of mortals, the women accused, tortured, led to the stake by the parish minister, and burned among the curses of the populace for the crime of witchcraft.

Again, in that scene where Davie Deans rejects, as advocate for his daughter Effie, all the glories of the Scottish Bar, he refuses a young kinsman of Mackenzie. "What, sir, wad ye speak to me about a man that has the blood of the Saints at his fingers' ends? Didna his eme (uncle) die and gang to his place wi' the name of Bluidy Mackenzie? and winna he be kenned by that name sae lang as there's a Scots tongue to speak the word?"

Again, we have that vision where Steenie, in " Wandering Willie's Tale" (*Redgauntlet*), sees the persecutors in their own place, with "the fierce Middleton, and the dissolute Rothes, and the crafty Lauderdale, and Dalziel with his bald head and a beard to his girdle; and Earlshall, with Cameron's blude on his hand, and wild Bonshaw, that tied blessed Mr. Cargill's limbs till the blude sprang, and Dunbarton Douglas, the twice-turned traitor baith to country and king, and Claverhouse, as beautiful as when he lived." And there was "the bluidy Advocate, Mackenzie, who, for his worldly wit and wisdom, had been to the rest as a god."

The echo of the popular voice prolongs itself in the notice of Mackenzie published in the modern Book of Doom, *The Dictionary of National Biography*. Thence the shuddering student learns that there was but one "redeeming feature" in Mackenzie's character, his love of literature!

To tell the truth, knowledge of History and of historical biography in Scotland long was, and to a great extent continues to be, not critical but traditional. In the cottages, till recently, the War of Independence was studied in the well-thumbed copies of Blind Harry's *Wallace;* modernised in a book dear to Burns in youth, Hamilton of Gilbertfield's poem on the Bruce. Information about the Covenanting period and the Restoration was derived from Peter Walker's uncouth but honest and entertaining cheap Lives of the Saints of the Covenant,—Cameron, Peden, Cargill and others;[1] from works like *Naphtali, The Hind Let Loose, The Cloud of Witnesses*, and the *Scottish Worthies* of Howie of Lochgoin.

Round the graves of the martyrs, too, traditions flocked and skirled, melancholy and vague as the cries of the whaups on the moor. Many farmers' families looked back to their forbears of "the Killing Time," to these men and women of indomitable courage, with as much pride, and often with better warrant, than noble Houses regard their Norman ancestors who "came over with the Conqueror."

In our own day popular books, and tracts, and religious services held by the graves of the martyrs, keep fresh the Covenanting tradition. But a critical knowledge of more than a century of war between the Kirk and the State, from

---

[1] The best edition is that edited by Mr. D. Hay Fleming, *Six Saints of the Covenant*. Hodder and Stoughton, London, 1901.

1559 to 1689, is rare indeed. The Early Fathers of the Kirk, and the Covenanters, are too commonly regarded as champions and martyrs of enlightenment, of liberty, civil and religious, of freedom of conscience, whereas religious liberty and freedom of conscience were to them abominations. Meanwhile nothing is remembered about Sir George Mackenzie, for example, except that he was "the bluidy excommunicate Advocate," and "a persecutor."

On the other side, inheritors of Cavalier traditions are apt wholly to forget Mackenzie, a man of the robe, while they cherish the memory of the equally "bluidy" but more romantically attractive Claverhouse, a man of the sword.

The interest of the career and character of Mackenzie, as of the famous Maitland of Lethington, a century earlier, is that in him we see a thoroughly modern man, one of ourselves, set in society and political environment unlike ours, and perverted by his surroundings. Had he lived in England, Mackenzie would have won a happier record. But Scotland was in an anomalous and wretched condition. Twelve years of religious wars, eight years of subjection to the Commonwealth, had perturbed society, and, with the Restoration, Scotland had again become an independent nation, under the same king as England, indeed, but under strange laws, such as England had never known, laws which made the monarch, or so Mackenzie believed, as absolute as Louis XIV. was in France.

For some ten years after the Parliament of Charles I. in 1640, Scotland was, for the first time, a constitutional monarchy; but she was at war with her constitutional monarch. She returned, in 1661, to her unconstitutional conditions, and the later part of Mackenzie's career was devoted to supporting, against a Church which claimed to be *jure divino*, a king who urged the same claim for himself. It was as if two bodies of equal weight encountered each other with equal momentum. There was a bitter struggle, waged by both parties with great stubbornness; on the royal side with persistent cruelty, on the ecclesiastical side with slowly bending fanaticism. In this contest Mackenzie was out of place, and his career was inharmonious with his nature, or rather, the times brought to the surface of his nature elements which, in a more settled age, would have lain dormant, and unsuspected by himself.

With all the courtesy and courage of the Highland character, Mackenzie had the fiery temper of the Celt, and more than once spoke unadvisedly with his lips, or wrote unadvisedly with his pen. Though his domestic correspondence is almost wholly lost, we have one brief and tender letter of his, when, with a heart wrung by recent grief, and in a spirit of "religious stoicism," he speaks of the consolations of faith, and of his indifference to a life wrecked by sorrow. His faith, of which he published a confession, was not lightly held; but he was always averse to the exorbitant claims and pretensions of priests and preachers.

The fatal error in his career was that, being, to quote his biographer of 1722, "a gentleman of pleasant and useful conversation, but a severe opponent of vicious and loose principles in whomsoever he found them," he became associated in politics with men whose principles were extremely loose and vicious. His enemies do not often attack his private character. Like Claverhouse, he is not charged by the sympathetic historians of the Covenant with sensual sins,[1] but he adopted, in an age of uproar, the policy of repression, when, as we shall see, the policy of concession was surrounded by insuperable difficulties.

The result of the clash between Mackenzie's *bon naturel*, in Queen Mary's words about herself, and his environment, was as tragic as in the case of the Queen of Scots herself. Hawthorne, perhaps, could have painted in words a true portrait of Mackenzie, and—

"Divinely through all hindrance found the man."

But the pen of one less imaginative, less keen to search in the dark places of conscience and of sin, shrinks from the task of judgment.

---

[1] "The hell wicked-witted, bloodthirsty Graham of Claverhouse . . . hated to spend his time with wine and women . . ."—Walker, *Six Saints*, ii. 64.

It is easy to describe the Advocate by antitheses in Macaulay's manner, thus: "The man who, in his *Discourse on Point of Honour* 'lighted this, though the smallest and dimmest of Virtue's torches, at Honour's purest flame,' was also the man whom his most unprincipled associate, the detested Melfort, spoke of as 'a useful tool,' a 'cat's paw to get us the chesnuts,' while Dundee writing to Melfort, just before Killiecrankie, styles Mackenzie 'a very honest man, firm beyond belief.' The man remembered as a ruthless oppressor had a heart full of pity for the poor, and pleaded earnestly for the practice of Christian Socialism. He who strove to compel the dour Presbyterians to 'make the laws of the country their creed,' in perhaps his last words written for the press, heartily applauded the most eccentrically aberrant wanderers from the fold of the Church, the Quakers. He whom Macaulay represents as only once entertaining a scruple was, to the last, full of scruples unintelligible to his associates in the government of Scotland. He whom Scott, and Davie Deans, so unhesitatingly consign to his own place, wrote, in his latest days, 'tho' the portion bestowed upon me be very small, yet I wish I may employ that one precious talent so as that I may have from my Glorious Master that only desirable Character, *Well done, good and faithful servant; thou hast been faithful in a few things, enter thou into the joy of thy Lord.*'"

His one precious gift was "right reason," and, when reviewing at its close the life which we are to study, he believed that the gift had been well employed. His wickedest associate was the chief of his traducers; his most intimate friend,—the great mathematician, Dr. Gregory,—wrote of him an eulogy ascribing to him all the virtues which a good man would most desire to possess. He was despised by Melfort; he was admired by Dundee, Dryden, and Evelyn, and was dear to all the learned of the University of Oxford.

In his life we see, as in a strange modern drama, *La Robe Rouge* of M. Eugène Brieux, "the working of the law to unjust ends through inevitable professional instincts, rivalries, practices, and traditions. Things that are life and death, or honour and dishonour, for the accused, are for the lawyers merely details of *le métier*."[1]

His professional and political career was to Mackenzie, *drama*, art, a thing with its own rules and conventions; his *life* was to him a thing apart, and from these twain which he would have kept asunder, was born his tragedy, mournful and inscrutable, true and incredible. As a legist, no man of his time was so sedulously careful in mitigating law, and protecting the accused; as a lawyer, no man was credited with more "diabolical alchymy," says Fountainhall, his contemporary, in transmuting, for State purposes, the gold of innocence into the lead of treason.

Such, without exaggeration, are the antitheses which mark the career and character of Mackenzie.

The learned minister of Eastwood, Mr. Wodrow, the author, (1721-1722) of *The History of the Sufferings of the Church of Scotland*, tells us, in another book, his *Analecta*, that Mackenzie was not without moments of remorse, as he confided to Mr. Matthew M'Kell, or Mackail. There are no traces of "this impure passion of remorse" in Mackenzie's works, or in his conduct. He seems to have been able to hold by the belief that he did no more than his duty. In the latest year of his life, when the dynasty which he had served, and the Cause which he had chosen, were overthrown, and he himself was an exile, he wrote his *Vindication* of the Government of Charles II. without regretting anything. (The publication was posthumous, and apparently the author had not checked it by documents.)

He had once been of another party in the State, a party which, however self-seeking and intriguing its leaders may have been, at all events fought against many intolerable grievances. But Mackenzie was moved, as we shall see, to change sides, by resentment of private wrongs, and by a dread of the extremes of popular passion, the haunting fear that the civil wars and anarchy of the Great Rebellion were returning. Once engaged, he was only too true to his Cause;

---

[1] Mr. A. B. Walkley in *Drama and Life*, 1907.

still, true he was, and he never deserted the sinking ship; he stood to his post with great courage, and retired, when retire he must, with dignity to his studies, and to Oxford, "that native city of his soul," that home of "impossible loyalties."

We wish that, like Archbishop Leighton, he had early abandoned a position which could not be held without smirches on the reputation, that he had gone back to his books and his garden. But he came of a fighting clan, he was of an ambitious nature: *enfin* he was a lawyer and a politician.

We shall have to examine the question, did he go beyond even the ferocious law of his country? but, to his praise or to his prejudice, it must be shown that, in the use of judicial tortures he acted against the grain of his character, which, though ambitious, was naturally honourable, considerate, and rather that of a man of letters than of a man of action. In short, like Lethington, this later flower of the wits of Scotland was born out of due time.

He played his part in what was not wholly a losing game, though he, like his king, "died in his enemies' day," and in exile. Neither party in the strife was entirely victorious. The Presbyterians restored their Church, *Nec tamen consumebatur*, but they abandoned the dream of thrusting their Church on England. Scotland was no longer to be furiously agitated, and was not at all to be governed by the clergy of the Kirk. The Cavaliers lost their beloved dynasty, but not before they had crushed the claims of the preachers to be prophets and judges and rulers.

The Government of the Restoration, under an absentee king, and under politicians almost incredibly profligate, was, apparently, a necessary moment in the education of Scotland. The country had to be weaned from a dream of a century's duration, the dream of a Theocracy like that of ancient Israel; a Theocracy under Prophets and Judges, namely the preachers who inherited the doctrines of Knox and Andrew Melville. The process of awaking was cruel, but the result was salutary.

One man alone could have saved the country, if even he could have saved it ; he whom Mackenzie revered—

"Montrose, his country's glory and its shame."

But he, happily for himself, had fulfilled his promise ; he had "carried fidelity and honour with him to the grave."

CHAPTER II

THE BURDEN OF THE RESTORATION

Why did the Restoration persecute?—The Struggle of the Restoration—
Unintelligible to English visitors—Why was Episcopacy restored?—
Not "because Presbytery was no religion for a gentleman"—Old
relations of Scotland and the Church—Exorbitant claims of the
Reformed Kirk—Struggle between Church and State—James VI.
introduces Bishops as a matter of police—Charles I. brings in the
Liturgy—The Covenant—Covenant imposed in violation of conscience
—Civil war—Clerical claim to interpret Covenant—The Kirk rent in
twain—Remonstrants, Resolutioners, Malignants—Result, Cromwell's
conquest of Scotland—The Restoration has to deal with impracticable
claims—State of parties before the Restoration—Clerical pretensions
unabated—Baillie's remedy, exile of Remonstrants—*Que faire ?*—Greed
and profligacy of the nobles—An impossible task in incapable hands.

WHY was there any persecution in Scotland after the
Restoration ? That question could only be duly answered
in a History of Scotland from the birth of Mary Stuart to
Oak Apple Day in 1660. Apparently the subject will never
be understood by the readers and writers of popular works
on Scottish affairs.

The struggle of the Restoration was a struggle to impose
Episcopacy on one side, and to restore Presbytery on the
other. Most Scottish children used to be taught this amount
of knowledge, but they were not taught what Presbytery
then meant, and for what political reasons Episcopacy was
imposed. They supposed Presbyterianism to be no more,
in the old days, than the peaceful religion in which they
were bred, and they wondered why men were hunted and
hanged, tortured, and sent in crowds to the West Indies,
for wishing to do without Bishops, and teaching the Shorter
Catechism, which, in fact, *was* taught under the Bishops.

English visitors to Scotland during the Restoration, could

no more understand than could little Presbyterians fifty years ago, what the trouble was about.   The Confession of Faith of 1560 was still the standard of the Church, the worship in the churches seemed identical,—save for the use of the Doxology and one or two other trifles,—with that of the Presbyterian meeting-houses in England. English tourists asked why there were risings, murders, hangings, and torture, all about nothing?

Why, then, was there such a frenzy on the part of rulers who despised Bishops to thrust Episcopacy on a Presbyterian people to whom prelacy seemed "a limb of Antichrist"?   Charles II., himself a Catholic by conviction, "was indifferent in the matter," as Lauderdale said, writes Bishop Burnet.[1]

The learned Dr. M'Crie explains that the maxim of Charles was that Presbyterianism "was not fit for a gentleman, his dissipated and irreligious courtiers were of the same opinion, *and therefore Episcopacy was established."* [2]

This is a flippant and frivolous, though popular, account of the reasons for the establishment of Episcopacy at the Restoration.   Really Episcopacy was established as a measure of police, and with the hope of preventing the renewed outbreak of the hundred years' war between Church and State.

Scotland, till the Reformation, had, of all countries, been least dominated by the Church, and was most regardless of Interdicts, and most cavalier in her treatment of the Pope. The troubles of the persecutors and persecuted, in the reign of Charles II., can only be understood if we go back to their origin a hundred years earlier.   Mackenzie himself was taunted with a pedantic affection for ancient history when, in 1678, he traced the causes of the turmoil back to 1648. We, unluckily, if we wish to understand, must go back to 1559, to the Reformation.   Before the Reformation Scot-

---

[1] Burnet saw a long letter on the subject, which Lauderdale wrote in 1660 to Lady Margaret Kennedy, who later married Burnet, *History of His Own Times*, vol. i. p. 198 : 1833. Ed. 1897, Pt. i. vol. i. p. 196.

[2] My italics . *cf.* M'Crie, Works, vol. iv. p. 17.

land had been, as we said, singularly exempt from the war of State and Church: her Parliament and kings were "Erastian" and kept the clergy in due subjection, from the days of St. Margaret onwards.[1]

After the Reformation, on the other hand, after 1560, the Kirk was not, like Rome, remote and almost *négligeable*, but planted in the heart of the country; and the Kirk, from the first, endeavoured to be, in a nation, what the Calvinist Church was in a small city state, Geneva. Her aim was theocracy, with preachers as interpreters of the will of God. Her preachers claimed the Keys of St. Peter, as Mackenzie himself observes, even when they were deprived of the Sword. Knox, from the first, averred that the preachers could "bind or loose, on earth, what should be bound or loosed in Heaven." By her power of Excommunication, the Kirk did not merely prevent men from approaching the Holy Communion, did not merely reduce them to a condition in which it was questioned whether they might, or might not, be poisoned with impunity! In the regular formula, she "handed" the excommunicated person "over to Satan." The civil magistrate was obliged to enforce the Kirk's decree by secluding the victim from all intercourse with his kind, except the members of his own family. The victim was *caput lupinum*.

The preachers could always refuse to obey the king on the ground that "God is to be obeyed rather than men," and as they were the only judges of what God's commands were, in any case, they could resist the State whenever they pleased.[2]

With more explicit claims went a vaguer pretension of the clergy to direct inspiration by the Holy Ghost. In Knox's Book of Common Order the preacher is directed to pray for the assistance of "God's Holy Spirit, as the same shall move his heart." If the preacher, after emitting a violent political attack on the civil power from the pulpit, chooses to say that he has spoken what "the Spirit" put into his lips,

---

[1] See *Statutes of the Scottish Church*, Dr. Patrick's Introduction, pp. xxxix, xl

[2] This pretension was a corollary from a Genevan formula. *Cf* Mitchell, *The Scottish Reformation*, pp. 100–102.

how is he to be taught his proper place? He is certain to refuse secular jurisdiction, till he has been tried by these "prophets" and "judges," his brother ministers. Their professional pride, and their consciences are almost certain to acquit the preacher, and the case having been decided in the spiritual Court, the secular Court has no *locus standi.*

Sir George Mackenzie has stated the secular view of this particular pretension in the case of a minister, Mr. James Guthrie, who was hanged in the dawn of the Restoration, long before Mackenzie was in office. "He was accused," says Mackenzie in his *Memoirs of the Affairs of Scotland*, "of having preached treasonable and seditious doctrine," and, against Charles II. and the Council, at Perth, in 1651, "he declined his Majesty and his Council, as Judges, in the first instance, to what he preached, affirming that the presbytery, or provincial assembly, were the only judges competent in the first instance, to what a minister spoke in the pulpit. This was the rather insisted on, because this principle had not only vexed King James (VI.), and was the foundation of much rebellion with us, but by the ministers' conniving with one another's crime and treasonable and seditious expressions, (which might probably be expected from them,) they were secure against the secular power, and might safely contemn the royal authority." [1]

Thus treasonable agitation, threats from the pulpit against the Government of the day, (threats which had a knack of fulfilling themselves,) could be safely organised and uttered from the sacro-sanct shadow of the pulpit's sounding-board, and under the ægis, as it were, of "the spreit of God."

It cannot be denied, again, except by the ignorant or the dishonest, that Knox had also introduced a doctrine rejected both by Calvin and by the French leader of the early Huguenots. This was the theory that the private citizen, if conscious of a divine "call," might righteously "execute judgments" on "idolaters," might assassinate "the enemies of God" as he found opportunity.[2] Against

---

[1] *Memoirs of the Affairs of Scotland*, p. 50.
[2] Knox's Works 1. 309, 328, 329. The opposite view, iii. 194; *cf.* ii 441 *et seq.*

this unhappy theory, borrowed from Knox by the Covenanting author of *Jus Populi Vindicatum* in 1669, and carried into practice by his disciples; against this legacy of the great Scottish Reformer, the Government of the Restoration had to contend.

It is impossible in these pages to trace in detail the history of the war of Church and State from the days of Mary Stuart to those of her great-grandson, Charles II.

It must suffice to say that James VI. triumphed over the pretensions of the Kirk by methods of cunning and violence. He was not content with reducing the preachers, on the whole, to abstention from interference with the State. He introduced modifications, such as kneeling at the Holy Communion, and the observation of Christmas and Easter, which galled the consciences of the godly. Charles I. wrecked himself in the effort to bring in, tyrannically and of his own mere motion, the Laudian Liturgy. Under the Covenant, 1638, the preachers became the authorised interpreters of that document; they had their turn in enforcing it by persecution; they ruled the State for some twelve years; they ruined the effort of the estates to release the imprisoned king; they divided the country, "purged" the army; brought on Scotland the Cromwellian conquest; and split into two hostile parties,—the fiercer, the Remonstrants; the milder, the Resolutioners.

Twelve years of the Covenant as interpreted by the preachers had led Scotland, State and Kirk, to these extremes of disaster. But time had taught no lesson to the Remonstrants. They were still the interpreters of the Covenants; still convinced that these treaties with Jehovah were eternally binding; still, (some of them at least,) persuaded that Charles II. was bound by oath to impose presbyterial government on England, and they were still the darlings of their flocks. Mr. Hume Brown has reckoned that the majority of ministers were Remonstrants or Protesters, but it is not easy to find trustworthy statistics.

When the Restoration came, in a General Assembly held

to admonish Parliament of its duties, (as was the custom,) they would carry their proposals.

Could Charles II., when restored, permit the existence of General Assemblies, and their Commission, and the re-opening of the old quarrel between the claims of theocratic preachers and the rights of the State? Was the experiment feasible, and, if not, where was Presbyterianism without a General Assembly? It was where Cromwell placed it, nowhere, and was innocuous; but it was no longer what the preachers desired.

Mr. Robert Law, minister of East Kilpatrick, expelled from his pulpit in 1662, shows the excellent results of Cromwell's policy in crushing the General Assembly. He says "from the year 1652 to 1660 there was great good done by the preaching of the Gospel in the west of Scotland, more than was observed to have been for twenty or thirty years before; a great many brought in to Christ Jesus by a saving work of conversion, which was occasioned through ministers preaching nothing through all that time but the Gospel, and had left off to preach up parliaments, armies, leagues, resolutions, and remonstrances . . ."[1]

These were the happy consequences of the policy of Cromwell. The Rev. Mr. Kirkton adds his testimony to the same effect. During Cromwell's time, the wilder party, the Remonstrants, or Protesters, had dealt with the Protector. Argyll, who had welcomed him on the Border after he smote the army of the State at Preston, "was judged to be the Protesters' agent in London," in 1656.[2] Mr. Guthrie, and the fierce fanatic, Johnstone of Waristoun, and others, had interviews with Cromwell in 1657, and obtained leave to renew, in a platonic way, the Act of Classes.[3] Their opponent was Mr. James Sharp, later the apostate Archbishop of St. Andrews.

In the spring of 1660, before the Restoration, Sharp was in London, watching events in the interest of the more moderate clerical party, the Resolutioners, men like Baillie

---

[1] Law's *Memorials*, p. 7   [2] Row's *Blair*, p. 329.
[3] Baillie, iii pp. 330, 354.

and Douglas, with whom he corresponded. Both were as keen as ever for the Covenant. Sharp, however, assured Douglas that the cause of "rigid Presbyterianism" was hopeless, and he insists on the phrase, in spite of Douglas's remonstrances.

Douglas, in turn, from Edinburgh, assures Sharp that "the new upstart generation" in Scotland, (men of Sir George Mackenzie's status) "bear a heart-hatred to the Covenant," and "have no love to Presbyterial Government, but are wearied of that yoke, feeding themselves with the fancy of Episcopacy, or moderate Episcopacy. *Our* desire is that presbyterial Government be settled. . . ."[1] Supporting the Covenant and "rigid Presbyterianism" as they did, the more moderate party do not seem so very remote from the wilder Remonstrants, yet "no peace can be had with these men, but upon their own terms, how destructive soever to truth and order," says Sharp, in 1658. "Nothing will satisfy them unless they have all their will. . . ."[2] Yet Douglas, himself of the milder party, says that the Solemn League and Covenant, imposing Presbytery on England, "is the only basis of settling these distracted nations."[3]

For Charles to act on the principles of the Solemn League and Covenant, and impose the detested rigid Presbyterianism on England, meant civil war. Yet we find Douglas, a man of the milder party of the Kirk, insisting on this mad scheme, as the only basis of settlement, before the Restoration.

What, then, could come of the re-establishment of a Kirk in which the wilder men, perhaps the majority, were impracticable, while Sharp's employers, "not stumbling if the king exercise his moderation towards" the Remonstrants, "yet apprehend their principles to be such, especially their leaders', as their having any hand in affairs cannot but breed continual distemper and disorder."[4] Baillie suggested that the Remonstrant preachers should be sent to the Orkneys![5]

---

[1] Wodrow, i. p. 21.

[2] James Sharp to Mr. Patrick Drummond, 28 Aug. 1658. *Lauderdale Papers*, i. pp. 3, 4.   [3] March 31, 1660. Wodrow, i. p 14.

[4] Wodrow, i. p. 24, note to p. 22.   [5] Baillie, iii. p 459.

When a dying man, (April 18, 1661) Baillie, a resolute Covenanter, wrote to Lauderdale, "I ever opposed Mr. James
Guthrie's way ; but see none get the king persuaded to take the
ministers' heads. Send them to some place where they may
preach and live. . . ."[1] Thus, even to so keen a Covenanter
as Baillie, it seemed that the Remonstrant ministers must
be removed from their parishes to "some boundless con-
tiguity of space," some Highland wilderness where they
might preach, apparently to Gaelic-speaking congregations,
or to the Orkneys. Now these preachers at the moment filled
the pulpits of the south-western shires. There was no room
for them in the Orkneys !

Conceive, then, a General Assembly composed of the two
parties, both eager for the Solemn League and Covenant,
though Douglas and his allies were ready to drop *that* after
the Restoration,[2] both supporters of the Covenant, and both
intolerant of their opponents.

Even if Douglas and the Edinburgh preachers who acted
with him were prepared to abandon the effort to make England Presbyterian, this was not to the mind of Baillie, a Re-
solutioner, a relatively moderate man. After the Restoration,
on June 6, 1660, he writes to Lauderdale, "Your unhappy
diurnals and letters from London have wounded me to the
heart. Is the Service Book read in the King's Chapel? . . .
Has the House of Lords passed an order for the Service
Book ? Ah, where are we so soon !" With much more of
same sort.[3]

If defeated on a vote, the Remonstrants, as they had
done before, would form a separate party, and disallow the
lawfulness of the decision of the majority. If themselves in
a majority, the Remonstrants would be "neither to haud nor
to bind," and the furies of 1638 might be again let loose.

Our historians do not, as a rule, seem fully to understand
the difficulties of the situation which the Government of
Charles II. had to face. The position of the king was this:

---

[1] Wodrow, i. p 290.
[2] See their letter to Charles of May 8, 1660, Wodrow, i. Note to p. 22.
[3] Wodrow, i. p. 288.

in Scotland, if he renounced the Covenant, he was a perjured man; while in England a Dr. Crofts told him to his face, in a sermon, that God allowed him to be defeated at Worcester because he had taken the Covenants, an act injurious to the Church of England!

Que faire? Probably the Government should either have allowed matters ecclesiastical to stand as they did under Monk; with no General Assemblies and no civil penalties consequent on excommunication; or they should have granted a General Assembly on the lines laid down by Douglas, in a letter of July 1660 to Sharp, "After this, Assemblies are not to interweave civil matters with ecclesiastic, and he" (Douglas) "wisheth that the king were informed of this, that after our brethren," (the Remonstrants) "went from us, our proceedings were abstract from all civil affairs."[1]

Had a General Assembly been granted, the preachers could not have abstained from meddling with religion as established in England; that is certain. Bishop Burnet, in 1660 a young man of twenty, writes, "It would have given a great advantage to the restitution of episcopacy if a General Assembly had been called and the two parties had been let loose on one another. That would have shown the impossibility of maintaining the government of the Church on a parity and the necessity of setting a superior order over them for keeping them in unity and peace."[2] They would not have seen the necessity!

The Remonstrant preachers, who certainly would not have abstained from interfering with secular policy, might have been packed off, on Baillie's plan, to the Orkneys, or elsewhere, but they were so numerous, and their fiery flocks were so resolute, that probably new ministers would not have been received in the vacant parishes, conventicles would have abounded, all the troubles which actually occurred would have ensued. The Government, however, increased, by their disloyal and infatuated methods, the difficulties which, in any case, were serious, while the wild orgies of

---

[1] Wodrow, vol i. p 47.   [2] Burnet, vol. i. p 199. 1897.

Middleton and Rothes, the champion drinker of his day, brought discredit on all the measures which were conceived in their cups.

The Government was to be restored, as under James VI., to the nobles of the Privy Council, inspired by the Court in England, and inspiring the Court. Sunk deep in debt, as a consequence of the long civil war, the nobles, as Mr. Froude describes them at an earlier date, were like a pack of hungry wolves. They recouped themselves with "the spoils of office," they hunted for fines and forfeitures: some of them to recover their own, lost by their loyalty, some to win new fortunes. Like wolves they fought each other over the quarry, and, in the reaction from puritanism, profligacy was reckoned virtue.

It is now plain, perhaps, that the Government of the Restoration, incapable as it was, had a hard and complex task. It is easy to be easy-going, and ask, "Why did these nefarious men not respect the consciences of the people, and restore Presbyterianism?" But that measure, though it ought, at any risk, to have been ventured as an experiment, seemed impossible to men who, from first to last, were haunted by the belief that the renewal of presbytery meant the renewal of the recent civil wars.

Such, then, was the Burden of the Restoration. The Government's object was to prevent the Kirk from reviving her old pretensions, and embroiling Scotland in a civil war which might spread to England. The repressive measures of Government were, necessarily, deemed persecution, and when Mackenzie took office as Public Prosecutor, "King's Advocate," in 1676, he became a persecutor, *ratione officii*.

CHAPTER III

THE YOUTH OF MACKENZIE

Mackenzie's early memories—Montrose's army in Dundee—Defeats of
Dunbar and Worcester—Massacre of Dundee—Mackenzie's ancestry
—Kintail and Seaforth—His father Highland, his mother Lowland—
Simon of Lochslin—Date of Mackenzie's birth, probably 1638—
Sufferings of his clan for the King—His mother's father an Episco-
palian minister—Mackenzie enters Aberdeen University (1650)—Frugal
life—Goes to St. Andrews (1653)—Life at St. Andrews—Mr. Blair on
Golf and Theology—Mackenzie's cousin, Tarbat, at St. Andrews—
Mackenzie at Bourges—Returns to Edinburgh—Admitted to the Bar
—Energy of Mackenzie in law and literature—Publishes his novel,
Aretina—Plot of *Aretina*—"An up-to-date novel"—Account of the
Civil Wars and Restoration—Mackenzie's sympathy with the great
Montrose.

THE most disastrous period in the civil wars was within
the memory of Mackenzie. As a child of seven, or perhaps
of nine, in his grandmother's house at Dundee, he may
have watched the plaids of Montrose's Highlanders sweep
through the streets, and heard the ordered tramp of his
disciplined Irish musketeers. He may have seen Montrose
miraculously gather the scattered and intoxicated forces
in the dusk, and drive them out to that retreat which
French strategists deemed more wonderful than his victories.
Children, we know, interest themselves eagerly in war,
but we cannot tell whether Mackenzie rejoiced or wept
over the capture of Montrose and his execution. As a
young man he admired and praised in verse the great
Marquis; in childhood we know nothing of his sentiments.
He must certainly, however, have been saddened, as a
patriotic boy, by the national defeats of Dunbar and Worcester; he may have understood the miserable results of
the feud of Remonstrants and Resolutioners, concerning

which he cannot but have heard many a sermon. He was probably not in Dundee, but perhaps at his Highland home in Ross-shire, when Monk stormed the town, and wrought massacre in the streets (1651).

George Mackenzie was a member of the ancient Highland House of Mackenzie of Kintail. His grandfather, Kenneth, was raised to the Scottish peerage as Lord Mackenzie of Kintail, in 1609. He was succeeded by his eldest son by his first marriage, who later became first Earl of Seaforth. The first Lord Mackenzie of Kintail married a second time; his bride was Isobel, daughter of Sir Gilbert Ogilvy of Pourie, whose ancestor had been a famous Catholic intriguer in the early reign of James VI. By her Lord Mackenzie had sons, Alexander, who died without issue; George, who succeeded his half-brother by the first marriage, as Earl of Seaforth; Thomas, laird of Pluscardine, and Simon of Lochslin, with an ancient castle in the parish of Tarbat, Ross-shire; from its two massive towers, rent from roof-tree to ground, which still dominate the loch, there is but a distant view of the violet-tinted hills. Simon, by his marriage with Elizabeth, daughter of the Rev. Peter Bruce, (who was minister of St. Leonard's, and Principal of St. Leonard's Hall in the University of St. Andrews,) was father of George Mackenzie, later Sir George Mackenzie of Rosehaugh. He was of Highland and Lowland, Celtic and English blood: his maternal grandmother was a daughter of Sir Alexander Wedderburn of Kingennie, town-clerk of Dundee.

Of Simon we know little; he seems to have stood outside of the hurly-burly of politics when it was at its wildest, but he sat for Inverness-shire and Ross in the Parliament of 1640–41. On June 3, 1634, he "was added to the Burgesses and Brethren of the Guild" of Dundee, "for his numerous services to the State." He died about 1666, being succeeded in his estates by his son George.[1] Sir George Mackenzie was born in Dundee, (of which in 1661 he became a burgess,) in the house of his mother's widowed

---

[1] *Roll of Eminent Burgesses of Dundee*, by A. H. Millar, pp. 152, 153, 171; Barty, *Mackenzie Wharncliffe Deeds*, pp. 104, 105.

mother, wife of Wedderburn of Kingennie. The town
then deserved the name it bears in the old light-hearted
song "Bonnie Dundee," and the beautiful site on the Tay
was occupied by a small city with four chief streets, meeting
in the wide market-place, with its Cross. It was Sir Walter
who transferred to Graham of Claverhouse the style of
" Bonnie Dundee."

On the mother's side, Mackenzie was akin to Sir Peter
Wedderburn of Gosford, a Lord of Session, who had been
Clerk of the Privy Council in the beginning of the Restora-
tion. Mackenzie has left a Latin eulogy of Sir Peter, and
was on terms of friendship with him ; unluckily his letters
to Sir Peter are not among the MSS. of the Halketts of
Pitfirrane, in Fife, who represent the Wedderburns of
Gosford.

According to the Biography of Mackenzie published in
the folio edition of his Works (1716–1722) he was born at
Dundee in 1636. All accounts of him, including that by
Mr. T. F. Henderson, in *The Dictionary of National Biography*,
follow the anonymous author, (probably Ruddiman,) of 1716–
1722. But as Mackenzie himself, in his book, *The Religious
Stoic*, published in 1663,[1] declares that he is not yet twenty-
five, he must have been born not earlier than 1638 : the
contents of the book, for example the allusions to the eviction
of many preachers, and to their conventicles, prove that
it was written in the year of its publication. If Mackenzie
was born in 1636, not in 1638, it is not easy to account for
the long interval between the time when he left school,
which would be 1646, and the date when he entered Aberdeen
University (1650). The Registers of Baptisms at Dundee
are missing before 1648.[2] The birth date of 1636 is given
on the tablet of his sepulchre.

We know almost nothing about the influences that surrounded the boy in childhood. His father's name is inconspicuous in the history of the troubles. His father's eldest
brother, Lord Seaforth, had been now for the king, now for the

---

[1] Mackenzie, Works, vol. i. p. 71.   [2] Information from Mr. A. H. Millar.

Covenant. He was, like most of the nobles save Huntley, a Covenanter in 1638–1639, but when Montrose, in 1641, revolted against the influence of Argyll, Seaforth joined him in the "band" of Cumbernauld, which had no effect save to delay Argyll's dictatorship, and to cause the imprisonment of Montrose, his friend Lord Napier, and a few other Cavaliers. When the great Marquis began his year of victories (1645) and had left Inveraray, he found that Seaforth was to encounter him as he went north, while Argyll was to fall on his rear. He turned on his tracks, made a forced march through the snow-clad hills, and "discussed Argyll" in the crushing victory of Inverlochy. After Montrose won his hard fight at Auldearn, Seaforth came over to his cause. After Philiphaugh, fines were imposed on, but never paid, by the chief leaders of the Mackenzies, among whom Simon of Lochslin, father of Sir George, is not numbered.[1] Possibly he was busy with commercial undertakings, at Dundee, where Sir George was born.

In 1649, Seaforth joined Charles II. in Holland, and he was acting as Secretary for Scotland when Montrose, foreseeing his doom, went to "search my death," as he wrote to his unworthy king. On the Oykel, near which he was surprised and defeated, Montrose hoped to have been joined by Seaforth's clan, but, their chief being abroad, not a man came to his standard. In 1651 Seaforth died in Holland, while Secretary for Scotland for Charles II.

From the Mackenzies Sir George may have imbibed a dislike of the Kirk and the Covenant, which had driven the chief of his house into exile. If his mother was of the same ecclesiastical politics as her father, Dr. Bruce, Principal of St. Leonard's College, she was no stickler for Presbyterianism. Dr. Bruce, in 1629, resigned his Principalship, being then aged sixty-three : he died before 1631. Through the latest struggle of James VI. with the Kirk, he was a quiet follower of Archbishop Spottiswoode. In 1616 he received his doctor's degree: "this novelty was brought in amongst us without

---

[1] Barty, *Mackenzie Wharncliffe Deeds*, p. 4.

advice or consent of the Kirk," grumbles Calderwood. Dr. Bruce sat on the Court of Commission, which held a sort of inquisitorial powers, and he was usually in opposition to the ministers who were recalcitrant against the Articles of Perth. His death prevented him from being involved in the latter struggles, but he was of King James's Episcopal Kirk, and from his daughter George Mackenzie was not likely to learn fanatical opinions, though ladies were so eager for the Covenant that we have no certainty on this point. Thus the mother of Bishop Burnet, though the wife of a resolute loyalist, was an *enragée* Presbyterian. But she came of a fanatical family, that of Johnstone of Waristoun, whereas Mackenzie's mother's people were probably, like her father, conformists and loyal.

Mackenzie entered Aberdeen University in 1650. If born in 1636 he would be aged fourteen. At that age Bishop Burnet had graduated, and, as Mackenzie like Burnet was very precocious, he may, if born in 1638, have entered King's College, Aberdeen, as the Register of King's College proves, at twelve years of age. His name is not recorded in his own hand.[1] Mackenzie's boyhood was probably spent under frugal conditions. His father, says Mr. Barty, was apparently " in pecuniary difficulties, and had to beseech his very dear friend, Mr. Farquhar, to advance money for his son, . . ." whose board, for a quarter of a year, cost £40 Scots, that is, £3, 6s. 8d. sterling. His red nightcap cost £1 Scots.[2] In the autumn of 1653 he migrated, and joined the fourth and last year's class, or lecture, at St. Andrews, under a Mr. Jamieson as Regent, or college tutor. His own college was St. Leonard's, and on May 13, 1653, he graduated.[3]

Of Mackenzie's life at St. Andrews no records exist. We do not even know of what rank he was ; probably of that answering to " Gentleman Commoner." The University, as

[1] I owe the facts to the kindness of Dr. Cowan, Professor of Ecclesiastical History.

[2] *Mackenzie Wharncliffe Deeds*, p. 104.

[3] Mr. Maitland Anderson, Librarian to the University, kindly consulted th books.

it was the oldest in Scotland, was the most famous, and had numbered among its *alumni* the rival Marquises of Montrose and Argyll, the Earl of Rothes, and a Covenanter no less notorious than Mr. Daniel or Donald Cargill. Probably Mackenzie competed for the prize of archery, though, unlike Argyll and Montrose, he was not successful. Among the men who graduated with him not one has left a memory, or made any mark on history. We may presume that he, like Montrose and like James Melville, nearly a century earlier, played golf, a game then in so much favour that the eminent contemporary preacher, Mr. Blair, is said to have illustrated the relations of our Lord to the Church by a homely simile drawn from the club-maker's art, the whipping and the glue that unite the head and the shaft.

St. Leonard's, later, became a Jacobite college, and there is every probability that, at St. Andrews, Mackenzie's views would be remote from those of the wilder Kirkmen.

His *Life* says that Mackenzie went from St. Andrews to the University of Bourges, which was at that time, and indeed had been since the sixteenth century, chiefly devoted to the legal studies in which he took much pleasure. In a Catholic country he was remote from Presbyterian influences. Returning to his native land, he was admitted to the Scottish Bar in 1659, and, after the Restoration, readmitted, in 1661. The Bar was then the one avenue of young Scots not of the highest *noblesse* to wealth and public office. He had not, probably, seen much of Paris or London, and to him the Edinburgh of that day, scarcely larger than in Queen Mary's time, with the long central street from the Castle to Holyrood, and the many steep lanes of tall houses branching off, may have seemed a magnificent capital, though, in summer, "the most unpleasant and unwholesome town in Scotland." Mackenzie, at all events, would walk and talk in the long hall, with lads more idle than himself, for he worked diligently from the first, and was working, when Monk rode forth on his march to England, at his novel, *Aretina*.

In 1660 Mackenzie published this novel, which he must

have written in the stirring times when the country was gazing towards the rising sun of Charles II. His story is entitled—

ARETINA

OR THE SERIOUS

ROMANCE

Written originally in English

PART FIRST

EDINBURGH

Printed for *Robert Brown*, at the
sign of the *Sun*, on the north
side of the Street, 1660 [1]

The Dedication is :—

"To all the Ladies of this Nation.

"Fair Ladies,—I do, like Moses' trembling mother, leave this my first born upon the banks of envie's current, wishing that the fair hands of the meanest of your number would vouchsafe to dandle it in the lapp of your protection," and so forth.

The words "written originally in English" are meant to make it plain that *Aretina* is not a translation from the French of Monsieur or Mademoiselle de Scudéri, or any of their rivals, whose works, as Mackenzie says elsewhere, are "the darlings" of his generation. He opens with an Apologie for Romances, as no "excuses for mispending time,"—how can time be better spent than in the study of character? The style of "the famous Scudérie," especially of his *Clelia*, deserves imitation, "wherein he professes that he hath adapted all to the present converse of the French," with no pedantic archaism. Kings and shepherds of Babylon or Memphis are to talk and behave like Frenchmen of the age of *Les Précieuses Ridicules*, while, in the amazing mixture, the Giants, Fairies, Knights, and errant ladies of the *Mort d'Arthur* roam at large, holding

---

[1] British Museum press mark :—12614. ccc. 20

tilts and tourneys. This fashion " is really the mould wherein all true romances should be casten."

The world has not agreed with the critical opinion of Mackenzie, given at a moment when, as certain recommendatory verses inform us—

"Thy beardless chin high voicedly doth declare
That wisdom's strength lyes not in silvered hair."

Perhaps Mackenzie read as many romances as law books at Bourges. These romances are now totally unreadable except by such insatiable students as Sir Walter Scott was, and Mr. Saintsbury is. Writers on Mackenzie have been daunted by *Aretina*, and none of them has observed that in an episode, " The Wars of Lacedæmon," he gives a veiled account of the Civil War, or rather of the history of Scotland from the Union of the Crowns to the rejoicings at the Restoration. Thus *Aretina*, published in the year of the Restoration, was a " topical" and " up to date" novel, and its extreme rarity is due to the fact that it must have been thumbed to rags in such circulating libraries as, ten years earlier, consoled at Hull the captivity of that wandering knight, Sir James Turner. *Aretina* is no longer readable " for human pleasure," none of the romances *à la Scudéri* are readable. The characters are numerous as the grains upon the ribbed sea sands, and not one of them is interesting. The scene opens in ancient Egypt, of which Mackenzie necessarily knew nothing. The period is of no actual time, but post-Ptolemaic, and rather Hellenic than redolent of ancient Khem.

" Melancholy lodged herself in the generous breast of Monanthropus," lately Chancellor of Egypt. He frequented forests more than men ; Egypt being famous for her pathless woods. As he meditated in a sylvan glade he met two ladies, naked to the waist (a characteristic of Minoan female costume in Crete about 2500 B.C.). The dames were chained to each other, and thus heavily handicapped fled from two villains. Two knights rescued them, and Monanthropus offered them hospitality. They explained that they were the highly educated daughters of a Theban *savant*, and that they, after his

demise, had been sought in marriage by two unwelcome
suitors. These bad men, having found a venal astrologer,
made him announce that the ladies must leave Thebes for
Delphi, to appease Apollo. *En route* the wicked wooers killed
the ladies' *chaperons*, and lodged the maidens in the cave of
a witch. Moved by advice from the astrologer, the wooers
carried the ladies to Egypt, and entrusted them to a pair of
murderers, from whom they had now escaped. To their joy,
Monanthropus possessed an excellent library, but Philarites,
one of the knights, on beholding Aretina, daughter of Monanthropus, swooned at the sight of her beauty, and that day
they read no more.

Need we proceed ? Aretina dropped a scarlet ribbon, by
way of giving Philarites encouragement, and he wore his
lady's favour at the tournaments which were the favourite
recreation of the Egyptian gentry ; or while he sat by Aretina's
side in the coach of the recluse Monanthropus, who had everything handsome about him. They visited a local hermit, who
showed them the skulls of Plato and of Alexander the Great,
whereon tears came in rivers from the eyes of Aretina and
her conscious lover.

The story now wanders to the distracted and "lunatick
country" of Lacedæmon, (England,) where a gentleman
named Megistus imparts to Monanthropus a full history of
Scotland since the days of James VI., (Sophus,) and his
minion Paratus, (Buckingham). The Bishops are "Muftis,"
the Presbyterians are "Jovists," Hamilton is Autophilus,
accused of aiming at the Crown. Argyll is Phanosebus, "a
man of more wit than virtue, and of more cunning than
either." Little did the author dream that he would soon be
defending Phanosebus on a charge of treason ! Montrose
is "Oranthus," "a gentleman whom hundreds of years cannot
parallel," praise not too high for the great Marquis. He did
not gain all the hearts that would gladly have come to him,
"because the Jovists had placed domestic priests in each
family, for the service of their household gods, to remark
men's actions, or at least to tutor their wives. . . ." Montrose's

" endurance of hardships showed the world that, as his spirit was of gold, his body was of brass. Grass was his best bed, stones his ordinary pillows, and the heavens his continual canopy." But to his equals he was as haughty as he was urbane to his inferiors. Macleod of Assynt is "an ignominious rascal who sold that priceless gentleman," Montrose. Theopemptus is Charles II., "a gentleman of noble spirit, and well-limbed eloquence." Cromwell is "the most hateful tyrant who ever lived." Here we have a view of Mackenzie's political opinions in youth.

A short extract may suffice to convey an idea of the style of this romance.

It was the sweet month of May, and one morning Agapeta and Aretina arose early and went into the garden and there met Megistus and Philarites by a hedge. "Philarites would willingly have tendered his respects to them, but his heart, which did climb up his throat, as if it would have propined itself to Aretina, had already stopt the passage." The gentlemen and the ladies fall into mutual compliments on one another's beauty and accomplishments, which Aretina requests them to stop, and changes the discourse to the beauties of the morning.

" Observe, fair ladies," said Megistus, " how these red roses blush, and these tulips grow pale, through anger to see their beauty so outstript by yours, and how these cherries, albeit they be but hard-hearted creatures, yet understand their duty so well as bow downwards to do you obeisance, and would willingly throw themselves at your feet, if their stalks did not hinder them ; and how yonder pond hath drawn your picture, and placed it in its bosom, presenting it to you when ye approach, to indicate the high value it sets upon your beauty, and concealing it when you are gone, fearing lest any should rob it."

The book ends abruptly, as if the author were thoroughly tired of it, but Philarites is at least the accepted lover of his Aretina, whom, unknown, and clad in black armour, he has rescued from various inconveniences. Scott did borrow a

scene in *Ivanhoe* from one of the Scudéri romances, as
he says, and perhaps he owed the Black Knight to Mackenzie.

It is not thought prudent in a young barrister to dally
with *belles lettres*, but *Aretina* did not injure Mackenzie in
his profession.

CHAPTER IV

MACKENZIE'S DEFENCE OF ARGYLL (1661)

Mackenzie as counsel for Argyll—Argyll's visit to Court—Vain warnings—
Charles's reasons for hating Argyll—Arrested, sent to the Tower—
Sent to Edinburgh—Defences of Argyll—His offences after the
Indemnity of 1651—Aided the English—A Campbell messenger from
London disturbs the Court—A pardon expected—The Campbell "a
corby Messenger"—"Prophecies of the death of Argyll"—Mac-
Naughton's Revenge—Argyll's fatal letters to Monk—Historic doubts
concerning these—Doubts destroyed—Were the letters holograph?—
Mackenzie's speech for Argyll—Courage of Argyll—His death—
Mackenzie in full practice at the Bar—Note, "Argyll's Compromising
Letters."

THAT Mackenzie's genius for his profession was early recognised, is proved by the first great event in his public life.
He was chosen with John Cuningham, afterwards Sir John,
and several other advocates, as counsel for the unhappy
Marquis of Argyll, when accused before Parliament of high
treason (1661).

Charles II., after his Restoration, had not yet proclaimed
an indemnity for Scotland, when Argyll, contrary to all
advice, and despising the warnings of second-sighted men
and howling dogs, went up, uninvited, to kiss the king's hand
at Court. He had crowned Charles at Scone, but he had
offended the king as he had offended all parties. The air was
full of grudges against him, from the clans on his frontiers,
Macdonalds, MacNabs, MacNaughtons and Macleans, to the
Ogilvies, for his burning of the Bonny House of Airlie, and
the Grahams, who pined for vengeance for Montrose. Apart
from his leadership of the Covenanters in the Civil War, he
was accused of taking the lead in the sale, as it was called,
of Charles I. to the English; he had ruined the broken
army of the Engagers; he had helped to pass the Act of

31

Classes; if he had brought Charles II. back to Scotland, it
was across the dead body of Montrose, and at the cost of
the king's honour, for he was compelled to sign the
Covenant. Argyll was supposed to have entangled Charles
in some sort of engagement to his own daughter, Lady
Anne, though it was more probable that the idea of the
match came from the Royalist side, and he certainly, when
the king was in his power, and sorely bestead, made Charles
sign a promise to pay him a debt of £40,000. This sum
seems to be the unpaid portion of Argyll's share of the
arrears of the Scottish troops who served in England against
Charles I.: the first portion was paid when the king was
delivered over to the English at Newcastle.

All these facts made it highly imprudent in Argyll, who,
to add to his offences, was now allied with the detested
Remonstrants, to leave his lochs and impenetrable hills, and
present himself at St. James's. He knew, better than any
one, the part he had taken in aiding the leaders of the
English army of occupation, when they were opposed by
his own son, Lord Lorne, and by the Earl of Glencairn,
in 1653-54, after the general indemnity given by Charles II.,
early in 1651. He knew what letters he had written to the
English commanders, and though he had later furnished
Charles with money, the score against him was long and
black, and endorsed by Glencairn, Middleton, and other
Cavaliers who were in the royal favour.

He arrived in London, he went to St. James's; it is
said that in the ante-chamber Hyde (Clarendon) rebuffed
him; his last chance, for he might even now have escaped.
But he carried that stricken, sallow, soured face which his
latest portrait shows, and the gleyed eyes of one who, in
Evelyn's aviary, mistook turtle-doves for owls, into the light
of a hundred candles, a glittering crowd, and before the
eyes of the king. Charles was not by nature resentful or
cruel; he was too light-hearted, too *nonchalant*, too good-
natured. But that face of Argyll reminded him of un-
speakable shames, dishonours, and disgraces, of deliberate
perjuries, of the mangled limbs of Montrose, spiked on a

gate under which he had passed. He sent his visitor to the Tower, whence, in December 1660, the sometime dictator of Scotland was taken by sea to Edinburgh, where he was lodged in the Castle.

Mackenzie, and the rest of Argyll's advocates, though they knew it not, had a hopeless cause to plead. The Indemnity of 1651 covered their client's conduct, as we saw, up to that date, from the consequences of all his actions against the Crown from 1638 to 1651. After the Cromwellian occupation, he could plead that "compliance" with the English conquerors was due to *force majeure*: that all men were guilty, even Lochiel and Glengarry, who were present at the proclamation of Richard Cromwell at Inverlochy.

But the truth was that Argyll had run too cunning, and had committed himself. In 1653, when his eldest son, Lord Lorne, had ridden off to join the Highlanders and others in arms against the Cromwellian Government, Argyll had solemnly cursed Lorne, and had sent a copy of the curse to Lilbourne, the English officer. No doubt he was merely playing the old game, the father on one side, the eldest son on the other, though the loyalty of Lorne is beyond impeachment. But he did not succeed in "playing for safety." He assisted Colonel Cobbett to take Douart Castle, the strength of the royalist Macleans in Mull, so Glencairn reported to Charles. Lilbourne writes to Cromwell, Sept. 13, 1653, that by intelligence sent from the Marquis of Argyll, Sept. 3, Cobbett entered Mull, and took in the strong castle of Douart.[1] Argyll went far beyond passive compliance, and he thus dealt a stroke, which had terrible consequences for his son, at his old foes, the Macleans, while Charles II. was then aware that the English boasted of Argyll's assistance, and Charles told this to Lorne by letter. Glencairn, the leader of the Royalist rising, then asked Charles to proclaim Argyll a traitor, as having been with the English at the taking of Douart, and as having "hindered all this summer's service."

."The Marquis of Argyll is resolved to engage in blood

---

[1] *Scotland and the Commonwealth*, Scottish History Society, p. 221.

with us," Monk wrote to Cromwell, (July 17, 1654,) and Argyll's clansmen were in the pay of the English. "The hate of the country is heavy on Argyll," in 1659. Yet Monk detested him and thought him utterly treacherous. Two days before the Restoration, (May 29, 1660,) Argyll and Mr. Patrick Gillespie, a Remonstrant, whom Charles above all men especially detested, "with a world at their back," held a Communion of the wilder sort at Paisley.[1] On February 13, 1661, he was presented at the Bar of Parliament, and accused of treason by Sir John Fletcher, the King's Advocate.

In his indictment were many charges dating before the Indemnity of 1651, including the burning of the Bonny House of Airlie, the arrangement to hand over Charles I. to the English at Newcastle; the opposition to the rescue of Charles I.; advice to Cromwell and Ireton to behead the king, (this was certainly a false charge,) and the abetting and furnishing of arms to the English in 1653-1654.

He put himself at the king's mercy: this offer was refused by Parliament. He denied, or justified himself, as regards the mass of accusations, and, as to the affairs of 1653-54, "denies any joining with the English to oppose the Scots forces;" he was, he says, a prisoner in the hands of the English. The pay of his men by the English meant no more than keeping up what was later called "an independent company" to maintain order, and pursue cattle thieves. "Because his men did not oppose the Royalist forces in the hills Monk discharged payment," did not pay.

Wodrow, who is very copious in his account of the trial of the Marquis, does not know, or cannot bring himself to tell, the cause of his condemnation (May 25). The real facts were doubted or denied by his partisans in later history, though they were briefly indicated by Bishop Burnet in his *History of his Own Times*. The truth came out when, in 1821, a fragmentary historical work, *Memoirs of the Affairs of Scotland*, by Sir George Mackenzie, was published, and, since that date, some of Argyll's damning letters have been given to the world.

[1] Baillie, iii p. 404,

In the fragmentary manuscript, *Memoirs of the Affairs of Scotland*, Mackenzie tells the story of the defence of his great client. He and the other counsel for the defence protested "that as some things might escape them which might be interpreted as treason, what we pleaded or spoke might be no snare to us." Parliament did not admit the protestation. Counsel also asked that Argyll might be tried by a Justice Court; Parliament men were not his peers. Argyll put in this request; he was asked who had written it; he would not betray his advocate, "and at last *we* owned the paper. The bill was refused, but we were excused." The King's Advocate, by the king's desire, "restricted his pursuits to such acts as were done since the year 1651."

Lauderdale, then in London and in possession of the king's favour, was supposed, says Mackenzie, to have procured the document surreptitiously, to protect his own friends, and to "have shuffled it in among other papers," for Charles's signature, "when his Majesty was in haste." But the good-natured king hated to hang people, as he scribbled in a note handed to Clarendon at the Council table at Oxford; the notes are in the Bodleian Library, and have been published for the Roxburghe Club.

It was thought that Lauderdale, from respect to his own old cause, "the good old Cause for which the Marquis mainly suffered," says Mackenzie, and out of kindness to Lorne, would save Argyll. But Middleton, the King's Commissioner, himself a hard fighting cavalier, though he had been in arms for the Covenant before the Engagement, sent to Court Rothes and Glencairn, (who had wished Argyll to be proclaimed a traitor in 1653,) and Glencairn daily incensed Monk, while Rothes worked on Lauderdale, who might fear that Argyll, if acquitted, would renew an old feud with him.

The contest turned on Argyll's dealings in 1653-54. Sufficient proof was not produced; debate was closed; Parliament was about to consider its verdict, when a man of clan Campbell "knocked most rudely at the door," and handed a packet to Middleton.

There was a pause and a deep silence. Hope may have

risen in the heart of Argyll, if he merely heard that the
rude and hurried messenger wore the tartan of Clan
Diarmaid. But, if he saw the man's face, he must have
guessed the worst. All the Campbells were not loyal to
him, and this man served his deadly foe, MacNaughton.

As the bearer of the packet was a Campbell, Middleton
himself naturally supposed him to be an envoy, (probably
from Lord Lorne, who was pleading for his father's life
in London,) with a pardon for the Marquis. But this
Campbell was a retainer of MacNaughton, whose ruined
castle of Dunderawe stands on the shore of Lochfyne,
near Inveraray, and whose lands lay between those of
Argyll and those of the Campbells of Ardkinglas.

A scurrilous poem on Argyll, "to be sold at the new
Mercat of Inveraray, 1656," begins—

> " How now, Argyll, thinkst thou to stand
> With thy deep plots and bloody band?
> There must no house stand near to thee,
> But Ahab-like thy prize must be,
> If MacNaughton brooked on its raw
> For forged crymes he tholes the law."

The meaning is that Argyll used MacNaughton as Ahab
used Naboth, and MacNaughton had his revenge when his
retainer, a Campbell, brought the fatal packet.[1]

It really contained, says Mackenzie, "a great many
letters," written by Argyll to Monk while he commanded in
Scotland. Of these many letters a few, to Lilbourne and to
Monk's secretary, exist at Inveraray. Even they were enough
to prove that Argyll's conduct was complicity, not compliance, with the English.[2] They were by no means "private"

[1] The date of the poem, 1656, is intended to prove the rhymes to be prophetic:
they must be of 1661, so the Higher Criticism will aver. But it is not so certain,
for the prophecy contains an item never fulfilled. Argyll will beg in vain for the
original lands of his family, near Loch Awe.

[2] These letters came into the possession of the late Duke of Argyll on November
5, 1874, from what source we are not told (Sir William Fraser, in *Hist. MSS.
Com. Report*, vi. 607). They are published in the same volume, p. 617, in summary;
they were written to Monk, Lilbourne, and Clerk, Monk's secretary. In the article
on the Marquis of Argyll in the *Dictionary of National Biography*, Mr. T. F. Hen-

and friendly letters to Monk, who was accused of betraying friendship. "No sooner were these produced, but the Parliament was fully satisfied as to the proof of the compliance," and Argyll was convicted and condemned, "though his own carriage drew tears from his very enemies," says Mackenzie. "And I remember, that I having told him, a little before his death, that the people believed he was a coward, and expected he would die timorously, he said to me he would not die as a Roman braving death, but he would die as a Christian without being affrighted." Argyll's was not military courage, perhaps, but in his death he did honour to his name; and public sympathy veered round to the lately detested chief.

Mackenzie, pleading for Argyll, excused his own "unripeness both in years and experience," and discussed the question "Whether passive compliance in public rebellions be punishable as treason?" Unluckily Argyll's compliance had not been merely passive, as was proved after Mackenzie had spoken.[1] He hints no doubt, in his *Memoirs of the Affairs of Scotland*, that the "great many letters" contained sufficiently damning proof.

His sympathy was clearly with his client. In defending Argyll he pointed out to the Parliament, (as, indeed, did Middleton himself,) that the new Indemnity for Scotland had not yet been issued, and that, if they condemned Argyll for "compliance" they made a dangerous precedent against themselves, for all had, at one time or another, "complied" and been in Argyll's situation. If they were severe against Argyll, they, like the Earl of Morton, who brought a kind of guillotine, the Maiden, into Scotland, might be introducing an instrument for their own destruction. This argument, with others, might have saved Argyll, but no members of Parliament, probably, had compromised themselves as Argyll's letters to the English commanders in Scotland proved *him* to have done. In face of these Mackenzie's eloquence was

derson says that these letters are only known through Bishop Burnet's account of them. Burnet, pt. i. vol. 1, pp 224-225 (ed. 1897).

[1] *Works*, vol. i.; *Pleadings*, pp 80-84: 1716.

unavailing. He had shown ability, and courage, a virtue in which he never was deficient; but his defence of Argyll, though perilous, was only part of his professional work, and did not commit him to the party of covenanted Presbyterianism.

In 1661, as we learn from the Acts of Parliament, Mackenzie appeared in many important cases; for Montrose against the estate of Argyll, on which he asserted some claims; for the Argylls in other cases; for Mackintosh against Lochiel, and in many suits of less moment. He was in wonderfully good practice for so young a man.[1]

---

[1] ARGYLL'S COMPROMISING LETTERS.

I owe the following note to the kindness of Dr. Barty:—

"According to the present practice in trials with a Jury before the Scotch Criminal Courts no witness for the prosecution can be examined whose name is not contained in the list of witnesses served on the accused, and no article can be produced of essential importance that is not mentioned in the list of productions. It would be impossible, therefore, at the present time that such an occurrence as the production of Argyll's letters to Monk after the evidence for the prosecution had been led could happen. It seems, however, as far as one can see from Mackenzie's own book, not to have been thought an irregular or improper thing in the seventeenth century. I observe in Mackenzie's *Criminal Law*, page 524, (1678,) that he refers to the letters thus. 'And yet the Marquess of Argile was convict of treason upon letters written by him to General Monck, these letters being only subscribed by him and not holograph, and the subscriptions having been proved *per comparationem literarum* which were very hard in other cases; seeing *comparatio literarum* is but a presumption, and men's hands are oft times and easily imitated, and one man's write will differ from itself at several occasions.' Strictly speaking Monk should have been forthcoming as a witness, but they did strange things in those days in their criminal trials "

CHAPTER V

MACKENZIE AS A DEFENDER OF WITCHES

Mackenzie appointed Justice Depute (1660–1661)—Presides on Trials for
Witchcraft—Abates the frenzy against Witches—The frenzy during the
English occupation—Statistics of Witchcraft in 1661—Stereotyped
formula of confession—A "pricker" at once arrested—Confessions
extracted by illegal torture—Case of the Macleans—Later recrud-
escence of persecution—Temporary abatement due to Mackenzie—
Fountainhall's credulity—Mackenzie on the Law of Witchcraft—The
Judges condemned—Judicial processes—*Jugement del Pais*—Lairds
and Ministers accuse and try—Torture in most cases—Anecdote of
Mackenzie and a confessing witch—Mackenzie's defence of Maevia—
He does not deny possibility of witchcraft—His reasons—Humanity of
Mackenzie—Excommunicated for his humanity (and other offences)
—Letter to Lauderdale—Resigns his office—A later letter to Lauder-
dale—Judge in Criminal Courts—Introduces rules favourable to the
accused—Salaries of Judges very small.

MACKENZIE's defence of Argyll rather advanced than injured
him in his profession. In November 1660, the king appointed him and on July 25, 1661, he was promoted by
Lauderdale, to a judicial post, that of Justice Depute, which
was very poorly paid, at £50 a year, but gave him experience
and, I think, enabled him to do good service to the cause of
common sense, and of a humanity then very uncommon.

Mackenzie, with two other Justice Deputes, Alexander
Blair and John Cuningham, was ordered at once to hold
Courts at towns near Edinburgh, such as Duddingstone,
Musselburgh, and Dalkeith, to try the cases of "a great many
persons, both men and women, who are imprisoned as having
confessed, or witnesses led against them, for the abominable
sin of witchcraft."[1]

To stimulate the zeal of these young Judges, they were

[1] *Privy Council Register*, 1661–1664, pp. 11, 12.

actually promised a share of "the fines and escheats" of prisoners found guilty! This was a premium upon severity, but Mackenzie saved as many as he could of the unfortunate men and women whom he pitied ; and it seems probable that he, with his fellow Deputes, did much to abate the frenzy for accusing people of sorcery.

Few could guess at the heights to which that frenzy had risen. The English, while they occupied Scotland, were surprised and horrified by the tortures which the lairds inflicted, with the sanction and assistance of the preachers, on witches and warlocks. In one horrible case, reported by the *Mercurius Politicus* of October 23, 1652, the English judges "ordered the minister, sheriff, and tormentors to be found out, and to have an account of the ground of their cruelty." They had hung women up by the heels, whipped them, and placed lighted candles beneath their toes and in their mouths. These appear to have been the usual methods of extorting confessions. The English may have kept down the insane fury of witch-burning among a superstitious clergy, gentry, and populace ; at all events the numbers of those who had been tortured into confession and were lying in loathsome prisons awaiting judgment is amazing. In three-quarters of one year, (1661–1662,) I reckon that eighty persons were awaiting judgment in the regions of Duddingstone, Dalkeith, Musselburgh, Newbattle, Spott, Stirling, Queensferry, Inner-leithen, Eyemouth, Crichton, Forfar, Selkirk, Flisk, Inverkip, Falkland, Montrose, and so forth. Some had lain in durance for three years, others for shorter periods. Most of them had already confessed to a kind of formula which is stereotyped as to the central facts, but varies in details. The accused is always made to allege that she met the devil in the shape of a black man, that he laid one hand on her head and another on her feet, that she gave herself body and soul to him, and became his mistress, receiving from him a new name. There are eight of these confessions in the papers of the Privy Council, for May 28–31, 1661.[1]

---

[1] *Privy Council Register*, pp. 647–651.

How these confessions were extorted we gather from the *Privy Council Register* of August 2, 1661, just five days after Mackenzie and the other two Justice Deputes were sent to hold their court of inquiries. The Council orders the arrest of John Ramsay, "an ordinary pricker of witches, to answer for the pricking of Margaret Tait, *who immediately thereafter died*."[1]

Probably the Justices had informed against this man Ramsay. On April 1, 1662, we find John Kincaid imprisoned, "for taking upon him the pricking and trying of witches, whereby in all probability many innocents have suffered." Kincaid, by some influence or other, escaped punishment. On April 10, 1662, the Privy Council issued an Act to this effect: "We, being certainly informed that a great many persons, in several parts of this kingdom, have been apprehended and hurried to prison, pricked, tortured, and abused," under suspicion of witchcraft, forbid any man, without legal warrant, to arrest any one on this charge. Persons legally arrested are to be tried according to the known laws of the land, "without any pricking or torture but by order," from the Judges of the Court of Session, or the Privy Council. In issuing commissions for trials, torture is always forbidden. But it had already been *illegally* used to extort confessions.

We find a cause of torture on July 3, 1662,[2] when Maclean of Dowart enters a petition for a score of persons of his clan imprisoned by Chisholm of Comer, as witches, because he could not evict them from their lands by any legal process. He tortured the women by depriving them of sleep, hanging them up by the thumbs, applying fire to the soles of their feet, and dragging them at horses' tails. These were not Highland methods, they were borrowed from the Lowland practice, as we have seen. One woman has died, one has gone mad, "and all of them have confessed whatever they were pleased to demand of them." Such cases of people awaiting trial after confession swarm in the *Register*, but, before Mackenzie resigns his Justice Deputeship in 1663, they have ceased to

[1] *Privy Council Register*, p 198.   [2] Ibid.

appear. I therefore deem it highly probable that the reports of witch cases presented by him and his companions in office to the Government, had, for the time, discouraged the witch hunters, and had saved " many innocents," in the words of the Privy Council, from imprisonment, torture, and death at the stake.

Though the efforts of Mackenzie and his companions appear to have produced salutary effects, for a time, the fury of witch-burning was not exorcised. Fountainhall, in his *Historical Notices* for 1677, gives cases of great cruelty and absurdity: a hysterical or wicked girl brought a dozen poor wretches to the stake in that year in the west; several were burned at Haddington; two, in 1678, at Prestonpans; eight or ten were in another affair, and one poor woman complained of having been tortured by Gowan, a pricker. His defence was that he had been a pupil of the notorious Kincaid. The Council, of which Mackenzie was a member, caused the woman's innocence to be proclaimed in her parish church, and again announced the illegality of torture by those amateurs. They imprisoned the pricker.[1]

In 1662 the temporary disappearance of the usual commissions to ministers and country gentlemen for the trial of witches *who have already confessed*, must be due to the humanity and sense of Mackenzie, Cuningham, and Blair. This is a fair inference from Mackenzie's own statement of his opinion about witchcraft, at that time a matter of faith, as all the world knows, with Joseph Glanvil, F.R.S., and Sir Matthew Hale.

In his chapter on Witchcraft, in *Laws and Customs of Scotland in Matters Criminal*, Mackenzie argues as elsewhere in his speech for " Maevia." Though we hear so little of witchcraft in the history of Israel, still, as Mackenzie says, it is condemned in the legal books of the Old Testament; therefore " the most mysterious of crimes " must be an actual crime; moreover its existence is assumed by the laws of Scotland. In all cases, however, " the most convincing pro-

---

[1] Fountainhall, *H. N.*, I. pp. 143 *et seq.*, 197–202.

bation" should be demanded, "and I condemn, next to the witches themselves, these cruel and too forward judges who burn persons by the thousand as guilty of this crime." "The accused are usually poor ignorant creatures," the simplest are tried for the most mysterious crime: one poor victim, harried by torture and preachings, asked, " Could a woman be a witch without knowing it ? "

The usual process, as Mackenzie shows, and as the Register of Privy Council proves, arose in a *fama*, or public rumour, current commonly against a woman, though men were also burned, for curing diseases, practically, by suggestion. Then the Kirk Session took the matter up ; an ignorant laird or other busybody imprisoned the poor wretch, starved her, deprived her of sleep, tortured her, (wholly against law,) and had her extorted confessions recorded.

Mackenzie shows the worthlessness of these ravings, but the confessions are sent to the Privy Council, which gives a commission for a trial by burgh magistrates, preachers, or lairds, or all three. The accused is not represented by counsel. A threatening word, followed by any accident to the menaced person, is regarded as proof of witchcraft, then comes the burning. " I know for certain that most of all that were ever taken were tormented, and this usage was the ground of all their confessions ; and albeit the poor miscreants cannot prove this usage, the actors being the only witnesses, yet the Judges should be afraid of it, as that which did at first elicit the confession, and for fear of which they should not retract it."

Mackenzie, when Justice Depute, had constantly to attend witch trials, as we have seen. He tells how a poor old woman that had confessed, gave him her reasons. She wished to be out of a world where none would employ and defend her, and men would set dogs at her. Assizes of the neighbours hardly ever acquit, and ministers are "indiscreet in their zeal," as we learn from many an anecdote in Wodrow's *Analecta*. In a certain kind of cases, Mackenzie thinks conviction for witchcraft just, namely when the accused are *proved* to have exercised " sympathetic magic," as we call it, by burning or pricking puppets taken to represent persons whom they are *proved* to hold in hatred. Here we have the evil intention ; and often, by dint of suggestion, the resulting mischief. But tales of metamorphosis and other silly stories Mackenzie inclines to regard as purely impossible. As far as he dared, he counteracted the baneful superstitions fostered by the clergy in England and Scotland, and by judges like Sir Matthew Hale.

An example of the details of a case of witchcraft, in which Mackenzie was counsel for the defence, is that of " Maevia." Maevia, his client, was accused of laying a disease on a woman by a charm, and of taking it off by another charm. Probably she would have been condemned, for it was not denied that, after she had whispered to the woman, the woman was " distracted," and that after she had applied a plantain leaf to the patient's head, and a paper with the name of Jesus, the woman recovered. Maevia had harmed and healed by " suggestion," as we say now, by witchcraft, as they said then. Mackenzie argued that the disease must be proved to be *abnormal,* like disgorging fragments of broken glass, a very common symptom, due to hysterical trickery. The cool plantain leaf was a *normal* cure : the charm with the name of Jesus could not be a gift from the Devil !

The story, told by two penitent witnesses, that Maevia flew with them in the form of a dove was, in itself, " very ridiculous," an hallucination of " melancholy heads," sent by the Devil. Torture was used to procure false confessions. " Poor innocents die in multitudes by an unworthy martyrdom, and burning comes in fashion through the fancies of ordinary judges."

Mackenzie did not dare publicly to deny the possibility of witchcraft, first, because the Bible alleged it; next, because the law of the land proclaimed it; again, he does not know (as Faraday did) the limits of possibility; though he does think that a woman could not assume the shape of a bird. The confessions, being the result of delirium caused by want of sleep and food, and by torture, are not evidence. A preacher told a poor woman that "the Devil would challenge a right to her," after she was said to be his servant, and would haunt her, and so she desired to "confess and die." This explanation of her confession she gave to Mackenzie "when I was Justice Depute."

We may conceive the number of burnings, when we note eighty recorded cases of trials in less than a year, and remember that "I have observed that scarce ever any who were accused before a Country Assize of neighbours did escape that trial." In 1661–1662, eleven persons, in one small town, were awaiting judgment and the fiery death. Mackenzie inveighs against the arrest of a suspected witch by any one, without any warrant, almost in the terms of the Act of Council which, while he was Justice Depute, forbade these practices. He denounces as "villainous cheats" the "prickers" who searched for "anæsthetic areas," and though two were arrested while he was Justice Depute, another was active, and was seized, in 1666.[1]

Thus speaks "Bluidy Mackenzie." If we take another famous Scottish lawyer of this period, Lord Fountainhall, we find, as Mr. Crawford says, that he "frequently mentions torture, but without comment." However, if not in his *Journal* in his other works, Fountainhall makes comments enough. "Possibly he had some misgiving," adds Mr. Crawford.[2] He was deeply superstitious ; witch trials "gave him uneasiness," but he *published* no such plea for sense and mercy as Mackenzie offered in his book on Crimes, to which Fountainhall often refers in his notes on law cases.

Even prejudice, perhaps, can scarcely deny that Mackenzie displays, in reference to the most unfortunate class of the community, strong sense and sympathetic kindness. The so-called witches were usually old and poor, and from the boy in the street to the preacher and the laird, every hand was against them. A very marked decline, nay, a cessation of charges of witchcraft, followed the Proclamation of the

---

[1] Works, vol. ii. pp. 84–95.   [2] *Lauder of Fountainhall's Journals*, p xxxviii.

Council, the arrest of prickers, and the inquiry held on a witch-hunting preacher, during Mackenzie's brief tenure of the almost unpaid office of Justice Depute. He tells Lauderdale, in a letter, that he had no salary, and that some of the cases which he tried, "went against his conscience." In a later year, Mackenzie's efforts for the protection of poor people accused of sorcery were made one of the charges on which Mr. Donald Cargill excommunicated him !

Mackenzie scarcely ever dated his letters. We know that he resigned the office of Judge Depute on December 8, 1663.[1] But in his letter, dated "March 5" without date of year, he says that he "would like" to demit the employment of a Justice Depute, but is loath to abandon anything that is a mark of Lauderdale's favour. He has told the Council that he will reserve his "dimission" till he has Lauderdale's answer. He speaks of presenting to Lauderdale his MS. on "The Genealogies of the Families of Scotland."[2] In another letter to Lauderdale of 1667 (?), he mentions his arrears of pay (as Justice Depute) and his reorganisation of his Court. The letter is in terms rather obscure, and is appended in a note : others may understand the situation better than I do.[3]

---

[1] *Decreta*, p 437.   [2] *Malet Papers, Add. MSS.* 32,094 ; f. 260.

[3] Sir George Mackenzie of Rosehaugh *to* (address awanting, but evidently John, Earl of Lauderdale), 5th November (1667 ?)

"MY LORD,—The Exchequer recommended to his Majestie my petition wherin I crav'd the discharge of a thousand merks due by mee to them, and that in *satisfaction of all my arrears as Justice Deput* ; bot I lye at the poole becaus no man helps mee to get in ; and yet I could have as many recomendations from your friends as might satisfie the publisher of a booke, if I designd not to ow it, amongst many other favours to the Earle of Lauderdaill's generositie.

"I will not ascrybe to others your civilities nor desyr I to have two creditors for one debt. Neither wold I think this affaire worthie of your trouble if by not getting a favourable returne the Exchequer and others heer wold not conclud that I wer guilty of such crymes as might render mee uncapable of justice. For, seriuslie, the desyr of that petition was judgd most just becaus I had servd constantly, and if souldiers who killd on man at most in two years wer weel payd, should not I who killd hundreths" [this is unintelligible to me] "and more justly and without any self defence, as they did, expect som acknowlegment. I ordourd and establisht the reeling forces and brought the lousnesse of that court to som method ; and yet I dare not plead merit, albeit I might adde that I lost a hundreth pounds sterling yearly by wanting the employment of ane advocat.

"In the vaccance now I writ our criminall law in Latin and our criminall pleadings

Mackenzie was paid at last: we have his receipt of March 2, 1668. The papers are in the Laing MSS. (Library of Edinburgh University). "That Court" of which he speaks, I understand to be the Criminal branch of the Court of Justiciary. Mackenzie in his *Vindication* (1691) says that when he was a Judge in the Criminal Court "he ordered for the good of the people the remedy of Exculpation, whereby the Defendant, representing that he has some defences, a warrant is given to force the witnesses whom he names to appear," this order was turned into an Act (XVI. 3 Sess. Parl. 2, Charles II., Article II.).[1]

Mackenzie did not lose his practice at the Bar when Justice Depute, though his practice must have been impaired and interrupted. He would lose more as a Judge in the Criminal Court. Judges were very ill-paid, and eked out their salary, often, by receiving "compliments" from suitors. The Lord President of the Court of Session had a salary of £350, and Sir George Lockhart, when President, looked wistfully back on the Bar where he made a better income. The King's Advocate, before 1707, got but £550 annually.[2] Probably no barrister's practice was worth £700 a year.

in our own tongue, as the French writ ther pleadings   This I say to recomend me to your Lordships favoure, who is the true protector of your nation, and not to get my thousand merks, which I value not so much for any reason as that the world may know that you ar just and that you hav some kyndnesse for, Your Lordships' most humble servant,

(*Signed*)   "GEO. MACKENZIE.

"EDINBURGH 5 *November*."

[1] *Vindication*, p. 29 (1691)
[2] Omond, *Lord Advocates of Scotland*, vol. i p. 290.

CHAPTER VI

"THE RELIGIOUS STOIC"

Mackenzie publishes *The Religious Stoic* (1663)—Vivacity and style—
Contains his principles—Opposed to pretensions of preachers—Dis-
believes in speculative Theology—"Why stand ye gazing up into
Heaven?"—The Zealots derided—Wandering fires—Heretics are like
tops—Law must be obeyed—Bloodthirsty paganism of the Covenanters—
Persecutors amazed when persecuted—The Restoration did not persecute for Religion—Views of Mr. Taylor Innes—Mackenzie's view not
tenable by the Presbyterians—How far the subject may dissemble
his belief—Religious hatred concerning trifles—Belief changes with
the point of view—Piety preferred to speculation—"I make the laws
of my country my Creed"—In unessential matters—Mr. Taylor
Innes shocked—Where Mackenzie drew the line in submission—At
Catholicism—Scottish zest for persecution—"Man a statue of dust,
kneaded with tears"—*Instinctive* belief in Deity—Mackenzie a Christian
Stoic—Will not discuss the Fall—Answer of his opponents—Mackenzie
anticipates Pascal's bet—"Preaching no part of public worship"—Why
the heathen had no sermons—Claim of the preachers to miraculous
gifts—Prophecy, Clairvoyance—Mackenzie's theory of the supernormal—Anticipates that of Mr. Frederick Myers—Denounces Conventicles—Anecdote of Mackenzie and the Liturgy—"Wily Jamie
Stewart"—Really "a damned Macgregor"—Revenge of Gregarach.

IN 1663, before he was twenty-five years of age, Mackenzie
published his book, *The Religious Stoic.* Though it effer-
vesces with the high spirits of youth, though the soil
of the argument blossoms with a hundred lively tropes and
similes, now poetical, now fantastic, this work expresses
the principles to which Mackenzie was true, (with perhaps
a period of other ideas, indicated in his Memoirs,) to the
end. He had already speculated much on ultimate problems
of life, of government, and of religion. He had seen the
ruin that came from Knoxian ideas, and from clerical
pretensions. These things had waxed old as a garment,
their end was nigh. He practically abandoned speculative

48

theology as hopeless, and there is melancholy as well as gaiety in his glances at the ruins of so many systems.

He opens with "A Friendly Address to the Fanatics of All Sects and Sorts," and heads the address with the text, "Ye men of Galilee, why stand ye gazing up into Heaven?" Ye are not St. Stephen, ye shall not see heaven open, ye gaze in vain, the everlasting gates will not be unfolded, no mortal eyes will behold the Beatific Vision, no human scrutiny will discover the secrets of God. *Une immense espérance a traversée la terre;* we know enough for Faith, enough for Hope, enough for Charity, but we do not know and in this life shall never know enough for Curiosity.

Mackenzie unconsciously opens with two lines of blank verse—

> "The madcap zealots of this bigot age
> Intending to mount Heaven, Elias-like,"

unlike Elias, and like Phaethon, have fallen earthward in their flaming chariot; "and when they have set the whole world in a blaze, this they term 'a new Light.'" The furiously driving Jehu, full of zeal, did more harm to the House of God than Gallio, who cared for none of these things. The only members of the Apostolic conclave who desired to call down fire from heaven, were those sons of Zebedee, (and of Thunder) who desired the first seats, not in synagogues, but in the kingdom of Heaven. Fever-fits of unseasonable zeal, as of the Covenanters, the Brownists, the Quakers, all the sort of them, are a malady of the Church, which is "in a very distempered condition, when its charity waxes cold and its zeal hot." The trivial differences and the fury with which they are fought for, (as when a Kirk with the Confession of Faith of 1560, the Shorter Catechism, and extempore prayers, revolts against law on a question of Bishop or presbyter,) "is that *ignis fatuus* or wild fire, which is but a meteor patched up of malignant vapours, and is observed to haunt churchyards oftener than other places."

Mackenzie does not applaud individualism, and the sanctity of private judgment in religion. "I am of opinion,

D

that such as think that they have a Church within their own breasts, should likewise believe their heads are steeples, and so should provide them with bells. . . . Elias believed that the Church, in his days, was stinted to his own person," just as the Rev. Robert Bruce, about 1630, and the Rev. Donald Cargill, about 1681, are said to have regarded themselves as the only lawful ministers in Scotland. If Laws and Lawgivers did not make heretics conceited, "by taking too much notice of their extravagancies, the world should no more be troubled with these than they are with the Chimaeras of Alchymists and Philosophers. And it fares with heretics as with tops, which, so long as they are scourged, keep foot and run pleasantly, but fall as soon as they are neglected and left to themselves."

This is one of Mackenzie's best known sayings, and has been thought inconsistent with his later career as a persecutor. But he explains that while persecution for *religious* opinion is unjust, "God leaving us, upon our own hazard, a freedom in our choice," none the less " I confess when men not only recede from the canonised creed of the Church, but likewise encroach upon the laws of the State, then, as of all others they are the most dangerous, so of all others they should be most severely punished."

It was the firm belief of the rulers of the Restoration that rigid Presbytery was the mother of civil war, or at least of eternal unrest. For their opinion they had the experience of a century of troubles. The State therefore made laws which left religion where it had been, left worship where it had been,[1] save for the use of the Doxology and the Lord's Prayer, but placed the preachers under bishops, for the sake of the peace of the country. They did not thus ensure the peace which they sought, but they made its existence possible in the next generation.

---

[1] I may be in error, but I presume that the Confession of the Convention of 1560 had not been abolished. Kirkton, however, says that the restored Episcopal Church "owned no confession of faith," save a " a general and short" one, "both nonsense and heresy," in the Acts of Parliament. The young divines were so lost as to "plough with the heifers" of Sherlock and Jeremy Taylor, "and such." Kirkton, pp. 191, 192

The zeal of the Covenanters, said Mackenzie with perfect truth, "supposes our most merciful God to be of the same temper with these pagan deities, who desired to have their altars gored with blood." It was for the sake of cleansing blood with blood that the Commission of the General Assembly demanded the deaths of cavaliers taken under promise of quarter, and of women who had followed Montrose. It was in accordance with this pagan idea of purification by blood that the Rev. Mr. Nevoy, (who at this time fled to Holland,) urged Leslie to the massacre of Dunaverty.

There is no certainty so firmly based, says Mackenzie, that it "justifies so much violence in such things. Are we not ready to condemn to-day, as fanatic, what yesterday was judged *jure divino*. And do not even those who persecuted others for their opinions, admire why they should be, on that score, persecuted themselves?" He quotes the tenor of the Gospel, which is not that of the Koran, and "all this makes us admire why, in our late troubles, men really pious, and naturally sober, could have been so transported as to destroy whom they could not convince, and to persuade those who were convinced that Religion obliged them to destroy others."

Mr. Taylor Innes, in his admirable essay on Mackenzie,[1] writes, "His *Vindication* (1691) opens with the statement that 'the civil government in Scotland was never bigot' under Charles II., and on that account he thinks it unnecessary to consider either Episcopacy or Presbytery in themselves, neither of them having been held to be *jure divino*. We are inclined to think that the claim he here puts forward is a true one; nor perhaps is the other assertion which he goes on to make false, that 'the Governors of the time can truly and boldly say that no man in Scotland ever suffered for his religion.'" The religious opinions were a matter of indifference to the Government. "The standards of the Kirk" the confession of faith, were what they had been, unless a man chose to say, as men did say, that, according to their religion, "prelacy was a limb of Antichrist."

---

[1] *Contemporary Review*, vol. xviii. pp. 248–266, September 1871.

When Mackenzie writes, "As every private Christian should be tolerated by his fellow subjects to worship God inwardly according to his conscience, so should all conspire to that exterior uniformity of worship which the laws of his country enjoin." But there was no difference in exterior uniformity of worship among conformists and non-conformists, unless the latter thought it wrong to say the Lord's Prayer and to hear the Doxology. To the Government the quarrel was purely political; bishops were part of the Civil Service. To the thorough Presbyterian they were " priests of Baal."

This belief, and no other, was what Mackenzie thought that honest citizens might blamelessly dissemble. He himself would not have dissembled his disbelief in Transubstantiation; he would not even vote for relieving Catholics from penal laws.

Mackenzie could not help observing that "the meaner the subject" of contention "is, the heat is always the greater. Stand not some Episcopists and Presbyterians at greater distance than either do with Turks and Pagans." There is no use in religious controversy, he says. No man is ever convinced by argument. One man may account that a miracle which another looks upon as a folly, and yet none but God's Spirit can decide the controversy. "Matters of religion and faith resemble some curious pictures and optic prisms, which seem to change shapes and colours, according to the several stances from which the aspicient views them." Everything in our ideas of religion depends on the point of view. The right rule, in matters so fleeting, in a phantasmagoria so protean, is to regulate our conduct by "the Laws of our Country." Perhaps Presbytery is the best of Church governments, perhaps Episcopacy is; a wise man will accept, in matter so essentially trivial, the decision of the State in which he lives. "May not one who is convinced in his judgment that Monarchy is the best of Governments, live happily in Venice or Holland. . . . What is once statuted by a Law we all consent to, in choosing Commissioners to represent us in these Parliaments where the Laws are made; and so, if they ordain us to be decimated, or to leave the nation if we conform not, we cannot say when that Law is put into execution, that we are oppressed. . . ."

Yesterday, by the decree of the State (*de facto*) the Covenant was a thing of Divine Right; to-day, by the same decree, Royal Prerogative is of Divine Right, and the Covenant is a seditious rag.

"Since discretion opened my eyes," says Mackenzie, "I have always judged it necessary for a Christian to look oftener to his practice of piety, than to confession of faith . . . working out the work of his own salvation with fear and trembling, than standing still with the Galileans, curiously gazing up to heaven. True religion and undefiled is to visit the widow and the fatherless."

Mackenzie declares that, "in all articles not absolutely necessary for being saved, I make the laws of my country my creed," and adds, in a postscript, "By the laws of this country the author means that religion which is settled by law." By that he stands, "in all matters not absolutely necessary for salvation." Under the Covenant he was a Presbyterian, under the Restoration an Episcopalian. He did not think that the salvation of his soul was imperilled by one or the other form of Church Government, the religion, down to the Shorter Catechism, ("Proofs" and all,) being the same in both, and the worship identical, bar the use of the Lord's Prayer, (which cannot be dangerous,) and the Doxology, which seems orthodox.

After the Reformation the Scottish Protestants compelled, by many forms of persecution, the Catholics to accept for *their* Creed, the creed dictated by "the laws of their country." The Protestants did not regard this process "with loathing and indignation;" as we all do now: they thought it a godly process: "the idolater should die the death;" and, in short,—by fines, exile, disabilities, mob violence, oppression by Protestant landlords of Catholic tenants,—they very nearly extirpated the Catholic faith in their country.

The Government of the Restoration, by measures yet

more ferocious, left only "a misrepresented Remnant," true to the doctrines of Andrew Melville. This much may be said for persecution that, in Scotland as in Spain, it was successful. Catholicism and the Presbyterianism which attempted to erect an *imperium in imperio* were reduced to negligible quantities. We ought to regard with equal abhorrence the method which obtained both results.

Mackenzie now enters on his own doctrine of Christian Stoicism. "Albeit Man may be but a Statue of dust kneaded with tears, moved by the hid engines of his restless passions," yet he is a creature of boundless pride, who could never have admitted that there exists a Being greater than himself, if "a natural instinct . . . had not irresistibly bowed his faith to assent to a Deity." Religion is *natural* and inevitable.

Mackenzie's own religion is Christianity harmonised with what people called "natural religion," that of the Stoics, whom he regards as "perhaps a sect of John Baptist's," certainly an unhistorical position! His God is the God who revealed himself to Socrates, as to all men, in the "mirror" (so he calls it) of "instinct" and of "conscience." Like Tertullian, he thinks that the nations of old "*vocem Christianam naturaliter exclamant*," though many superstitions, in his own time, choke and confuse the *vox Christiana*. Revealed religion, that of Christ, restores and illuminates the instinct of faith. The mysteries of faith are not to be pried into. Borrowing an illustration from his favourite study, Heraldry, he says, "in religion as in heraldry, the simpler the bearing be, it is so much the purer and the ancienter." He desires as little theology as possible.

He declines to be drawn into those insoluble problems of foreknowledge and free will, that distracted Satan's Angels. He wishes religion to "drive at practice," to make men gentle, not ferocious. He will not discuss the Fall of Man, and "that forbidden fruit." "I think we should rather lament than inquire after so pitiful a frailty," as Adam's eating the apple. Mackenzie's attitude is the chief example, in Scotland, of the freedom which began to dawn with the Restoration after exactly a century of Presbyterian power.

He could now publish, in safety, doctrines "Arminian," "Latitudinarian," or what you will.

"The Fanatics inveigh against Presbyterian gowns. The Presbyterian tears the Episcopal lawn sleeves, and thinks them the Whore of Babel's shirt. The Episcopalian flouts at the Popish robes, as the livery of the Beast." Religion, he says, is, apparently, now old and dying; shaken by senile fever-fits. In the visible Church, "charity is cold, zeal is hot."

Mackenzie's book was certainly not apt to remove the prejudice of the godly against the Bar : he told ludicrous anecdotes of Puritan casuistry. A case of conscience among the godly was, "Is it lawful to use the herb tobacco on a Fast day ? " The answer was, tobacco may not be used in a pipe, for the smoke enters the mouth, but may be used in snuff, which is inhaled through the nose !

Mackenzie, admitting the difficulties of belief, anticipates Pascal's famous argument that, whether there be anything to believe in or not, belief is "safer." We ought, says Pascal, to put our money on belief ; it is even betting ; and Mackenzie avers that the death-beds of Atheists are awful warnings of the dangers of disbelief.

Mackenzie thought "preaching no part of divine worship." Few men can have suffered more than he from long sermons.. "The pulpit is a Calvary, whereon our Blessed Saviour suffers daily from scandalous railings," political, social, personal, and theological. The godly, after their twenty-two years of "ruling the roast," must have felt that Satan was unchained when such sentiments could be published in Edinburgh. Observing that the ancient heathen went to no sermons, Mackenzie supposes that the Legislator, in his wisdom, had forbidden harangues which were certain to prove inflammatory, and of perilous consequence to the State.. Of course, as a matter of fact, the nature of classical religion gave priests no chance of coercing the State by addresses to the populace. The priest of Zeus or Athene, however, was not believed to be inspired by the God, or to possess, what the Presbyterian preachers claimed, the "Power of the Keys."

What Mackenzie, and many men of his generation above all things desired, was a breathing space of peace in Scotland. From 1558 to the Restoration the country had been hurried up and down in religion through a mist of tears and blood, for the sake, not of Presbyterianism, but of the insane pretensions of the preachers. For bishops Mackenzie probably cared no more than Montrose had cared, that is, not at all; but the new generation, as Douglas said in his letters to Sharp before Charles II. returned, inclined to a moderate Episcopacy, manifestly in hopes of a quiet life.

But the pretensions of the preachers were backed, as we have seen, not only by their claim to possess the keys of St. Peter,—"those who offend them are sure to get it over the head with these keys," Mackenzie wrote,—but by the popular belief in their miraculous powers. Some of them were credited, and had been credited since the days of Knox and Bruce, with the gifts of prophecy, clairvoyance, second-sight, premonitions; with gifts of healing, and with marvellous visions. Hence came their perilous prestige. On this point Mackenzie writes, "Albeit the cessation of miracles be cried down," (he means "proclaimed,") "by many, yet do the most bigoted relate what miracles have been wrought by the founders of their hierarchies, and what prophecies they have oraculously pronounced." Thus Bishop Burnet tells us that Mr. Robert Bruce was credited with prophecies, but that his father had heard him frequently deliver oracles which never were fulfilled. Later, Peden and Richard Cameron were looked on as prophets, and there are many stories of clairvoyance and prediction, by preachers, especially in the case of Peden. The belief greatly increased the influence of these preachers among the people, and Mackenzie ventures on a theory of the phenomena, which he probably derived from the Neo-Platonists. It curiously resembles Mr. Myers's hypothesis of the "subliminal self," and he distinguishes between the "supernatural" and the "supernormal," though not in these terms. "I am almost inclined to believe," he says, "that prophecy is no Miraculous Gift, bestowed upon the Soul at extraordinary occasions only, but is the Natural though the Highest Perfection of our human Nature . . . since it must be Natural to the Soul, which is God's *Impressa*, to have a faculty of Foreseeing, since that is one of God's." Veridical dreams too, he says, are not "extraordinary," but "natural," and dying men sometimes show clear foresight, because "the soul then begins to act like itself."

Holding this theory, Mackenzie would neither burn a woman as a witch, because she was proved to be second-sighted, nor adore a preacher, because he had the second-sight. The faculty is no more than a natural faculty of the human spirit, which is *divinæ particula auræ*.

As for the conventicles of people who preferred the ministrations of an "outed" minister, to those of a conformist, "compared with our Jerusalem they resemble only the removed huts of those who live apart because they are sick of the plague." There could be no fair and useful discussion between Mackenzie and his adversaries ; indeed he maintains that all religious controversy is altogether vanity. No man looks for any useful light in his opponent's statements, he only seeks the readiest dialectical trick, or Biblical text, for their confutation. The preacher damns the lawyer, the lawyer accuses the preacher of treason. Both sides end by trusting to the arm of flesh, sword, musket and pistol, and the peace and quiet for which Mackenzie longed never visited Scotland during the Restoration. The contending parties had to destroy each other by a process of attrition. As vainly as Falkland, did Leighton "ingeminate Peace! Peace!"

In the confession of his *Religio Laici* Mackenzie does not indicate any preference for the Anglican or Laudian liturgy over the "conceived prayers" composed by the ministers. If we may believe a story in Wodrow's collection of gossip, the *Analecta* (iii. 257, 258), Mackenzie was opposed to a liturgy. Being in London in 1678, he, with a Scottish bishop, argued against an English bishop who stood up for the liturgy. Each party called in supporters, the Englishman brought two friends; Mackenzie brought a person whom he did not name, a person in a very negligent attire. The English bishop overcame the Scottish prelate in argument, Mackenzie was worsted, but the stranger interposed and triumphed all along the line.

He was James Stewart, "wily Jamie," a violent Presbyterian, who was in hiding, for he had been mixed up in the Pentland Rising of 1666, and was the author of a dangerous book, *Jus Populi Vindicatum.* We often meet him and his book in the following pages. Of his family, the Stewarts, Mackenzie is said to have exclaimed in court, after the trial of this scion, in 1684, that they were not Stewarts, they were "damned Macgregors!" Their father had chosen Stewart in place of "the name that is nameless by day."[1]

---

[1] Omond, *The Lord Advocates,* vol. i. p. 252. No authority is cited. The passage is from part of the *Coltness Papers,* written apparently by Sir Archibald Stewart Denham (born 1683, died 1773). I do not know who these Stewarts really were, but these old baronial claims were exploded by the learned Riddell, in the once famous Saltfoot Controversy. Naturally Sir Archibald Stewart Denham did not like Mackenzie, who had styled these Stewarts "bare-behinded Macgregors." Sir Archibald gives a lively character of Sir George, "A man of great vivacity and humour, but of undigested accomplishments. He pretended to know everything, and was superficial and vain-glorious, in all a perfect Proteous (*sic*) or a kind of cameleon," (like Maitland of Lethington in Buchanan's lumbering satire). "He changed figure, shape, and colour upon every whim and turn, he had no penetration, and what struck him first was his best thought. His governing passion was to make a land estate, and establish it from generation to generation in his Highland name, but Sir John Lauder of Fountainhall, Lord of Session, a good judge of men, (and from whose character of Sir George most said here is taken,) observes he laid a bad foundation by defrauding his father's creditors. . . ." Of this I find no evidence. Sir Archibald goes on to praise "the virtuous ingenious Earl of Argyll," "the martyr Earl of Argyll," who, according to this very Sir John Lauder of Fountainhall, constantly bilked and oppressed *his* father's creditors and his own It is unlucky to tell a Stewart that he is a bare-behinded damned Macgregor!— *The Coltness Collections,* The Maitland Club, pp. 75-80 (1842).

CHAPTER] VII

MACKENZIE'S HISTORY, POLITICS, POEMS, 1663-1668

Mackenzie's first marriage (1662)—His descendants through his daughters —His *History of his Own Times*—Comparison of Mackenzie with Bishop Burnet—Mackenzie's politics as traceable in his History— Singular fortunes of his History—A fragment discovered (1817)— Published in 1821—Character of its editor—When was the History written?—Lauderdale revised a History by Mackenzie—Could it be the Fragment?—Did Mackenzie write two Histories of which ours is the earlier?—His portrait of Middleton—His candour—Character of Lauderdale—Mackenzie on Lady Margaret Cassilis—Lauderdale in his night-gown—Mackenzie's sympathy with the poor—Episcopacy established—Expulsion of ministers blamed—Burnet's description of the ministers—Their parishes occupied by "owls and satyrs"— Middleton's attack on Lauderdale—Mackenzie of Tarbat is Middleton's agent—Probably he is the source of Mackenzie's information—"The Billeting Act"—Lauderdale saves the Earl of Argyll—Drives Middleton and Tarbat from office—Rothes in favour—His character—Mackenzie sympathises with Tarbat and Middleton—Execution of Waristoun— Oppressive policy of Rothes—Mackenzie dedicates to him a Moral Essay—Mackenzie corresponds with Evelyn—The south-west ready to rebel—Intrigues with Holland—Offers of Dutch aid—The Pentland Rising—Mackenzie defends the rebels—Rebels tortured—Mackenzie accused of responsibility for introduction of torture—The charge erroneous—Mackenzie's second marriage—Melancholy religious letter —Poem on Caelia—Letter to Evelyn—Verses on Montrose—Mackenzie's town-house.

BETWEEN the year 1661, when he defended Argyll, and 1663, when he published *The Religious Stoic*, Mackenzie's time was occupied by the discharge of his duties as Justice Depute, by his profession, and, more agreeably, by wooing and winning Elizabeth, daughter of George Dickson of Hartree, one of the Senators of the College of Justice. The marriage was in 1662. Of the children, the sons died young; from the eldest daughter descend the Marquis of Bute and the Earl of Wharncliffe.

These years of love-making were full of events, in which began the fierce ecclesiastical struggle of the Restoration. Concerning them, Mackenzie's opinions can only be divined dimly, through his fragmentary *Memoirs of the Affairs of Scotland.* He wished to be an historian as well as a legist, a moral essayist, a novelist, an authority on heraldry, a dramatist, and an orator. His play, to which he refers in a preface to his printed pleadings, is lost ; its very name is unknown. As an historian, he is acute and singularly impartial, he knows the inner wheels of the political machine, but he does not aim at the picturesque. We really are not in a position to criticise him as an historical writer, as will be seen when we presently examine the curious puzzle presented by his fragmentary work, styled *The Memoirs of the Affairs of Scotland.* It is by no means certain that he intended to give *this* work to the world ; not improbably he had decided to publish a more polished and literary composition.

As it is mainly from these Memoirs that we learn Mackenzie's opinion concerning public affairs in 1660 to 1663, and again from 1669 to 1677, it is necessary to explain, as far as possible, the singular fortunes of the book, and to discover the date of its composition.

The "proposals for" the publication, by subscription, of Mackenzie's collected works, were issued in 1714. They offered "many learned treatises of his, never before published," and the *Discourse concerning the three Unions between England and Scotland* was produced as an example of the fifteen manuscripts in the hands of Mackenzie's friends and family. But nothing like fifteen hitherto unprinted works are contained in the two folio volumes of 1716–1722, which also lack *Aretina* and *The Discovery of the Fanatick Plot* (1684), a folio now absolutely *introuvable.*

Among the fifteen manuscripts of the advertisement of 1714, mention was made of a *History of the Affairs of Scotland from the Restauration of King Charles II.,* 1660, *to* 1691. When the second volume of the posthumous folio edition (1722) of Mackenzie's collected writings was being printed, an advertisement announced that his History was in the hands of some of his relations, "who think it not ready for the press until it be carefully revised." The book was promised as an Appendix to the second volume of his works, after it had been "revised and transcribed by a good hand."

No more was heard of this History, till a century later, when in 1816 or 1817, a grocer of Edinburgh found a MS. book in a mass of waste papers "purchased by him for the humblest purposes of his trade." The grocer placed the MS. in the hands of the learned Dr. M'Crie, the biographer of Knox and Andrew Melville, who briefly describes it in *Blackwood's Magazine* for June, 1817. The book was in the writing of a copyist of the seventeenth century,[1] but had been corrected in Mackenzie's own hand. Dr. M'Crie gave extracts from this treasure, but unluckily he did not edit the whole, which was published, anonymously, by Mr. Thomas Thomson, in 1821. The contents, from 1663 to 1669, had been excised or lost, with all that followed 1677, if that part were ever completed, (as from the advertisement it appears to have been,) and there are other gaps in the volume, and lacunæ where documents were to be inserted.

The editor, Mr. Thomson of the Register House, was a man of great learning, but confused in his affairs, apt to procrastinate, and singularly averse to adding introductions and notes to his editions of old manuscripts. He meant to have written an introduction on Mackenzie's literary character, and the historical value of the Memoirs; and to have added an appendix of documents; so he wrote to Sir James Mackintosh (March 30, 1821).[2] But he never carried his good intentions into practice, and, what is worse, the original MS. which he meant to place in the Advocates' Library, cannot now be found there. Probably it filtered back from Mr. Thomson's house into a chaos of waste paper.

Mr. Thomson, in a brief preface to the Memoirs, says, "At what particular periods of time the several parts of the following work were written, it would not be easy to ascer-

---

[1] Dr. M'Crie says, of the eighteenth century, but this must be an error, as it is said to be corrected in the hand of Mackenzie, who died in 1691.

[2] *Memoirs of Thomas Thomson*, pp. 171, 172.

tain," but he presumes that it "was done progressively, during the course of the author's political life, though perhaps at considerable intervals. . . ."

This is a probable inference, for the book shows curious waverings in opinion. Mackenzie says, in his second page, that he has been an actor in, or witness of the events which he records, "especially since the year 1677," when he became King's Advocate. But this statement is, as Dr. M'Crie apparently supposed, a Preface, an Introduction, an afterthought. It is true that, in 1680–1681, we find Mackenzie asking Lauderdale for copies of papers of 1663, for the purposes of a History, portions of which Lauderdale has revised. But this can scarcely be identical with the work of which fragments survive.

The difficulty is that, as every reader of the Memoirs must see, Mackenzie could not have submitted that work to Lauderdale's scrutiny. It is far too frankly critical of his patron. Are the Memoirs, as they stand, an early draft, and did Mackenzie, about 1678–1680, begin a quite different new history, which Lauderdale read and criticised ? It is impossible to solve this problem. If Mackenzie began a new history, no trace of it has been discovered.

It must be confessed that Mackenzie's *History of his Own Times*, as it has reached us, lacks the liveliness of Burnet's, and, up to 1663, where it breaks off, not to begin again till after a gap of six years, gives us little information about his own opinion of men and affairs. He does not, like Burnet, open with a series of vivacious portraits of the chief characters in the drama ; he draws only one of them, the Earl of Middleton, a good soldier, but a very bad representative of Royalty in the early Parliaments. This portrait may be cited, because it shows much sympathy with Middleton, as a man, though no sympathy is expressed for his measures.

"The Earl of Middleton had by his valour raised himself from the condition of a gentleman to be Lieutenant Generall, *in anno* 1648, under Duke Hamilton ; and continued in the same employment *in anno* 1651, when his Majesty was in Scotland : but these armies being dissipated by his Majesty's unkind fate, rather than his ill conduct, he after a wonderful escape from the tower of London, followed his Majesty in his exile, and was sent *in anno* 1653, General into Scotland. He was by his heroick aspect marked out for great things, and was too liberal to be a private person ; but this too munificent humour, which made him value the services of those whom he esteem'd above all rewards, made him ofttimes disoblige such as were not virtuous enough, by promising to them what he hoped to obtain, though he fail'd in the undertaking; by which great men should learn to surprize their dependers with favours, for thereby the benefit is more welcome, and their own reputation is less hazard. His natural courage and generosity made him likewise less jealous both of men and events than a great person ought to have been : but his greatest weakness was, that he prefer'd such to offices of trust as were unfit to serve him in them, regarding therein rather their interest than his own. Nor did he attend his Majesty so frequently as was convenient, but made his addresses ordinarily by Chancellor Hyde ; whereas all Kings and great persons love to have their servants depend immediately upon them ; and it was observ'd that nothing endeared more any person to his Majesty than personal acquaintance. He was really a man of a manly eloquence as well as aspect ; happier in his wit than in his friends ; and more pitied after his fall than envy'd in his prosperity."

Nothing is said here about Middleton's schemes of extortion. Tarbat, a cousin of Mackenzie, was a prime favourite of Middleton, Mackenzie obviously was informed by Tarbat, and naturally dwells on the best side of Middleton. Had Mackenzie drawn in this manner the other leading nobles in the struggles of the Reformation, we should better understand them, and better understand himself.

Mackenzie frankly attributes the troubles which arose to greed for the spoils of office, and to jealousies on the part of the nobles who had adopted the Royal cause in 1648–1651. He states that Clarendon, as a Cavalier from the first, made another Cavalier, the Earl of Middleton, Royal Commissioner, practically Viceroy of Scotland (a post for which

his careless temper, habitual intemperance, rancour against
the Kirk, which had excommunicated him and made him
do humiliating penance, and his desire of money, rendered
him hopelessly unfit). But Middleton detested Presbytery,
and Clarendon, to keep Lauderdale, a Presbyterian, out
of Scotland, had Middleton selected as Charles's representative. This suited Lauderdale at the time, for he preferred to stay at Charles's side as Secretary for Scotland.
Of him, who had evil influence on Mackenzie's career,
a brief account must be given.

The Earl of Lauderdale, of old a vehement Covenanter,
a man most active in handing over Charles I. to the English,
and a foe of Montrose, was, after 1647, an anti-Montrosian
supporter of Charles I. and Charles II. He was of infinitely
greater ability in civil matters than Middleton. He came of
the house of Maitland of Lethington, in which talent, literary
and political, was eminent and hereditary. Moreover, he
still retained or professed a tenderness for " the good old
cause " of the Covenant, with all the contempt of prelates as,
at best, serviceable tools, which marked his caste in Scotland.
The freedom of the Restoration, coming to Lauderdale after
a long period of imprisonment in England, debauched his
naturally sensual temperament ; he was brutally profligate,
his conversation, Mackenzie says, was " bawdy " and blasphemous, and, before his death, his coarseness and his dull
attempts at humour ended by alienating Charles II., as Lord
Ailesbury proves by anecdotes not easily to be quoted.[1]
But when Ailesbury knew Lauderdale, the Scottish duke
was old and was losing his memory.

He certainly was a very remarkable man. In earlier days,
he had been dear to the erudite Baillie, not only as an ardent
Covenanter and godly youth, but as an accomplished scholar
in Latin, Greek, and Hebrew. He had been, as we saw, one
of those opponents of Charles I. who came over to his side
after he had been sold to England ; and he was none the
less dear to the Resolutioners, because he urged Charles II.

---

[1] *Memoirs of Thomas, Earl of Ailesbury*, vol i. pp. 14, 18. Roxburghe Club,
1890.

to perjure himself by taking the Covenant, and to rejèct the honourable advice of the great Montrose. Charles II. delighted in his society for many years; in a pamphlet he is called " the king's buffoon " ; he is said to have dissipated the king's melancholy by draping his bulky form in petticoats and dancing a skirt-dance before his Majesty, and his skill in political intrigue was only equalled by his intense desire to set the king, in Scotland, above law. Though he offended the Presbyterian clergy, as Mackenzie says, by his conversational delight in blasphemy and obscenity, yet, even after his policy wavered from concession to suppression, and back again, the Presbyterians could not rid themselves of the idea that his heart was true to their cause. He was, at least, able to please an honourable Presbyterian virgin like Lady Mary Margaret Cassilis. Her letters to him, innocent indeed, and much occupied with efforts to gain Lauderdale's protection for suffering "professors," display a shy fondness of affection ; she uses cyphers to disguise the phrase "my dear."

Lauderdale is well spoken of, for his national patriotism and his ability, by oppressed preachers and historians, Mr. Law and Mr. Kirkton. He could win men, and, at last, he won Mackenzie. While Lauderdale kept close to the king's ear, at Court, Middleton, as Commissioner to the Parliament in Edinburgh, found that, in Mackenzie's words, "Never any Parliament was so obsequious to all that was proposed to them." They instituted an oath of allegiance, to be taken by all before admission to any public judicatory, and by this oath the king's supremacy was asserted even in matters ecclesiastical. The Earl of Cassilis was alone in declining this oath, so obnoxious to Presbyterians. The Covenant was declared to be an unlawful oath, "upon which the ministers did begin to thunder after their usual manner," a phrase which suggests that Mackenzie did not relish their thunders. They resolved to remonstrate in their provincial assemblies, but Rothes, Atholl, and others were sent to bring them to order. By Mackenzie of Tarbat's device, aided by Archibald Primrose, the Acts of

E

Parliament, since 1640, were rescinded, save in private legislation, and all constitutional advances that had been made were swept away, leaving the king as absolute as James VI. had been. The Parliament voted to Charles a sum of £40,000 yearly, mainly from excise of beer and ale. Lauderdale cried out against this, "and yet so strange and dangerous a thing is advancement" that "when he became Commissioner he would not abate a penny of it."

"So strange and dangerous a thing is advancement!" These words of Mackenzie's sum up the tragedy of his own career. The tax which tried "to rob a poor man of his beer" had the pernicious effect of "lowering the price of victual." Mackenzie shows his wonted tenderness of heart by exclaiming, "Pardon me, reader, to entreat thee that if ever thou become a member of Parliament, then consider what curses are daily poured out by many poor, hungry, and oppressed creatures, upon such as are in accession to the imposition of taxes." The poor creatures suffering from cheap bread, were thirsty rather than hungry.

Going to Court with his proof of Parliamentary obsequiousness, Middleton moved for the restoration of Episcopacy, against Lauderdale, who had been a rigorous Presbyterian, knew that the country preferred Presbytery; and wished, according to Burnet, who had read his letters to Lady Margaret Cassilis, to keep Scotland in the best humour, as a counterpoise to the English Parliament. It was the dream of Lauderdale to avenge Scotland for her Cromwellian defeats, and to lead an army of loyal, contented, Presbyterian blue bonnets over the Border. Charles himself, though he thought Presbyterianism "no religion for a gentleman," was not eager, Burnet says, to enforce Episcopacy. He knew the Scots very well, moreover he had solemnly promised to restore Presbytery. Crawford was passionate on this side; Hamilton, too, backed Lauderdale; but the majority of the Scottish Council held in town was for Episcopacy, or so the king said, and he struck the Privy Council in Edinburgh dumb, (September 5, 1661) by bidding them inhibit the synodical meetings of the ministers, and by later restoring the government of the Church by bishops.

Every one knows how, in the Parliament of 1662, the Royal commands were obeyed; how in "the drunken Council" at Glasgow, ministers were given a short day to accept bishops or leave their parishes; how a longer reprieve was given, when the extent and vigour of resistance was understood; and how, in 1662–1663, nearly four hundred preachers abandoned manse and kirk. Mackenzie says that "all wise and good men" heartily disapproved of these reckless measures, which deprived of their pastors . a people who "were fond of their ministers," and placed at the head of the Church a Primate, Sharp, who was undeniably an apostate, and was believed to have slowly and warily betrayed, from the first, the sacred cause of Presbytery. It will be remarked that Mackenzie speaks with grave disapproval, in his History, of a revolution which he welcomed with a light heart in *The Religious Stoic* of 1663. We must infer that he wrote this part of his History in a graver mood, perhaps at the time (1665) when he commended, in a dedication of one of his moral essays, the resolution of the Earl of Crawford, who resigned public employment rather than take oaths of ever increasing anti-Presbyterianism.[1] "Your Lordship's condition makes you almost the only Person who deserved" (the Dedication) "at all, and altogether the Person who deserved it most." When Mackenzie affronted persons in power by this dedication to a recalcitrant, he must have been under some Presbyterian influence which is unexplained. That influence ceased to direct him in 1666, but again revived for a while: so much is plain; the rest is obscure.

To replace the "outed ministers," young men of little education, of morals declared to have been odious, and of preaching powers very inadequate, were foisted on aggrieved parishioners. To be sure Burnet tells us that the deprived

---

[1] See Works, vol. 1. p. 75   The Dedication of the Essay *Solitude Preferred to Public Employment*.

ministers, at least the Remonstrants, had many faults. Their
parishioners were often addicted to morbid casuistry, he says,
were spiritual hypochondriacs, "and they fed this disease of
weak minds too much." Kirk discipline as to sensual sins,
Sabbath breaking, and we may add the crying sin of witchcraft,
was very severe. The preachers were indiscreet, passionate,
and "too apt to fawn upon and flatter their adherents. . . .
Their opinions about the independence of the church and
clergy on the civil power, and their readiness to stir up the
people to tumults and wars, was that which begat so ill an
opinion of them at this time in all men, that very few, who
were not deeply engaged with them, pitied them much,
under all the ill-usage they now met with." [1]

These preachers being succeeded by a hastily gathered
crowd of "curates," "Ignorance, scrupulosity, and censure
ordinarily go together, especially in so dark an hour as this,"
(says Wodrow, speaking of other events,) "and now came
"one of the first handles to the common people to censure"
ministers who showed any signs of acquiescence in the
decrees of the Government.[2] The curates cannot have
been so black as they are painted by their adversaries ; but
Burnet says they were the worst preachers he ever heard,
ignorant to a reproach, and often openly vicious. Leighton
also reprobated the careless haste with which they were
selected and introduced. They were pelted with stones and
insulted by their parishioners, who flocked to the "outed"
preachers in their field conventicles. These large assemblages
were dispersed by force ; fines were imposed on their attendants and on absentees from church. The outed preachers
were placed under the "Scots Mile Act," and curates informed against their own parishioners.

Henceforth the contest was between the defenders of two
prerogatives, "the prerogatives and Crown honours of Christ,"
with the Covenant, and the prerogative of Charles II. Unhappily both parties, as we see them in the perspective of
time, were in the wrong. It was an error, on the Presbyterian side, to think that the claim of preachers to interfere

[1] Burnet, i. pt. i. pp. 272–274 (ed. 1897).   [2] Wodrow, i. p. 286.

in secular affairs, to be free from the secular law of libel, and to make the Covenant eternally binding, was a "prerogative of Christ." It was no less an error, on the other hand, to stretch the prerogative of Charles, as Mackenzie later did, by straining the terms of Scottish laws passed under James VI., at a time when the Tudor ideas of absolutism, and of Royal right divine, were passed into legislation.

The Covenanters, between 1641 and 1649, had abolished the power of the Lords of the Articles, (a packed Committee dominating parliaments) had acquired the right to control the king's choice of ministers and officers of State ; and had abolished lay patronage of livings. It was one of the prerogatives of Christ, that the people should elect their own preachers. The early parliaments of the Restoration restored patronage, allowed the king to choose his own ministers and officers of State, restored the power of packed legislative Committees, the Lords of the Articles, and made Charles supreme over all persons and causes.

The Revolution of 1688-89, at last, made an end of the Lords of the Articles, reduced patronage, restored Presbytery, but did not restore the full Crown Honours of Christ, and the Covenant. This result was only rendered possible by the brutal struggle of extremists of both parties, who, during the Restoration, wore the strength of each other down into weakness, and made compromise welcome.

We study the early portion of the Memoirs, not to find traces of Mackenzie's part in politics, for at that time he had no opportunity of playing any part, but to discover his opinion of the various measures, and the leaders of parties. He was well informed, we saw, by his cousin, Mackenzie of Tarbat, who, in the complicated intrigues of 1663, stood by Middleton for " the Cavalier interest" in Scotland, which Lauderdale, at Court, was thought eager to ruin.

Burnet describes Tarbat, who, at one time, had so much ousted Lauderdale from Royal favour, that the king, says Mackenzie, would shut the door on the Secretary, while he conferred with Middleton's envoy. " He was a young man of great vivacity of parts, but full of ambition and very crafty, who has had the art to recommend himself to all sides and parties by turns, and is yet alive, having made a great figure in the country now above fifty years. He has great notions of virtue and religion, but they are only notions, at least they have not had great effect on himself at all times." He was son of Sir John Mackenzie of Tarbat, his father was a brother of the first Lord Mackenzie of Kintail (later the title became Earl of Seaforth). Tarbat died in 1714, being then Earl of Cromartie.

This statesman was Middleton's chief agent with Charles for his purpose of exacting fines from hundreds of persons in Scotland, for their compliances with Cromwell, and for depriving a dozen eminent men of capacity for public office. They were selected, on Tarbat's suggestion, by an unheard-of process of secret balloting, called " Billeting " in Parliament. Members were bribed or threatened into voting in accordance with a list dictated to them.[1] Middleton hoped to shelve Crawford, Sir Robert Murray, and Lauderdale, among others. The king, informed by Lauderdale of this plan, which he had never sanctioned, was irritated by the Athenian mode of Ostracism, a strangely impudent innovation, and told Tarbat that he would not accept the advice, but would not disclose the secret of the voters. Tarbat in vain said that only by the dismissal of Lauderdale could the Scottish cavaliers escape ruin. Charles dismissed Tarbat ; who advised Middleton to hurry to Court (February 1663), and at Court Lauderdale and Middleton fought out their battle.

Mackenzie does not insert Lauderdale's written speech, apparently he did not obtain a copy, but describes it as " the great masterpiece of his life." (Mr. Thomson inserts the papers in the printed Memoirs.) Middleton, argued Lauderdale, had invaded the Royal Prerogative in an unheard-of . way, by passing, without the king's approbation, the Act for

---

[1] The whole complicated intrigue is well described by Mr. Osmund Airy in " Lauderdale and the Restoration in Scotland," *Quarterly Review*, January to April 1884, pp 407-439.

Ostracism. Such conduct, if allowed, made the Commissioner a despotic ruler in Scotland. Middleton, for example, had, without instructions, touched with the Royal sceptre and ratified an Act prohibiting the king from pardoning the sons of men recently forfeited. Thus, for example, Middleton had made it impossible for Charles to restore the son of Argyll to his estates.

The truth is that Middleton wanted them for himself, and Lauderdale, who was of a surprising loyalty to the House of Argyll, did restore the young earl in 1669, without taking the vote of a Parliament most hostile to the proceeding.

Lauderdale next exposed the craft of Tarbat, (as he called it, Mackenzie disagrees,) who had tried to "juggle" with two different copies of an Act of Oblivion, and with the Act of Billeting, or Ostracism. This, said Lauderdale, is a mode of secret voting only heard of among the Athenians, "*who were governed by that cursed Sovereign Lord, the People.*" Mackenzie was right in admiring the tact and logic of "Lauderdale's masterpiece."

Middleton's speech was much longer, and was able enough, but "full of palpable falsehoods," says Mr. Airy. From the constant citations of precedents, of Roman legists, of passages in Scottish history, and from the style, I am tempted to think that Mackenzie himself had a hand in its composition, though Tarbat also was skilled in law. But the king was justly dissatisfied: recalled Middleton's commission, took from him the all-important command of Edinburgh Castle, and gave it to Lauderdale.

In this affair Lauderdale had made great use of the Earl of Rothes, son of him who had at first been the great leader of the Covenant. Rothes was young, almost uneducated, as was said, and in addition to his natural wit, applauded by Mackenzie, he possessed a strength of head which enabled him to see one set of boon companions under the table, and then renew the bacchanalian conflict with fresh combatants. He was so profligate that he carried with him a young lady of good family, dressed as a page, when he rode about the country. His face, as shown in an admirable miniature, is that of a very dark man, with an evil glance, much like Charles II., and bloated with high living.

A great favourite of Charles, Rothes increased his hold on the king, says Mackenzie, by arranging that his wealthy niece, the Duchess of Buccleuch, should marry Charles's favourite bastard, James, Duke of Monmouth. Both were very young, and Monmouth's heart was given to Lady Henrietta Wentworth. Charles now made Rothes Commissioner, and Parliament condemned themselves for their Billeting Act.

Mackenzie makes it evident that his own sympathies are with his cousin, Tarbat, who, he thinks, did not juggle with and deceive both Parliament and the king. Lauderdale would have proceeded further against Tarbat, but he had something " up his sleeve." He possessed old letters written, in 1647, by Lauderdale, " wherein he persuaded them " (the Scots) " to deliver up King Charles I., with many severe reflections upon the King's person." Lauderdale, being informed that Tarbat would produce these letters, wisely ceased to assail him. So Mackenzie says, but from the Lauderdale papers it seems that the compromising letters were copies, not originals.[1]

A gap in the manuscript of Mackenzie's Memoirs occurs at the end of the Parliament of 1663, and the narrative is not resumed till 1669. It ceases after the statement that the fanatic Covenanter, Johnstone of Waristoun, (executed on July 22, 1663) " had been a man of [*eminent parts and more eminent devotion*]." These words are a late addition to the MS. and appear to indicate an appreciation of Waristoun's furious superstition which is surprising in Mackenzie. The sentence goes on, " But his natural choler being kindled by his zeal had been fatal, first to this kingdom, and then to himself."

The nature of Mackenzie's Memoirs continues to puzzle their readers. Can they have been shown, as we have them,

---

[1] Compare Memoirs, pp. 49, 131. On p. 49, Middleton possesses the letters. In any case Tarbat was consigned to private life till 1678

to Lauderdale, as shown some History certainly was ?   How are we to understand the apparent tenderness for Middleton, Tarbat, and the extreme Episcopal party, in combination with the admiration of Waristoun's "eminent devotion," and the disapproval of the measures against Presbyterian ministers ?

Once more, the career of Rothes, when he was at once High Commissioner, High Chancellor, Lord President of his Majesty's Exchequer and Council, and Commander-in-Chief in Scotland, was notoriously reckless and oppressive. Between 1663 and 1667, Scotland was governed by Rothes through the bishops, who re-established a Court of High Commission to detect and punish nonconformity, and by the army.

The Remonstrant counties of the west and south-west, Dumfries and Galloway, with the shires of Lanark, Ayr, and Renfrew became ripe for rebellion, vexed as the gentry and peasantry were by fines, and by the military license of the few men commanded by Sir James Turner, a gallant and learned soldier, and most amusing writer, who lent some traits to the picture of Dugald Dalgetty.   Sir James, to judge by his diverting Memoirs, was a man of a tender heart, but he admits that "drink brought me into many inconveniences."   Though he undeniably acted more gently than his orders commanded him to do, when in liquor he was furious, and his men, in his absence, were extortionate and cruel.

Yet, while Rothes accumulated offices in an unprecedented way, (the death of Glencairn had left the Chancellorship vacant,) Mackenzie dedicated to him his essay, "Moral Gallantry," proving that "The Point of Honour, abstracting from all other ties, obliges men to be Virtuous, and that there is nothing so Mean, or unworthy of a Gentleman, as Vice."   The vices of Rothes may not yet have come into perfect flower, but the dedication would seem ironical, if Mackenzie did not say, "My obligations to you are such as may excuse real passion in a Stoic, and seeming flatteries in a Philosopher."

What can these obligations have been? Perhaps the honour of knighthood was among them.

"No paper, nor anything else except the heart which sends you this, is capable to contain or express that kindness it feels for you." These are Mackenzie's "last words," as a Moral Essayist, "I confine my thoughts for the future to my ordinary employment."[1] We can date this effusion, by aid of the following letter of Mackenzie to John Evelyn :—

EDINBURGH, *February* 4, 1666-7.

SIR,—I have written two letters which, with my last moral discourses, now lie before me because I want your address. This I have at last ventured upon, which will assure you of a friendship as zealous, though not so advantageous as you deserve; as a testimony of which, receive this inclosed poem written by me, not out of love of poetry, or of gallantry, but to essay if I might reveal my curiosity that way. I could wish to know the censure of Sir William Davenant or Mr. Waller upon it; and in order to this, I beg that you will present this letter and it to Sir William, and if he pleases it, to give copies of it, or use it as you please. I wish he sent me an account of its errors, and as a penance I promise not to vomit any new one. I had sought my security in no other approbation than your own, if your friendship for me had not rendered you suspect. Dear sir, pardon this imprudence in

Your most humble servant,
GEO. MACKENZIE.

The "last moral discourses" are "Moral Gallantry" with others. The poem on which the author wants the opinions of Waller and Davenant is unknown. However, we find Mackenzie deeply obliged to Rothes, and perhaps, attempting to win him to virtue as the only course for a gentleman, in 1666, the year when the misgovernment of Rothes produced the Pentland Rising. Here is an unexplained

---

[1] Mackenzie, Works, vol i. pp 99, 100.

departure from the tone of the dedication to the disgraced Crawford, in 1665.

England was at war with Holland, and in June 1665, after a naval battle with the Dutch, Government treated several of the leading western gentry as the Government of Anne and George I. treated the Jacobites in troubled times, locked them up to keep them out of mischief. Conventicles continued to be held, and the Covenanting chiefs not in durance turned for aid to Holland, just as the Jacobites, later, turned to France.

From Neuport (August 5, 1666) some one writes to Lauderdale that there is talk of a Dutch landing in Ireland or Scotland, "hoping in God that your Lordship tell His Majesty, that our gates and frontiers be provided, that our poor country be not a prey, and the seat of war." From Antwerp came news that de Witt "makes the people believe he has Scotland with all the Scots in Ireland at his devotion for driving Charles Stuart out of his dominions." [1]

Possibly Government knew that the Covenanters, acting through violent exiled preachers like Mr. MacWard, resident in Holland, had laid a plot, in July 1666, to seize the castles of Edinburgh, Stirling, and Dunbarton. The States-General (July 15) in a secret resolution say that the "friends of religion" in Scotland have announced to them their intention of seizing fortresses. As soon as they have succeeded, the States will send them 3000 muskets, 1000 matchlocks, 1500 pikes, swords, and ten field-pieces, with 2000 brace of pistols, 1000 carabines, and 150,000 gulden in money. MacWard writes to another preacher, Brown, about this transaction, in September and October, 1666. [2]

In the camps of rebels, Jacobite or godly, there are usually traitors; Government perhaps knew about the doings of "the friends of religion" and the Dutch, so when the Pentland Rising began on November 13, 1666, Government supposed that "the turtle had popped its head out of the

---

[1] Information from letters from Holland printed by Mr. W. del Court

[2] M'Crie. From MacWard MSS. in the Advocates' Library. *Life of Veitch*, pp 363, 378, 379

shell." In fact the rising began in the remote clachan of St. John's town of Dalry, in the Glenkens, (at a field conventicle, Mackenzie says,) and was not premeditated. The country people, according to most versions, rose against the cruelty of three or four soldiers; country gentlemen like young Maxwell of Monreith, and preachers like the Rev. James Mitchell, (who later shot at Sharp,) Mr. Veitch, (who later perhaps knew more than befitted a clergyman about the Rye-House Murder plot,) and others flocked to their standard. They went to Dumfries and caught Sir James Turner. They walked about the country, getting very wet and renewing the Covenant; they approached Edinburgh, where they received no assistance; and on, November 28, tired and discouraged, they were driven to all the winds by Dalziel of Binns, at Rullion Green. Fifteen preachers were denounced as traitors in connection with this raid, and some eighty prisoners were put in gaol in Edinburgh.

It was urged in their favour that they had received quarter, at least in many cases, from commissioned officers. Not much had the plea of quarter availed to screen captured cavaliers: after Philiphaugh, in 1645, the Covenanters executed gentlemen taken under promise of quarter. The precedent was awkward for Captain Arnot and other prisoners of Rullion Green, who were tried before one of the Judges, and a Justice Depute on December 4, 1666. The Privy Council allowed them, as Counsel, Sir George Lockhart, an eminent advocate, and Sir George Mackenzie, already knighted, with two others.

To the lay mind it may seem that quarter given to rebels, guilty of high treason, on the field of battle, merely means sparing their lives, and letting them have their chance with the law. Mackenzie argued that in war, civil or international, every soldier has a right to give quarter, and that the quarter remains valid, seeing that, but for this promise of life, as it were, men, being desperate, might fight to the death, and do incalculable injury to the Royal forces. Quarter, in fact, is regarded by lawyers as a *transaction* (so Grotius. Claudius de Cotte, Paris de Puteo). The king's forces with Glencairn in the hills, (1653–55) and Cromwell's English forces acted on this principle, when the English were rebels. "Wilt thou take the life of those whom thou hast taken by thy bow and sword?" asked Mackenzie.

The judges took the view that, quarter or no quarter, none can remit treason but the king, and the prisoners were hanged. The same principle appears to have been applied to some prisoners of war in 1745, by the English Government. Mackenzie had not a likely cause to plead, on this occasion.

A consequence of the Pentland Rising, and perhaps of the Covenanting intrigues with Holland, was the use of torture to extract evidence from two of the prisoners, the Rev. Hugh Mackail and Neilson of Corsack. For perhaps thirty years judicial torture had been in desuetude, but henceforward it again became familiar.[1]

The extreme scarcity of Mackenzie's private letters, and the deplorable loss of his Memoirs for 1663–1669, make it impossible to follow his career during these years. He had a low opinion of their literature. "It hath been well observed, that it would seem now, that none but mad men write or censure" (criticise). These words occur in his preface to *Pleadings before the Supreme Courts of Scotland*, published in 1672. He may have been thinking of fiery Covenanting books like *Naphtali* and *Jus Populi Vindicatum ;* at all events the age was not propitious to literature. It has been "kind to his own writings," he says, "beyond his merit and expectation."

Of Mackenzie's private life, at any time, very little is known. A single brief letter lights up a melancholy moment. He married, as we saw, in 1662, and by his first wife he had three sons and two daughters. These must have been born years before 1670, when he was married again, to Margaret Haliburton, daughter of Haliburton of Pitcur, whose brother fell at the battle of Killiecrankie. From the births of five children by the first wife, in less than eight years, she must

---

[1] The author of the notice of Mackenzie in the *Dictionary of National Biography*, has made *him* "chiefly responsible for the introduction of torture." It is easy to disprove this.

have died not later than 1667–1668, and, if there were three sons, two of them must also have died. These were heavy sorrows, and it was probably in 1668 (?) that he wrote as follows to his friend, Sir Peter Wedderburn of Gosforth. The note was obviously written in the sorrow of bereavement, and in bad health, while contemplating the difficult journey into Ross-shire. " I am now forced to go north, though somewhat tender, and if anythings ails me, I hope you will look to the little children. I have left a disposition of my estate to the boy, and failing him to the elder lass, and failing her, to the other, and an exact account of my effects. Your Lordship may call for them from Colin " (his brother). " Think me not apprehensive but cautious in this, for truly I fear not death now in the least. My thoughts are, God be praised, very much of my Maker, and I live as much out of duty as inclination." [1] Was this the period when, according to Mr. Cargill, Mac-kenzie " began a profession of godliness " ?

Mackenzie must have been rising in his profession. In 1665, he was chosen as Advocate for the town of Dundee, his retaining fee being the moderate sum of £46 (Scots). It is to be hoped that he received "refreshers" when he spoke in the cause of the good town.

What follows is, to some extent, conjectural, but it is possible that, probably towards the end of 1668, Mackenzie had begun to think of a consoler in his bereavement. He writes to John Evelyn, dating " Edinburgh 1668," to the following effect :—

I did, Sir, in my greener years believe that our lofty and more wingy thoughts could not be forced into rhymes or submit to the rules of poetry. But I attribute this partly to the rudeness of my ear, which the storminess of the place where I live fashioned from my infancy to take notice of no sound less loud than winds or thunder, and thus I undervalued poetry as soldiers accustomed to the noise of drum and cannon contemn the softer airs of the viol or lute.

---

[1] *The Wedderburn Book*, i p 138. Mr. Wedderburn quotes from a published text of this letter ; once the MS was at Pitfirrane. Lady Halket kindly informs me that none of Mackenzie's letters are now in the papers at Pitfirrane

But being at last released from this error, I resolved to choose for my essay a theme which (like her for whom the poem was intended) would not look ill in any dress, and in which my duty might excuse my want of wit. This poem being the first fruits of my muse, I have sent to you as to whom it was due, being Apollo's high priest. Your eyes can ripen everything they see, and if there be any lameness in its feet, your touch can miraculously cure it. Your approbation is a sanctuary unto which if these lines can once get they will be secure, nor dare the avenger follow them; and your bays are branches enough to secure them against the heats of envy, though they need, I fear, more the pity than the rage of more exalted heads. I desire rather your assistance than your censure, and I fear as much the one, as they need the other. Pardon the rudeness of this address from

Your humble servant,
GEO. MACKENZIE.

P.S.—If you favour me with a return, direct it to Sir Geo. Mackenzie, Advocate, in Edinburgh.

The poem to which Mackenzie refers as "intended for" a lady "who would not look ill in any dress," is probably "Caelia's Country House and Closet." His Muse is that, for the moment, of friendship:

"Friendship ! that wiser rival of vain Love
Which does more firm, but not so fiery prove."

He can raise his thoughts in the direction of the Sublime, he says,

"but cannot raise my Theme,
There's too much merit in her charming name"!

He describes the avenues of elms, and the tranquil lake beside Caelia's home, a lake where, if the swan does not "float double, swan and shadow,"

"The birds at once here and above do fly."

"But when those waters show their Lady's face
The world can boast of no such picture-case."

The country, (with Caelia,) is preferred to scenes of ambition,

> "What courts, what camps, what triumphs may one find
> Displayed in Caelia when she will be kind!"

Leaving wood and lake the poet reaches the gate, which was adorned by a statue of Caelia's father, who was not a lawyer, but a military man. The garden boasts images of Nereids, and "an artificial rock," and fountains.

> "O happy country life, pure like its air,
> Free from the rage of pride, the pangs of care!
> Yet all these country pleasures, without love
> Would but a dull and tedious prison prove."

The poet next invades the gallery, wherein are sacred pictures and portraits. Among these we remark Charles I.,

> "His life was the best law a king could make.
> Much liberty he gave, but none did take:
> Above all martyrs in this magnified,
> They for religion, but it with him died."

The ideas of *The Religious Stoic* are repeated in verse,

> "Fretted religion sickens into zeal,
> That holy fever of the Commonweal.
> By this sweet name fierce men their rage baptize,
> And not to God but Moloch sacrifice."

After describing busts of Roman heroes, the poet comes to a modern fit for Plutarch's pen,

> "*Montrose, his country's glory and its shame,*
> Cæsar in all things equall'd, but his fame,
> His heart, though not his country, was as great
> As his, and fell yet by a nobler fate"

From these lines we gather, at least, that Mackenzie appreciated the greatest character of his age.

Caelia's books are next celebrated: they are the poems

of Tasso, Cowley " whose melting works are new," Denham, Waller, " toiling Johnson" (Ben), " easy Fletcher,"

" And Donne, into whose mysteries few pry,"

but Shakespeare is strangely absent. The lines give us some idea of Mackenzie's tastes, and are on the level of contemporary amateur verse.

In the course of 1669, Mackenzie was consoled, and was wooing a daughter of Halyburton of Pitcur, whom he married on January 14, 1670. Of this lady we know little, but concerning her the following story is told. Mackenzie's country house, within reach of Edinburgh, was Shank, which "is said to have stood on Shankpoint, a beautifully wooded promontory in the grounds of Arniston, formed by the confluence of the Gore water and the Esk."[1] Very early one morning, Lord Tweeddale rode to Shank, to consult Mackenzie on legal business of importance. He was ushered into the lawyer's bedroom, and found him in a fourpost bed, with the curtains drawn. From behind the curtains Mackenzie's voice delivered all his lore, and Lord Tweeddale approached the couch with his fee, when a *lady's* hand slipped forth, and took possession of the gold. Lady Mackenzie appears to have taken charge of her lord's finances.

In Edinburgh, at this time, Mackenzie occupied the old town-house of the Abbots of Melrose, on the south side of the High Street, in the alley now called Strichen's Close from a later judge, Lord Strichen. The house had a garden which ran down to the Cowgate. In 1847 there was a small quadrangle, and the gable was surmounted by a curiously carved fleur-de-lys, while the gutter of the roof ended in a grotesque gargoyle of the period of the Abbots. Mackenzie's estate of Shank, not far from the town, and his other property, Haughead, then produced a rental of less than £100.[2] The lands of Rosehaugh came into his possession in 1668, 1669; he was generally known by the

---

[1] *Journal of Jurisprudence*, ix. 194, *note*.   [2] Barty, pp. 70-72.

territorial title of " Rosehaugh," in the county for which he sat in Parliament, in 1669, and later. His most important estates were in Perth and Angus. They had been the personal property of Robert Bruce, and were conveyed by him to an Oliphant.[1]

---

[1] Barty, in *Mackenzie-Wharncliffe Deeds*

CHAPTER VIII

MACKENZIE IN PARLIAMENT

Policy of conciliation after the Pentland Rising—Conciliation fails—
Government wavers—An Indulgence contemplated—Mitchell's attempt
to murder the Primate—Some ministers are indulged—Ferocity of
Covenanting literature—*Jus Populi Vindicatum*—" Hang all Bishops :
exterminate all the ungodly."—The maxims of Knox on assassination
accepted—Mackenzie opposed to these doctrines—Parliament of 1669
—Procedure described—Dictatorship of Lauderdale—Opposed by the
Duke of Hamilton—His character—Queensberry, Perth, Argyll—
Lauderdale's Instructions—An Union proposed with England—Royal
Supremacy Act—Militia Act—Question of Forfeitures—Measures of
Conciliation—Mackenzie opposes the Union—Criticises the Lords of the
Articles—Speaks against haste as to the Union—Act of Supremacy—
Both religions coerced—Mackenzie on the preachers—Sons of ser-
vants and farmers—Mackenzie on Leighton—On Presbyterian insolen-
cies—Opposes Militia Bill—Anger of Lauderdale—Opposes Salt Tax
—Opposes forfeitures of rebels in absence—Lauderdale illegally re-
stores Argyll to his estates—Parliament of 1670—Armed conventicles
—Mackenzie opposes compulsory evidence on oath—Outrages by
Presbyterians—Burnet's evidence—"Clanking Act"—Lauderdale and
Lady Margaret Kennedy—Lauderdale's second marriage—Rapacity
of his wife—Mackenzie opposes new taxation—Civic jobbery of Lauderdale in Edinburgh—Provost Ramsay's corruption—Mackenzie defends
the town—Called a John of Leyden by Lockhart—Fountainhall's
defence of the Provost—*Autres Temps, autres Mœurs.*

MACKENZIE first entered public life as member for the county
in which his clan was predominant, the shire of Ross, in
1669. His Parliamentary career, while in opposition, is
perhaps the least interesting and characteristic period of his
life. He is no longer the gay philosopher and stylist; no
longer the poet ; and he is not yet the picturesque persecutor,
still less the mournful Jacobite and premature Socialist. In
him we see a familiar figure; the earnest young Liberal
member of Parliament, whose mind is full of "the House,"
of divisions and debates about questions settled long ago.

To understand the proceedings of this Parliament, the first since 1663, it is necessary to look back at the events which followed the defeat of the western rebels at Rullion Green in 1666.

The prisoners of the Pentland Rising, according to Burnet, "might all have saved their lives if they would have renounced the Covenant," but they refused, and rejoiced in their sufferings. We cannot but respect their ill-guided consciences, but their consciences, and those of the fiery exiles, like MacWard of the Dutch plot, still kept the country disturbed. The bishops were more than ever loathed. Gilbert Burnet accuses his namesake, the Archbishop of Glasgow, Wodrow and popular rumour accused Sharp, of keeping back a Royal letter that ordered the cessation of executions. Burnet, if any one, was the offender. Popular passion was stirred, Government was in the mood to make concessions, Sharp was "snibbed," reduced to abject submission, and Sir Robert Murray came down from London in 1667, to see that "things were managed with more temper." Rothes ceased to be Commissioner, Commander-in-Chief, and Treasurer, becoming Chancellor, while Lauderdale, at Court, was more powerful and inclined for peace in the country.

Murray cried "peace, peace," where there was no peace, for the curates in the west were attacked and robbed by the godly. Sir James Turner was deprived of his command, but attempts at lenity were met by fresh outrages from the blades of the Covenant, whose consciences permitted them to "rabble" conformist ministers but not to arraign them before their bishops for their misdeeds. The king was anxious to be tolerant, all the more as he was trying to be secretly reconciled to Rome, and desired to protect Catholics, who, like Quakers, were persecuted by all parties. They had no right to own consciences!

Leighton attempted to reduce episcopal powers to the shadow of a name, but the preachers cried "taste not, touch not, handle not." MacWard, safe in Holland, persuaded the preachers not even to sign a bond "to keep the peace."

There was an *impasse*, a deadlock. There could be nothing else. No concessions short of restoring Presbytery and the Covenants would satisfy, and the Government knew what such a concession meant. Orderly firm repression was impossible, without police, without a standing army, and, above all, without ready-money and supplies for the troops. The few regiments that the king had in Scotland were on the point of mutiny for their pay.[1] The method of free quarters inevitably led to abuses and increased discontent. Government wavered between "Indulgences"—which divided the brethren among themselves, but were followed by an increase of conventicles—and the infliction of penalties too severe to be executed save in a spasmodic fashion. Leighton, in an undated letter, justly says that the mischief arose in bereaving a large district of its clergy at a stroke, in 1662–1663, "and then stocking again that desert we had made with a great many owls and satyrs" (the "curates"). "We have still been tossed betwixt the opposite extremes of too great rigour and too great relaxations and indulgences; well made laws too severe to be executed and, for a counterpoise to have executed almost none of them, except by exorbitant fits and starts that by their extremity made all men sure of their short continuance."[2]

An Indulgence was to have been proclaimed in 1668, when James Mitchell, one of the preachers implicated in the Pentland Rising, carried out a favourite tenet of John Knox. Having "a call," and being armed with two pistols of large bore, he fired at Sharp, in his coach in the Blackfriars Wynd, and shattered the arm of the Bishop of Orkney (July 1668). Mitchell fled to a house, changed his clothes, borrowed a perruque, and walked away to a safe hiding-place. In face of this outrage the scheme of "Indulgence," of filling vacant pulpits with tame Presbyterian preachers, was postponed. In 1669 it was put into practice, forty-two tame preachers were planted in parishes, under various hampering restrictions. The precise parishioners avoided, condemned, and

---

[1] Hamilton to Lauderdale, Nov. 14, 1670, *Hist. MSS. Com.*, XI., 6, p. 140.

[2] *Ibid.*, p. 149.

deserted them. The indulged preachers then took to evading
the restrictions, but Indulgences, renewed at intervals, broke
the Kirk into two irreconcilable factions, weakened her, and
ended by leaving a wild " Remnant" alone true to the ancient
clerical pretensions.

In 1669 a fanatical manifesto was issued, *Jus Populi Vindicatum*, by James Stewart, then a fierce Presbyterian, later an
extremely shifty politician. Stewart fled to Holland, leaving
his mine to explode behind him. His book, says Mackenzie,
"had made the killing of all deserters from Presbytery seem
not only lawful, but even duty, amongst many of that profession, and, in a postscript to *Jus Populi* it was told that the
sending the Archbishop of St. Andrews's head to the king
would be the best present that could be made to Jesus
Christ." .

This is not strictly correct, but *Jus Populi* did ask Charles
to hang all the bishops, and all his ministers who aided and
abetted them, to renew the Covenant, and to unite England
and Scotland by forcing Presbytery on England. The
fanatics were as eager as ever to renew the Civil War.

As every one is not familiar with *Jus Populi* it may be
convenient to quote the frantic words of a writer who, after
being the closest associate of King James's worst minister,
Melfort, later became King's Advocate of William III.

"Let his Majesty . . . execute justice on the Apostate
Prelates, by hanging them up before the Sun . . . and on
all others who have been authors and abettors of this horrible
course of defection, and unparallelable apostasy, which makes
these lands an hissing and a byword to all nations; and let
him honestly and with an upright heart prosecute the end of
these holy Covenants, *and with that Godly King enter into a
Covenant, that whosoever will not seek the Lord God of Israel
shall be put to death, whether small or great, whether Man or
woman.*"[1]

This appears to mean that every one who does not take
the Covenants "shall be put to death." The fanaticism of
these people had to be suppressed. Sharp was adjured to

[1] *Jus Populi Vindicatum*, pp. 376, 377 (1669).

send his own head "as a propine, in a silver box, to his Majesty,"[1] and assassination was advocated, under a cloud of words and quibbles.

In *Jus Populi Vindicatum*, the author accepts Knox's arguments in favour of such "executing of judgements" as Phinehas, that favourite model, practised. Lethington, in controversy with Knox, had said that, "the fact was extraordinary, and not to be imitated." Knox replied, "I say that it had the ground of God's ordinary judgement, which commandeth the idolator to die the death; and therefore I yet again affirm, that it is to be imitated of all these that prefer the true honour of the true worship and glory of God, to the affection of flesh and wicked princes." Lethington answered that "we are not to follow extraordinary examples unless we have the same warrant and assurance." Knox replied that it would not do to rob because the Israelites robbed the Egyptians, for theft is contrary to the Decalogue. "But where the example agrees with the Law, and is, as it were, the execution of God's judgement, expressed within the same, I say that the example approved of God stands to us in place of a commandment."[2]

The author of *Jus Populi Vindicatum* accepts Knox's position, overlooking Knox's repudiation of it, when to repudiate it was useful. He says, "Sure I am this fact of Phinehas was according to the Law, and to the express mind of God, and why then might it not be imitated in the like case? What warrant, command, or commission had Phinehas which none now can expect?" It is not proved that no man can now have such a "call" as that of Phinehas. The author would not say that the example of Phinehas is "a binding precedent in all times to all persons, unless it be every way so circumstantiated as it was then."[3]

---

[1] *Jus Populi Vindicatum*, p. 572.

[2] *Ibid.*, p. 418, citing Knox; *History of the Reformation*, p. 390, folio edition.

In my *Knox and the Reformation*, I dwelt on Knox's occasional encouragement of assassination, his anarchism; and a Scottish Professor of Church History denied that Knox promulgated such views. I give my authorities for the fact in Appendix B.

[3] *Jus Populi Vindicatum*, pp. 418-426

In effect, the fanatic who thinks he has the "call" to murder constitutes himself judge of the case and the circumstances. Mitchell did so, so did the later murderers of Sharp, and of other persons. However much the writers of books like this work of 1669 might shift and wriggle, Knox spoke plainly enough in his discussion with Lethington, to the encouragement of fanatics.

We now understand part of Knox's legacy to Scotland, and perceive the difficulties which would have beset a much better ruler than Lauderdale, in conducting a much more sagacious policy than that of "the king's buffoon" ever was. On one side the statesman had to do with the exiles in Holland and their adherents at home, zealous even unto slaying for the Covenants. On the other side were the Presbyterians who were ready to accept the Indulgence, and to wait peaceably for better times. To restore Presbytery fully and freely, yet without the Covenants, which could be renewed without civil war, was to leave the fanatics and the milder party engaged in a death struggle, while the conformists, deserted, would have been at the mercy of the extremists. The Church party in England, against whom Charles II. was powerless, would have interfered, and a chaos at least as bad as the actual misery of Scotland would have reigned. At no time did Mackenzie lean to the side of the fanatics.

We now arrive at the autumn of 1669, a critical moment, for a Parliament began to sit, with Lauderdale as Commissioner representing the king. Here commences the political career of Mackenzie. A few preliminary remarks may make the conditions of politics and of parties intelligible. The Members of Parliament, the Spiritual Estate, six prelates, the "Lords of Parliament," from dukes to the barons (sixty-five), the members for shires (fifty-six), and the sixty members for boroughs, sat all in one room, distinguished only by their appointed seats, while members of both parties, (as far as there were any party divisions,) crowded together without distinction.

A division of party could not yet be said to exist; there

was no Parliamentary "party" worth mentioning till 1673. Lauderdale, as Commissioner, ruled everything after his own pleasure, the House was merely "obsequious." Business was done, in the old Scottish manner, by the Lords of the Articles, a Committee of eight members from each of the Estates. The Articles were "packed," and produced such Acts as suited Lauderdale, while the House accepted these without much debate.

Yet the House contained many men adverse to Lauderdale, in Church policy, (though on this they were usually mute,) and in regard to Lauderdale's inveterate jobbery. The chief of the nascent party of resistance to Lauderdale was the third Duke of Hamilton. This peer was a Douglas, eldest son of the first Marquis of Douglas by his second wife. In 1646, Charles I. created him Earl of Selkirk. In 1656 he, being still a very young man, married Anne, Duchess of Hamilton, eldest daughter of James, first duke. He had been out with Lorne, Glencairn, and the last of the loyal, against Cromwell, in 1654. In 1660, Charles II. made him Duke of Hamilton for life. His main object was to obtain, as he did in 1673, the arrears of the debts of Charles I. to his wife's father. But from the first (1663), Hamilton lay under suspicion of "not being forward in Church business, as Lauderdale told him."[1] He held large lands in the districts abandoned to the practice of field conventicles, and his letters show a reluctant obedience to the drastic rules imposed on his tenants. His real sympathies were with them, and his wife was sincerely Presbyterian, not from any speculative ideas about the scriptural warrant of either form of Church Government, but because the Presbyterian ministers were better men and better preachers than the conformist curates. If we read *Presbyterian Eloquence,* and the retort by *William Laick,* and believe both books, we must suppose that the sermons of both parties were inconceivably grotesque, while many of the curates, as Leighton said, were "satyrs" of the worst description. Their amorous exploits are incredibly

[1] *Hamilton Papers, Hist. MSS. Com.,* XI., 6, p. 139

lewd, and remind us of those attributed to the monks by Boccaccio, and in the mediæval *fabliaux*.

Between the influence of his wife and his sympathy with his tenants, Hamilton was certainly "not forward in Church business," indeed, in Parliament, the Presbyterian cause was not supported ; Lauderdale's political profligacy and personal tyranny came to be the objects of attack. With him, later, was William, third Earl of Queensberry, also a Douglas, who, after the fall of Lauderdale, and in the years 1682–1686, was to be powerful in the Government, and a persecutor. But, for several years, the Earl of Perth, and his brother, John Drummond of Lundin, were mainly of the Hamilton party, while Argyll stood by Lauderdale who had rescued him, after the death of his father, the Marquis, from a perilous situation, and, in December, despite the clamour of his countless creditors, had him restored to his estates, and backed him in his main desire, the conquest of Mull and Morvern, the territory of the Macleans. In these days Argyll was nothing less than a "phanatick," but was bent on retrieving his family's fortunes, extending their domination and estates, and avoiding his creditors.

The earls, as a rule, were of the Cavalier party, as were the members for shires, on the whole. Sir John Cochrane of Ochiltree much later appeared as an actual conspirator against Government, while Mackenzie himself was foremost in opposition to Lauderdale, till 1675. Of the earls, Kincardine, a man much esteemed, stood by Lauderdale while he could, but was to join Hamilton after a private quarrel with the burly and bullying dictator.

Mackenzie must not be regarded as an eager sympathiser, in 1670, with the oppressed Presbyterians. If ever he "made profession of godliness," as Mr. Cargill declared when excommunicating him, his godliness was a matter of his private religion, and he was revolted by the tenets of the left wing of the Covenanters.

Lauderdale, as Commissioner in 1669, had instructions (1) to propose union with England, (2) the Royal Supremacy over the Church, (3) the establishment of a Militia, (4) the consideration of the Forfeitures, (5) and measures of Conciliation.

In his Memoirs, Mackenzie treats, first, of the Union. Men of intelligence could not believe that it was really desired either by the king or the statesmen. As matters stood, Charles could play off one kingdom against another; and, indeed, the constant policy of Lauderdale had been, from the first, to raise an armed force in Scotland by which the king might coerce the English Parliament. His one idea was to establish Charles's absolute power, and to raise himself on that foundation. To merge Scotland into one kingdom with England was, for Charles, to lose his strongest base of power.

Lauderdale, again, had of all men most to lose if Scotland and England became one nation, "because his absoluteness over Scotland would cease," the English would have control over him. This is so true that Lauderdale in a private letter confessed his aversion to Union; he only worked for it in obedience to the Royal command. Meanwhile the people of Scotland, as in 1706, suspected that the nobles were bribed to consent, and were patriotically averse to the proposal of Union.

Describing the opening of Parliament, Mackenzie speaks of the Lords of the Articles as "a grievance with us";[1] the time came when he regarded "the Articles" as the very foundation of Prerogative, and valued them in proportion, even after the Revolution of 1688. Parliament, though entirely puzzled by the proposal of Union, instantly produced an obsequious and hasty letter of acceptance. Mackenzie rose, and, in his maiden speech, asked for the decency of delay and mature consideration. He was seconded by Sir George Gordon of Haddo, who, much later, was created Earl of Aberdeen. The delicate question of the Succession, (Charles being childless,) was raised, for "the lines of succession in Scotland and England were different, and would there divide" if the king died "without

---

[1] Memoirs, p. 142.

succession." Lauderdale "rose in a great passion," a spectacle to which Mackenzie became well accustomed, for, in 1669–1673, he was a leader of opposition, and in opposition was sometimes alone. "How could any gentleman be so bold as to inquire into the succession, upon a supposition that his Majesty and all the present line should fail?" A lawyer like Mackenzie, accustomed to deal with "tailzies," entails and the accidents incident to them, could not but observe the difficulty which failure of succession must cause, if the countries were made one kingdom without reflection. Hamilton made excuses for the two lawyers, Mackenzie and Haddo. "In him this excuse was thought imprudence, *because the doubt was started in his favour:* the family of Hamilton pretending to be next to the Crown of Scotland, if the succession of king James should fail." Their claim went back to James II. of Scotland, and for many generations had ruled the policy of their House. Perhaps in 1669, though Hamilton did not head the Opposition till 1673, Mackenzie sided with him as the only possible opponent of Lauderdale, and his practical sovereignty.

The letter of Parliament on the Union was read next day, (October 22) and Mackenzie again spoke. (He gives his account of those debates in his Memoirs.) He did not mean absolutely to gratify these popular delusions, "against the Union, but he did desire mature consideration in so great an affair, that the English may be convinced that we are as jealous of our liberties as they could wish us." *Their* Parliaments "do not pass any Law till it be proposed and debated several days." Now, in Scotland, there had been almost no debate, the Lords of the Articles practically prepared the Bills which Parliament merely accepted. So much did Mackenzie's opinions alter, under the later stress of the life official, that, in 1689, we shall find him warning William III. against the desire of his first Scottish Parliament to suppress "the Articles" and have free debate.

Mackenzie pointed out that Parliament was placing the selection of the negotiators of the Treaty of Union in the

hands of the king, (in 1706 the selection was given to
Queen Anne,) and Scotland, by the Parliamentary letter,
was "taking three steps before England meet us in one."
Debates and votes were necessary before taking each of
these steps. "Let us remember that Nature hath bestowed
ease and riches upon others, leaving us courage and honour,
by which we made ourselves oft masters of the other two;
and when honour was in the field, our veins and purses
were open upon all occasions; and therefore though honour
seems but a punctilio to others, let us be careful of it, as
were our predecessors."

The nomination of negotiators should be in the hands,
not of the king, but of the House. He went into details,
adding that, in the attempted Treaty of Union of 1604,
Parliament named the Commissioners, and recommended,
to James VI. and I., "the preservation of our liberties,
laws, and privileges." The Parliament of 1669 should be
as careful. He was saying that he hoped the House "will
suffer this tediousness to pass as zeal," when Tweeddale
cried that "such long discourses were intolerable," especially
where "they were intended to persuade Parliament not to
comply with his Majesty's desires."

The Duke of Hamilton, among shouts of "Privilege,"
moved that Tweeddale should go to the Bar of the House,
but Mackenzie urbanely said that "he had not been interrupted." In him we seem to see a vindicator of open Parliamentary debate, and his speech was cautious in its language,
as Lauderdale remarked with annoyance. He had given no
handle to the Dictator.

Charles presently dropped the scheme of Union, after the
Commissioners for a treaty had met. Mackenzie's remarks
on the plan, in a tract on the subject, balancing advantages
and disadvantages, prove that he would have been, from
patriotic motives, on the side of Lockhart of Carnwath and
Fletcher of Saltoun, against the Union, had he lived to take
part in the debates of 1706.

As to Church matters, he observes that Lauderdale, an
ex-Covenanter of 1637–1647, had been bred in aversion to

Episcopacy, and that the Presbyterians, which is strangely true, were devoted to his interest even when he "seemed to persecute them." Lauderdale was not more ready to persecute Presbyterians than to "snib" bishops. Sharp, who had amazed mankind by saying, in the first sermon preached before this Parliament, that "there were three pretenders to supremacy, the Pope, the King, and the General Assembly," was coerced by the suspension of Archbishop Burnet of Glasgow. He and his clergy had lifted up their voices against the Indulgence, "nor was this paper less seditious than the Remonstrance, nor the Archbishop more innocent than Mr. James Guthrie," writes Mackenzie, "for both equally designed to bar the king from interposing any way in the affairs of the Church." [1]

The Act of Supremacy was passed on November 16, and Mackenzie does not say that he made any opposition. The Act was so drastic that Wodrow "sees nothing to hinder the king, acting according to this power, from establishing a new religion, and palming a new Confession of Faith upon Scotland." James II. did not find that the Act availed him to that extent. But, says Mackenzie, "Most of the Lords of the Articles" (who were simply chosen from the list given by Lauderdale) "inclined to the motion, because by this all the Government of the Church would fall in the hands of laics, and especially of Councillors, of which number they were. And the nobility had been, in this and the former age, kept so far under the subjection of insolent Churchmen, that they were more willing to be subject to their Prince, than to any such low and mean persons as the clergy, which consisted now of the sons of their own servants and farmers."

There were many exceptions to this rule among the *Presbyterian* clergy, often cadets of very good old Houses, but the social standing of the curates was low indeed. Mackenzie's remarks on Bishop Leighton, who for some time took the place of Burnet at Glasgow, are worth quoting :—

"It was easily found, that the Bishop of Dumblane was

---

[1] Memoirs, pp 158, 159.

the most proper and fit person to serve the state in the church, according to the present platform of government now resolv'd upon ; for he was in much esteem, for his piety and moderation, amongst the people, and as to which, the Presbyterians themselves could neither reproach nor equal him ; albeit they hated him most of all his fraternity, in respect he drew many into a kindness for Episcopacy, by his exemplary life, rather than debates. His great principle was, that devotion was the great affair about which churchmen should employ themselves ; and that the gaining of souls, and not the external government, was their proper task ; nor did he esteem it fit, and scarce lawful to churchmen, to sit in councils and judicatories, these being diversions from the main. And albeit his judgement did lead him to believe the Church of England the best modell'd of all others, both for doctrine and discipline, yet did he easily conform with the practice of the Christians amongst whom he liv'd, and therefore liv'd peaceably under Presbytery, till it was abolish'd : and when he undertook to be a Bishop himself, he oppos'd all violent courses, whereby men were forc'd to comply with the present worship, beyond their persuasions ; and he had granted a latitude and indulgence to those of his own diocese, before the King had allow'd any by his letter."

How the popular Covenanting book *Naphtali* spoke of Leighton may be illustrated by an extract. Of this "angelic man," as Burnet calls him, it is written, "It is true indeed that Mr. Leighton, prelate of Dunblane, under a jesuitical vizard of pretended holiness, humility, and crucifixion to the world, hath studied to seem to creep upon the ground, but always up hill, toward promotion and more places of ease, honour, and wealth ; and as there is none of them all hath, with a kiss, so betrayed the cause, and smitten religion under the fifth rib, and hath been such an offence to the godly ; so there is none who by his way, practice, and expressions, giveth greater suspicion of a popish inclination, affection, and design." [1]

---

[1] *Naphtali*, p 301 (ed. 1667).

No sooner had Lauderdale discomfited bishops by the
Act of Supremacy, than he consoled them by bestowing his
attention on Presbyterian recalcitrants. Mackenzie writes,
"Upon St. Andrews's day, he past two Acts in their (the
Bishops') favours; one to make the parishes liable for the insolencies committed against ministers; and another, containing severe certifications against such as paid not Bishops'
duties, and Ministers' stipends. The first of these Acts was
enforc'd as necessary, because Ministers, to the great contempt
of religion, had their houses robbed, and were nightly pursued
for their lives, in all the western shires; so that they were forc'd
to keep guards, which exhausted their stipends, and abstracted
themselves from their employments: and albeit those shires
pretended that this was done by highway men, who showed
their insolencies under the pretext of religion, calling themselves Presbyterians, and enveighing against the poor
Ministers whom they robb'd, in the language of that sect;
yet it was concluded, that these insolencies were committed
by those of that persuasion, who were known to think that
all injuries done to Episcopal Ministers, were so many
acceptable services done to God: and it was most probable,
that the same zeal which carried them on to plunder,
imprison, and execute all such as differ'd from them,
in the last rebellion, and to shoot at the Bishop of St.
Andrews upon the street, might incite them to great
outrages, when they were countenanc'd, as they thought,
by authority, and under silence of night, when they might
hope for impunity: nor was ever the West country known
to be infected with robbers at other occasions, so that they
were connivers at least in those crimes, and therefore de-
serv'd to be fin'd upon such occasions." As to the outrages,
Mackenzie's evidence is amply corroborated by Burnet.

Lauderdale next introduced a scheme for "a constant
militia" of 22,000 men. Already, on riding from the Border
to Edinburgh, Lauderdale, as Mackenzie says, had reviewed
the militia with satisfaction. As he wrote to the king he
had seen five troops of horse, and six admirably drilled
regiments of foot, "those you may depend on to be ready

to march when and whither you please," that is, across the Border if the king needed them. Mackenzie says that the world quite understood the aim at a standing army, "to make Parliaments unnecessary."[1] But the militia did not prove useful against insurgent Covenanters. The Militia Act was opposed by Mackenzie, in a clause permitting the men to be quartered on "deficients" in tax-paying. He denounced quartering "as a word odious to the people," not foreseeing his own later use of the process. He also stood out against a tax on salt, which hampered the fishing trade of his constituents, till Lauderdale stood up in wrath and swore that "he would, by virtue of his Majesty's prerogative pepper the fishing"—give them pepper. "After a long and deep silence," Mackenzie rose, and spoke thus :—

"He believed that prerogative granted to the King, of disposing upon our trade with foreigners, would not authorise his Majestie's Officers of State, nor any else, to impose arbitrary customs ; the design of that Act being only, that his Majesty should, during the interval of Parliaments, regulate our trade with England, in order to the treaty of commerce which was to be settled betwixt us ; at least it could not warrant the taking away a privilege, granted to the fishers, in the same Parliament wherein this prerogative was granted : but without debating what his Grace might do in other cases, the Parliament would here desire the vote, whereby it would appear what was the opinion of the Parliament, who were his Majesty's great Council ; and if thereafter, his Majesty should think fit to burden trade, his subjects would succumb to all his royal commands." The votes were declared to be equal, twice, and Rothes, as Chancellor, gave his casting vote in favour of Lauderdale.

In short, by constant opposition, notably in favour of free elections in the burghs, Mackenzie "made his Grace swear that he would have that factious young man removed from the Parliament," as not "a free Baron," not holding his lands direct from the Crown. But Primrose, the Register, pointed out "that this would make the people jealous of

[1] Memoirs, p 167.

some close design to overturn their liberties, which, as they believed, that gentleman defended upon all occasions."

It was next Mackenzie's business to oppose a motion for forfeiting rebels who did not appear when summoned to trial. They had been so forfeited, after the Pentland Rising, with the sanction of the judges. Mackenzie spoke against the desired Parliamentary sanction : it permitted witnesses to give evidence which they would not dare to utter if confronted with the accused. Many years later, when public prosecutor, he had unwelcome proof of the correctness of his argument. The Act, however, was passed. Passed, too, by Lauderdale's violence, without a vote, and in face of the opposition of the innumerable creditors of the Earl of Argyll, and of his debtors, clan Maclean, was an Act restoring Argyll to all the lands that his father had forfeited. The consequences, as we shall see, were the ruin of Argyll, in 1681.

The Parliament in 1670 met on July 22. " The fanatics, encouraged by the Indulgence," had held many conventicles, especially a great armed conventicle at the Hill of Beith, in Fife, "being all armed," and insulting some of the Guards. Mackenzie says that Rothes exaggerated the facts, in letters to the king, in order to decry the Indulgence, and the Earl of Tweeddale, its author. The Church party in England blamed Lauderdale, who thereon passed Acts fining non-conformists, and making preaching at field conventicles a capital offence ; a law more severe in words than in fact, like the similar law inflicting death for the third hearing of Mass, passed by the Protestant Convention of 1560. Witnesses were obliged, under arbitrary punishment, to answer, on oath, all questions proposed by the Council.

This measure was regarded by Mackenzie as " a new Inquisition," and illegal. Tweeddale thought it severe but necessary. Something was necessary. Burnet says in 1672, " Conventicles abounded in all places of the country. And some furious zealots broke into the houses of some of the ministers, wounding them and robbing their goods, forcing some of them to swear that they would never officiate any more in their churches." Burnet visited some of these condemned men in prison. One went further than John Knox, and justified himself by the looting of the Egyptians by the Israelites.[1]

In 1673, on an unlucky day for himself, Burnet published his *Vindication of the Church and State in Scotland.* He was then a familiar of Lauderdale, whom he praises in fulsome wise in his Dedication. In his *Vindication* he says, " How many of the (conformist) ministers have been invaded in their houses, their houses rifled, their goods carried away, themselves cruelly beaten and wounded, and often made to swear to abandon their churches, and that they should not so much as complain of such bad usage to those in authority. . . . Their wives also were beaten and wounded by those accursed zealots, some of them being scarcely recovered out of their labour in child birth." A Presbyterian, in the dialogue, replies that " our honest ministers express their horror at such practices," to which it is answered that, notorious as the outrages are, and heavy as are the stolen articles, no evidence against the perpetrators can ever be extracted. The west, (as in "an island celebrated for its verdure and its wrongs,") was terrorised by village ruffians, whose pastors did not aid in detecting the authors of outrages.

Now came a quarrel between Lauderdale and Tweeddale, and the rising influence over Lauderdale of the Countess of Dysart, whom he married six weeks after the death of his neglected wife (1671). The daughter of Will Murray, who had been whipping-boy to Charles I., and was behind all the darkest intrigues of the Civil War, the Countess was said to have sapped the rigid virtue of Oliver Cromwell! She was regarded as unscrupulously avaricious, and driving Lauderdale on to greater excesses of tyranny. This marriage, according to Mackenzie, had strange consequences.

" Lauderdale had, of a long time, entertain'd with Lady Margaret Kennedy, daughter to the Earl of Cassillis, an intimacy which had grown great enough to become sus-

[1] Burnet, i. p. 621 (1833).

picious, in a person who lov'd not, as some said, his own
Lady. This Lady had never married, and was always
reputed a wit, and the great patron of the Presbyterians,
in which persuasion she was very bigot; and the suspicion
increas'd much, upon her living in the Abbey, in which
no woman else lodg'd; nor did the Commissioner blush
to go openly to her chamber, in his night-gown : whereupon
her friends, having challeng'd her for that unusual commerce,
and having represented to her the open reprehensions and
railleries of the people, received no other answer, than that
her virtue was above suspicion; as really it was, she
being a person whose religion exceeded as far her wit,
as her parts exceeded others of her sex." The rest of the
story, with its consequences, is to be given later.

Lauderdale's brother, Charles Maitland of Haltoun, took
Tweeddale's place with him, and Haltoun was as greedy
and unscrupulous as the new duchess herself. She was
forty-five years of age, but, says Mackenzie, "Her wit was
not less charming than the beauty of other women, nor
had the extraordinary beauty she possessed, whilst she
was young, ceded to the age at which she was then
arrived."

Lauderdale was now created a duke by the king whose
"creature" he professed himself to be, and he passed an
Act making the ordaining of young ministers by deposed
ministers, a capital offence. Such ordinations, as Mackenzie
says, *ad ministerium vagum*, were "against the Acts of
their own Assemblies." Mackenzie appears to have supported Lauderdale, for once, in his desire to abolish the
Summer Session, through which "June and July, the only
pleasant months, wherein gardens and land could be
improved, were spent in the most unwholesome and unpleasant town in Scotland." However, Lauderdale changed
his mind, and the town was supposed to have bribed his
duchess. But "after exact inquiry, I found these" (the
charge that the change was proposed in order to exact
bribes from the town) "to be mere calumnies."

Mackenzie again showed his courage when Lauderdale

passionately declared that the member for Inverurie should be sent to prison, and to the Bar of the House, for suggesting that, as in England, members might make extra-parliamentary addresses to their constituents.   Though Mackenzie and others "offered to appear for him," the member for Inverurie gave in his submission, "and was brought to the Bar and then to his knees, but without any vote of Parliament. . . . And here did many begin to repent their former pusillanimous compliance, and to accuse themselves of having betrayed the privileges of their native country."

Backed by the advocates and the burghs, Mackenzie next spoke against burdening personal, as contrasted with real property, with taxation. He was outvoted, and again, when he resisted an Act regulating, and reducing, the fees of advocates. "At best the Act will but tie such as fear an oath, and enrich such as contemn it, and thus you will seem more careful of the people's money than of their souls." The advocates, on whom Lauderdale had imposed four ignorant judges, including Ramsay, Provost of Edinburgh, turned to popular courses, and, in all societies, "most of them being idle, though men of excellent parts," criticised and ridiculed the Commissioner. Dalrymple of Stair, then Lord President, suffered from their tongues in Lauderdale's company.

We have a letter of Mackenzie to Lauderdale dated Edinburgh, Oct. 15, 1672. At that time he was opposing the "obliging minister." The occasion of this letter of October 15, 1672, is stated in his Memoirs. The Provost of Edinburgh, Sir Andrew Ramsay, was becoming, to all appearance, Provost for life. He had been elected ten times, and, by gaining £10,000 for Lauderdale in civic jobbery, was much in his favour, and led the votes for him in Parliament. Lauderdale procured for him an annuity of £200, and £4000 on his "comprising of the Bass, a rock barren and useless." In fact Lauderdale and Ramsay had established what the Americans, in the technical language of municipal corruption, style "a graft."

The reader must remember that Mackenzie tells us all this in his History, and that, about 1680, he was polishing the style of his History, under Lauderdale's "superintendency." We cannot sufficiently admire his candour, and Lauderdale's good nature unless Mackenzie had begun a *new* History on very different lines, a work of which nothing has ever been heard.

In "working the graft," Ramsay invented new patent places for his partisans, "applying the Common Good" (the municipal funds) "to himself and his friends." In 1672, he was opposed, two of his followers voted "*non liquet*," a case was put before the Chancellor and President, and it was decided that no man should be Provost for longer than two years in succession.

Ramsay wrote to Court that a riot had occurred during these proceedings, and the Privy Council were commanded to inquire into the tumult and its authors. The Council examined witnesses, in the absence of the accused, which was illegal (except, apparently, in the case of attendants at preaching conventicles). There really was no riot, but some unusual proceedings by men in Ramsay's own livery; and two bailies, who said that there was a riot, confessed that Ramsay had coerced them by threats. An important municipal politician, Rocheid, was judged without being heard : Ramsay was "so much dreaded that none dared oppose him," and under protection of Royal favour, was re-elected.[1] So Mackenzie writes in his Memoirs of Scotland. To Lauderdale, on the date already given, he writes as Advocate for the town : the letter is given in summary.[2]

EDINBURGH, 15 *Oct.* 1672.

To THE DUKE OF LAUDERDALE.—The neighbours of the good town of Edinburgh would have presented the Duke with an earlier address, but their business was not ripe enough for so eminent a person : they would have pre-

---

[1] Mackenzie, Memoirs, pp 246-250
[2] *Add. MSS*, B M. 32,094 (*Malet Papers*, f. 270).

sented a letter with many thousands of hands but feared to seem "tumultuary." Therefore as Advocate, in their behalf he sends an account of their differences with Sir Andrew Ramsay with a tender of their respects.

The town being desirous not to "jusle" with Sir Andrew Ramsay but finding his re-election would overturn their privileges, dealt with him to refuse the employment, on condition of securing to him all that had passed under his hands and continuing the clerkship to his son. On his refusal one of the number moderately and respectfully protested against his eligibility: even two of the voices numbered for him were only conditional: there was no tumult as represented. The people, who groaned under his perpetual dictatorship, by their looks expressed more sorrow than any one magistrate's interest is worth. He wonders how Ramsay can think it dishonourable to quit an employment which no subject can keep by law. Moreover, the Lords of Session are displeased at one of their members (Ramsay) being abstracted from the common service by extrinsic employments. The "factious" protest of which he complains that Mackenzie drew it up, is the foundation of a new "libell" before the lords, who finding anything censurable in it, he will forfeit his gown. The Chancellor found there was no tumult, and in Lauderdale's name promised the town a fair trial for their privileges. To pretend Sir Andrew is still a "marchand" is a cheating of the law. On behalf of his clients he begs that the Duke will inform himself through the Chancellor.

It is clear that Mackenzie stood in no fear of Lauderdale. His letter to that minister, who, for the purposes of the "graft" had made Ramsay a judge, a "Lord of Session," is in the same spirit as the passage in his History (Memoirs). On February 3, 1673, Mackenzie pleaded for the town, Sir George Lockhart was counsel for Ramsay. Mackenzie argued that Ramsay, as a Lord of Session, and no merchant, ought to be declared incapable of being elected as Provost, for all time coming. He described Ramsay's conduct in the Town Council in words which applied precisely to that of Lauderdale in Parliament. "He tyrannously threatened and abused, with most scandalous and opprobrious language," offering to imprison opponents without trial. Every listener must have noted and smiled at the parallel to Lauderdale. Just as Lauderdale made the untrained and ignorant Ramsay a judge, so Ramsay made his son, "a mere child, Town Clerk, and uplifted the profits."

Sir George Lockhart, the greatest advocate of his day, in reply, likened Mackenzie to "a John of Leyden, a Masaniello, an enraged Venner the cooper, and his Fifth Monarchy men." Sir George Mackenzie would "throw all into confusion, rebellion, and anarchy," and establish Annual Kings as in *The Golden Bough!* "He threatened to reduce the world to a second Babel, if not to the first Chaos." The judges seem to have laughed, for Lockhart says, "I pray you to be serious in so important an affair."

Fountainhall, then a junior at the Bar, later a judge, is wholly on Lockhart's side, against that "sneaking" anarchist, Mackenzie, and his riotous clients, who threaten to "de Witt" Ramsay, to tear him to pieces. Ramsay, in fact, is "a storehouse of virtuous actions." Among other good deeds, he obtained an annuity of £200 for the Provost;—scarcely unselfish, as he meant to be Provost for life. He did not succeed, for provosts, by Rothes's decision, were henceforth never to hold office for more than two years.

An instructive thing to mark is this attitude of Fountainhall, then Mr. John Lauder, of Fountainhall. He was an honest man, granting the state of society in which he lived. But he had married a daughter of this jobbing tyrannical Sir Andrew Ramsay, and he gives a flourishing report of his many virtues. His title as an amateur Lord of Session, or Judge, was Lord Abbotshall. Among the factions of Hamilton, Rothes, and Lauderdale, "Abbotshall, *who could make a very judicious choice,* did strike in with Lauderdale, and upon his bottom reared up the fabric of his ensuing greatness. For by his favour he was both maintained in the provostry of Edinburgh, and advanced to the Session, Privy Council, and Exchequer." Fountain-hall regrets that, when Ramsay appointed his own son, a boy, to the town clerkship, "his death, some few years after, made the design of this profitable place abortive!" He complains of the "envy and malice" of the citizens, when Lauderdale, through Ramsay, obtained "yearly, large donations and gratifications, besides they longed to have a share in the government of the town, which they saw monopolised by Sir Andrew and his creatures." Thus Sir Andrew, like Themistocles and Coriolanus, says the egregious Fountainhall, became the victim of popular in-gratitude.[1]

Such are the opinions of Fountainhall, the pink of respectability, and when Mackenzie, later, "made a very judicious choice," "struck in with Lauderdale," and "upon his bottom reared up the fabric of his greatness," he did a thing which we must regret and condemn, though, in the eyes of the contemporary moralist, his conduct was "very judicious."

Autres temps, autres mœurs!

[1] Fountainhall, *Journals*, p 306.

CHAPTER IX

MACKENZIE'S CHANGE OF SIDES—THE "OUTED" ADVOCATES

Mackenzie's boldness in bearding Lauderdale—How his party began to suspect him—In 1673, Church affairs neglected by both parties—Private aims of Hamilton—Mackenzie defends the burghs—Organised parliamentary opposition to Lauderdale—Lauderdale gives up monopolies—Mackenzie's secret interview with Lauderdale—Who falsely says that he betrays his party — His party believe Lauderdale — Irritation of Mackenzie — Quarrel with Lockhart — Resentment of English interference—Dread of danger from popular excitement—Lauderdale attacked in English House of Commons—Hamilton seeks their aid—Mackenzie's patriotism hurt—Turns against Hamilton as avaricious—Repeated Conventicles—Riot of Presbyterian women—Sharp hustled and threatened—Mackenzie disgusted—Affair of the suspension of advocates—Mackenzie sides with his profession—Believes that Lockhart intrigues for his ruin—Mackenzie breaks his leg—Accused of perjury—His defence—He and his friends to be brought to trial—Finds that Lockhart is betraying him—Makes his submission in deference to his Prince—His example is followed—Changes sides in politics—His mixed motives—Becomes an ally of the Duchess of Lauderdale.

So far we have seen in Mackenzie a young Liberal politician full of promise. He was not to be daunted ; he spoke with grace and studied moderation. He resisted and denounced the corruption, the public robberies, under Lauderdale's administration. In all matters, says Mackenzie, "the public good is made subservient to the meanest interests, and is overruled by the most inconsiderable and unworthy persons." Lauderdale, he says, consulted nobody, and passed all his measures by bullying and violence. He lost his esteem among the Presbyterians "by his bawdy discourses and passionate oaths," but "he knew not what it was to dissemble." We know Burnet's portrait, and

Lely's, of the flushed angry face of Lauderdale, which
terrified most of the members of the House, but had no
terrors for Mackenzie. In opposing Lauderdale he spoke,
as that politician says, in terms of honeyed urbanity, but
he was *tenax propositi*, resolute in support of his opinion.
The change in Mackenzie's attitude began, at first unper-
ceived by himself, in the next session of Parliament. In
opposing Lauderdale he had carried on the feud of his
cousin, Tarbat, against the statesman who had driven
Tarbat from office, for Mackenzie was a good clansman.

In October 1673, Lauderdale, who was now obnoxious
to the English House of Commons, again came down as
Commissioner. In this session, Mackenzie was suspected
by his party of deserting them: he gives his own defence
against that charge. In 1673 a set of politicians called
"The Party," consisting primarily of the Duke of Hamilton,
Queensberry, and Rothes, was deliberately formed against
Lauderdale. Of this party, Mackenzie, already distinguished
in opposition, was a member. On Lauderdale's side were
Argyll (the "martyr" of 1685), Kincardine, and Stair, the
godly President of the Court of Session. It would be a
mistake to suppose that Mackenzie's activity in the Opposition committed him to the cause of the Presbyterians.
Kirkton says "all the time of this great strife, (though
some expected it would have been otherwise) neither of
the sides mentioned the name of religion, either for dis-
tress or danger. . . . And this made the lovers of religion
to be less concerned for either of the Dukes, since neither
of the two owned the most noble interest, which was in
great hazard." The party divisions "emboldened the dis-
contents," the Presbyterians.[1] The "Party," as Hamilton's
group was called, was *not* a party formed to befriend the
Presbyterians. Letters that passed between Hamilton and
Lauderdale show that Hamilton was full of private grudges,
and anxious for money and public employment. He wants
a very old family debt repaid, he wants the Garter, and
the command of the castle of Dunbarton. He wishes

----

[1] Kirkton, p. 342.

(June 9, 1673) to decline a commission to keep order in the west, as dangerous. It is too like the commission that brought Sir James Turner into trouble.[1] It was not from a party aiming at the restoration of Presbyterianism that Mackenzie, later, retired.

Before Lauderdale's arrival in Edinburgh, in 1673, the burghs continued their course of agitation for free election of provosts, and were advised by Mackenzie. Burnet arrived in Edinburgh from London while the Party were discussing their tactics, the night before Parliament met; Lauderdale declined to let him come to his presence at Holyrood; and supposed, correctly, I think, that the Party were acting on encouragement and advice from Shaftesbury. Consequently Lauderdale, as he writes to Charles (Nov. 13, 1673) "was met with such a spirit as I thought never to have seen here," for, when he proposed that the Lords of the Articles should answer the King's Message, Hamilton, and more than twenty other speakers, demanded that their grievances should first be stated and considered. Morton, Eglintoun, Cassilis, Roxburgh, and Queensberry, with others, followed suit. Sir Francis Scott denounced the war with Holland; Hume of Polwarth moved for a Committee of Bills, that is of Grievances, and for a debate as to whether they were a Free Parliament. (This Polwarth, later Earl of Marchmont, is the Whig whom Macaulay hated worse than some Tories.)

The result was that Lauderdale called a large meeting at Holyrood, where he removed the monopolies on salt, a perquisite of Kincardine's, brandy, and tobacco, popular grievances. "This would certainly have satisfied," says Mackenzie, "if the design of such as managed the whole affair had not been, not to suffer Lauderdale to be reconciled to the people, and to persuade the Court that he was not able to serve the king here."

Emphatically he was not: Mackenzie's own Memoirs prove that, but his Memoirs now begin to take a new ply. He tells us what he did, after the failure of Lauderdale

[1] *Hist. MSS. Commission*, XI, Part VI, pp. 139–146.

to secure peace at the Holyrood meeting occurred. When the assembly broke up, "Sir George Mackenzie, finding that their differences reached further than was at first designed, resolved to try, in a private conference, if Lauderdale would consent to a rectification of some other abuses; and [they] having met privately upon that design, his own friends grew jealous that he was to desert them; and Lauderdale, that he designed only to pump him. And thus his love to his country drew upon himself that hatred which he endeavoured to lessen in both against one another. And these who would not believe Lauderdale, even when he spoke truth, seemed to believe him when he said, in policy only, that Sir George had offered to betray them: albeit they found that this was a mere Court trick, for Sir George had at that time refused to be Justice Clerk, and had adhered very vigorously to them thereafter; in resentment of this injury" (the charge that he was betraying his party,) "done him by Lauderdale. And Lauderdale entrusted him thereafter with all affairs of the greatest importance and secrecy, which certainly he had never done, if he had found that Sir George had betrayed his old friends." This part of the Memoirs must have been written, or the passage was interpolated, after 1677, when Lauderdale made Mackenzie King's Advocate.

When once Mackenzie had digested his grudge against Lauderdale for traducing him, he was on the way to change parties. This may seem rather extraordinary. He opposes Lauderdale's measures when Lauderdale is in the height of his power, and comes over towards that ruler when he is in considerable peril; when "the Thanes fly from him;" when Tweeddale, and Kincardine, and Sir Robert Murray, his most reputable supporters, fail the Commissioner, and when Gilbert Burnet reports to the English House of Commons, private remarks of Lauderdale very apt to involve him in the doom of Strafford.

A person enamoured of "solitude" and averse to "public employment," like Mackenzie in his essay of 1665, would not now have acted like Mackenzie. We shall see

that he changed sides partly in the irritation caused by
what he deemed the unjust treatment of himself by his
associates; partly in wrath against his insolent rival, Sir
George Lockhart; and, again, (if the partiality of a
biographer does not delude me,) because he resented
English interference in the affairs of his country; and
mainly because popular passions, on the Presbyterian side,
seemed to threaten great dangers to public peace, and to
Royal prerogative, then regarded by him as the only
bulwark against disorder.

It is my conjecture that Mackenzie, as a stalwart patriot,
was cooled in his aversion to Lauderdale by English
interference with the affairs of Scotland. "The Party,"
according to Lauderdale, was "advised and fomented at
London, you know by whom" (Shaftesbury) and is headed
by Tweeddale, Hamilton, "and their two or three lawyers,"
doubtless Mackenzie was one of them. Their aim was
to attack the existence of the Lords of the Articles, whom
Lauderdale, as we saw, nominated himself, to carry his
purposes. In Lauderdale's opinion, as he told his brother,
the English Whigs wanted him to be superseded by
Monmouth, who declined to meddle. The Whigs, early
in 1674, were stirring against Lauderdale in the House
of Commons of England. In their opinion, based on
Gilbert Burnet's revelations, Lauderdale meant to use
Scotland, as Strafford had meant to use Ireland, as a base
of attack on the English Parliament. Ever since the
Restoration this plan, the use of a Scottish force to invade
England, had been present to Lauderdale's mind. The
English had defeated the Scots; he wanted a stroke at them.

He was to be removed from Charles and his place,
"this vote pleased the factious party here exceedingly,"
but Charles had assured Lauderdale that he would stand
by him. The Party wished to send Rothes, Primrose, and
Nisbet, King's Advocate, "to transact the affairs of Scotland
at London without me," so Lauderdale wrote to the king.
(Feb. 1, 1674.) Kincardine, however, (February 10) wrote from
London to Lauderdale that he had refused to be questioned

by the English House of Commons, for "since they could pretend no jurisdiction over Scotland, I could not be answerable when I should return to my own country, if I should answer to a committee of the Parliament of England, on any affair which was only proper for Scotland." [1]

Lauderdale's faction argued that their opponents were bad Scots, unpatriotic courtiers of the English Whigs. The Duchess writes, "Their carriage is most detestable to all honest and sober men, but the longing desire," (in England,) "of such a conquest as would be the cantonising of Scotland, makes them respected by only those who will be the most ready to sacrifice them. . . ." [2]

When Lauderdale adjourned the Scottish Parliament (January 17, 1674), Hamilton, Tweeddale, and General Drummond went to London with their complaints, and raised a storm against Lauderdale in the English House of Commons. [3]   Burnet says that Charles sent for them, intending to back their party if he could get supplies from Parliament and so prosecute the Dutch war.   He failed, and returned to confidence in Lauderdale.   However this may be, it is clear that the English Parliament was interfering in Scottish affairs, and accusing Lauderdale of having said, in Council, that *The King's Edicts are as good as Laws.* [4]

Now Mackenzie was "a Scottish man," first of all, and had the greatest jealousy of English interference with Scotland.   It may be, then, that this jealousy of English interference first inclined him to hold late in 1673, or early in 1674, his private conference with Lauderdale.   His natural and professional aversion for the high-handed conduct of the English House of Commons, which Charles prorogued after signing the peace with Holland, may also have influenced him.   Certainly Mackenzie did not now come over to Lauderdale wholly.   The Convention of Burghs, in

---

[1] See *Lauderdale Papers*, vol. iii. pp 20–34; *State Trials*, vol. vi. 1026–1034.

[2] *Letters of Lady Margaret Kennedy*, Appendix, p 105.

[3] Memoirs, p. 263

[4] *State Trials*, vi 1028   Also Kincardine to Lauderdale, 12 Feb. 1673-4, *Lauderdale Papers*, vol. iii. p. 34.

August 1674, petitioned Charles for a new Parliament, (the previous Parliament had been dissolved by Lauderdale). Three provosts were thereon imprisoned: the rest were called before the Privy Council, and, when asked who was the author of their petition, the Provost of Glasgow "indirectly let fall that Sir George Mackenzie was the man." Their leaders were heavily fined, but nothing was done to Mackenzie.[1]

His Memoirs now begin to show an aversion to the Duke of Hamilton, whose party was, for long, the only drag on the wheel of despotism. Lauderdale (March 24, 1674) issued a Royal proclamation discharging all penalties due by penal statutes, and all bygone loss, and suspending all exaction of annuities. "The very men who had so passionately craved this . . . treated it in ridicule, lest it might make some kind impression upon the people for Lauderdale; and though Duke Hamilton had very earnestly pressed for this discharge, yet he would not consent that the proclamation should discharge the taxation 1633, because he pretended a right to them (sic)." Hamilton "forced the Council to discharge that part of the Act of Grace," and lost favour with the public, as an avaricious man.[2] He was fighting for repayment of the debts to his wife's father, incurred by Charles I.

It seems probable that Mackenzie and his party leaders first quarrelled, when Lauderdale, "out of policy," accused him of betraying them; and that then Lauderdale, "put at" as he was in England, thereafter ingratiated himself slowly with Mackenzie.

The year 1674 was remarkable for many conventicles, even in Lothian, and "the Magdalen Chapel in Edinburgh was broken open" for "outed" preachers. Mackenzie says that "many hundreds of women" with a petition, filled the Parliament Close, and threatened the life of Archbishop Sharp. "Some had conspired to set on him, when a woman,

---

[1] Law's *Memorials*, pp 72, 73.

[2] Memoirs, pp. 266, 267. See Hamilton's contention, that the discharge by a Royal letter was unconstitutional. *L.P.*, iii. 38–40.

whom I shun to mention, should raise her hand on high as a signal." Rothes, however, "entertaining the woman with insinuating speeches all the time as he passed to the Council, did divert that bloody design."[1] Charles Kirkpatrick Sharpe avers that Mrs. Livingstone, widow of a preacher and daughter of the fanatic Johnstone of Waristoun, was the woman, and refers to "Wodrow and Kirkton."[2] Wodrow says that Mrs. Livingstone "presented the petition to the Chancellor," Rothes ; so probably she was the lady on whom Rothes bestowed his blandishments.[3] Wodrow tells us that he received the petition civilly, read it, "and patiently heard what she had to add. He talked and jested a little with some of the rest." Some of the women (among them was Gilbert Burnet's aged mother, with two of his lady cousins,) called Sharp "Judas," and others "traitor," and one of them laid her hand upon his neck, and said, "Ere all was done that neck behoved to pay for it ; " but no further violence was done. We know what the sex are when they go on the warpath ! Sharp, an Episcopal Orpheus, was in danger of being torn to pieces by the Presbyterian Mænads ! Wodrow merely takes his anecdote, with verbal changes, from Kirkton.[4] Where Mackenzie got the story of the signal for murder we do not know. The ringleaders in the riot were punished, but to kill Sharp was the burning desire of the fanatics, male and female, indeed a woman put the slayers on his track at the last.

We have observed that among the grievances which Mackenzie had argued against in Parliament, were not named those of Presbyterians deprived of their favourite ministers. He probably adhered to his early opinion, given in *The Religious Stoic* (1663) that the subject, in matters of Church government, must obey the laws of the country, and,—as Leighton was peaceable under Presbyterian sway, though attached to "the beauty of holiness,"—be peaceable, though of Presbyterian sentiments, under legalised Episcopacy.

[1] Memoirs, p 273.   [2] Law's *Memorials*, p. 67, *note.*
[3] Wodrow, ii. pp. 268–269.   [4] Kirkton, pp. 344–345.

H

Such things as armed conventicles and riots of women, were not apt to make Mackenzie more tender towards the cause of Presbyterians, though he disapproved of the expulsion of many ministers from their parishes.

Events now occurred which, in their effects, led to Mackenzie's definite change of party. The suspicion in which he was held by his faction, on account of his private interview with Lauderdale, and Lauderdale's charge against him of betraying his associates, probably rankled deeply in his mind. Meanwhile (in May, 1674) Mackenzie's hated rival, Sir George Lockhart, had advised the Earl of Callendar, in a suit against the Earl of Dunfermline, to appeal to Parliament against a decision of the Court of Session. Mackenzie says that Lockhart, knowing Callendar to possess in Parliament the influence of his father-in-law, Hamilton, hoped that his client would thereby triumph, while Parliament would be glad to be recognised as the final Court of Appeal. "This appeal displeased most sober men," for ignorant members would have, in the subtlest points of law, votes overriding those of the expert judges. Lauderdale showed Charles that, while the king, (really Lauderdale himself,) chose the judges, the king did not elect the members of Parliament. The king, Lauderdale, and the judges were all interested in preventing appeals to Parliament.

The judges cited Callendar for making this appeal, which they regarded as an affront, and Mackenzie, with Lockhart and two other advocates, drew up a paper in which Callendar declared that he did not "appeal," but merely "protested for remedy of law," a delicate distinction ! Examined before the judges, they adhered to this declaration, though why that course then pleased Mackenzie which "displeased most sober men," and was, he says, part of an intrigue of Lockhart to become President of the Court of Session, he does not tell us, beyond saying that Lockhart, for his own purposes, beguiled him into it. The judges were mostly in Lauderdale's interest, and gave him a kind of testimonial to the legality of his proceedings. Armed with this, and accompanied and backed by the President,

Dalrymple of Stair, he went to London, and complained against the advocates. They regarded the crafty Stair as their chief foe, and persecuted him with printed pasquils, to be found in Maidment's collection. Charles, in a letter to the judges (May 19, 1674), approved of their doings, and expressed his "abhorrence of appeals." He bade the judges forbid such appeals, and command the advocates to disavow them on oath, under penalty of disbarring, and of imprisonment. Charles also forbade the burghs to elect members who were "gentlemen or noblemen's servants." The burghs conceived that they would thus be deprived of representatives learned in the law, though such elections were contrary to their old rules.

Mackenzie drew up for them a reply to the king, which Lockhart and a Mr. Pringle carried to their committee. But they so altered Mackenzie's draft as to change it from "a discreet and dutiful" to "a most indiscreet and unpolished paper," for the purpose, so Lockhart told James Stewart, of "making Sir George Mackenzie unpardonable." This Stewart, author of *Jus Populi*, was an unscrupulous mischief-maker, and it is not necessary to believe the charge against Lockhart which he seems to have revealed to Mackenzie. The Committee of Burghs, believing the altered paper to be Mackenzie's, sent it up to the king, who was angry, and fined and imprisoned the provosts of Aberdeen, Glasgow, and Jedburgh.

Lockhart and Sir John Cunningham being now called before the judges, owned that *formal* appeals were contrary to an Act of James II., but said that *protestations for remedy of law* might be allowed. They were disbarred; and the junior counsel followed them out of the court in a "tumultuary" fashion. They were ordered to leave Edinburgh, and some of them went to Haddington, some to Linlithgow. Lockhart thus had sharers in his disbarment, and "diverted early from himself that great hatred which was so justly conceived against his insolence and his avarice; two crimes which were more eminent in him than his learning." His insolence we have seen in his grotesque

attack on Mackenzie, when he spoke for the freedom of
the election of provosts of Edinburgh. Burnet also says
that Lockhart was "a covetous, an ambitious, and a
passionate man," though a most learned pleader and
accomplished debater.

Mackenzie, at all events, having been in opposition to
Lauderdale, was supposed to have devised the appeal. Really
Lockhart had drawn him into it, telling him that, in his
parliamentary opposition, he would have the aid of the advocates in general, and that the appeal was contrived for this
very purpose. Mackenzie was not averse to receiving such aid
against Lauderdale, he says, till he found himself opposing
his Prince, who, by Proclamation, announced that all
advocates who did not submit by a given day should be
for ever disbarred.

In November, 1674, according to the Biography prefixed
to his Works (1722), Mackenzie addressed the judges on
the whole question, in a speech which is published. He
said that he was resolved to withdraw and not to plead,
"because of my indisposition," he refers, perhaps, to an
accident in which he broke his leg.[1] He cannot therefore
be asked to "declare"; his meaning is not obvious, unless
the declaration was that he disavowed the late appeal, and
would never more be concerned in an appeal to Parliament.
He never means to plead, if he does not plead he cannot
appeal, and therefore cannot be asked to forswear appeals.
But his profession is his "life rent right," "his plough
or his ship," and cannot be taken from him if he commits
no crime. Now there is no law declaring appeals to be
criminal. Express Acts of Sederunt have allowed Protests
for Remedy of Law; if his law is wrong, he is mistaken,
not criminal. A new Act against Appeals can be made,
and will be obeyed, and the advocates are ready to promise
not to appeal in future. They are also asked to disown

---

[1] This broken leg is rather mysterious. In an undated letter to Archbishop Sharp,
written apparently in 1675, Mackenzie says that his enemies "have broken his leg,
and are trying to break his reputation." How did they manage to break his
leg?—*Add. MSS.*, Brit. Museum, 23,138, f 53.

what they have done ; they are disbarred for a mere word ; "and no gentleman would disapprove what he hath done."

Mackenzie's Life avers that this speech was held satisfactory, "the Advocates returned to Edinburgh, and were admitted to plead."[1] This is erroneous. On November 24 Mackenzie, "who has been sick before," was required to disown his appeals, he did not give satisfaction, and was disbarred.[2] The king (December 18) called on the advocates, on pain of perpetual disbarment, to petition the judges for readmission before January 28, 1675.[3] Mackenzie says in his Memoirs that he "did so much tender the reputation" of his king, "that being bedridden by a broken leg," he did not attend in Court when the rest were disbarred, or "publicly own the appeal." He wrote a letter to his brethren of the Bar in which he promised not to practise till the others were readmitted. Lockhart insisted that he should have himself disbarred, so he "owned the appeal with a very undaunted courage." To his letter of promise to abstain from practice till the rest re-entered, he added a postscript, "But if I enter, and put myself in the same position with the rest, I do declare this letter, and all the obligations therein, to be void and not obligatory. This is that letter from which the Party" (that is the Opposition, Hamilton's allies, called "the Party") "concluded Sir George Mackenzie to be guilty of perjury, in having entered before the rest; dispersing copies of the letter, without the postscript, because they knew the postscript destroyed their malicious pretences."

It is not easy to follow his reasoning.[4] I give in a note the whole passage.[5] Mackenzie next reluctantly signed,

[1] Works, vol. i pp. ii, iii, iv. [2] MS. Books of Sederunt, November 24, 1674.
[3] MS Books of Sederunt. [4] Memoirs, pp 278, 279.
[5] "And though it was most unfit to cause the King promise this, upon the word of a Prince, yet Sir George Mackenzie did so much tender the reputation of his King, that he, having been bedrid of a broken leg when the rest were debarr'd, shun'd to have himself debarr'd, or publickly to own the appeal ; though to secure such as had, he declar'd that he would not return to his employment without them. Which not satisfying Sir George Lockhart, who prest still that Sir George Mackenzie should be debarr'd, he was content, in a letter under his

with Lockhart and twenty-eight others, a long address to
the Privy Council. They disclaimed a "combination," or
trade-union, and professed their loyalty, begging the Council
to send the paper to Lauderdale. They stated the reasons
why they could not "disown protestations for remeid of law,
as unlawful in general." They discriminated between
"appeals" and "protestations." Protestations are permitted
by an Act of Session of 1567, and by precedent under
James III., V., VI., and so on.

The Council declared this paper to be seditious, and
Lockhart with two others went to town, to mollify the
king, promising that if Mackenzie and the rest were
prosecuted for the address, they would return, and concur
in their common defence, which Mackenzie drew up. It
occupies thirteen pages, and is interrupted by a gap in
the MS. After the gap, Mackenzie says that he suspected
Lockhart and his companions of deserting him and the
advocates. He intercepted a letter in which they told
their "confidents" that, contrary to their promise, they
meant to wait in England till they saw how the process
against Mackenzie went. If he were absolved, so were
they; if he were found guilty, "the malice of their pursuers
would be blunted before it reached *them.*" "*This gross dis-
ingenuity did so confirm his former aversion for these principles,
which, he daily discovered, had inflamed the ignorant people
beyond his first inclinations, that he resolved to submit to his*

hand, to oblige himself in those terms; but this letter not having satisfied, and he
being prest, merely to satisfy Sir George Lockhart's private humour, he call'd
for his former letter, and wrote in a postscript these words · "But if I enter, and
put myself in the same condition with the rest, I do declare this letter, and all the
obligations therein, to be void and not obligatory ' And having own'd the
appeal with a very undaunted courage, *did from that hour despise that party which
had jealous'd him*, after so many proofs of his courage and fidelity, to please a
little creature, who had never follow'd them, but his own passion; to which he
and they were become such slaves, that they had thereby lost the glory and
reputation of impartial reformers, which had so much recommended them at
first, whilst they followed Sir George Mackenzie's disinterested advices. This
is that letter from which the party concluded Sir George Mackenzie to be
guilty of perjury, in having enter'd before the rest; dispersing copies of the
letter, without the postscript, because they knew the postscript destroy'd their
malicious pretences."

Prince." [1]   These words contain Mackenzie's reasons for leaving "the Party" of Hamilton.

He called together the advocates, denounced Lockhart and his companions as "cowardly rogues," said that the advocates, as a body, must not be "martyrs for any faction," nor set to their successors the precedent of, as we say, "going solid" for any political party. "It was no dishonour to submit to their Prince." Tumults tended to sedition, and sedition to war, "in which advocates not only became losers, but insignificant." All present, save one, then signed a petition to the king, "which was allowed by his Majesty: and though the four who were at London decried it, as insinuating an acknowledgment of guilt because they had submitted to his Majesty's clemency as well as his justice, yet themselves did shortly follow their example." [2]

Matters were not, in fact, so readily concluded; and we must glance at the facts as recorded in the manuscript Books of Sederunt.

The affair is puzzling. On January 28, 1675, some advocates obeyed the Royal will, they sent in petitions, and these were transmitted to Lauderdale. Other advocates had entered their petitions as early as January 15, and they were readmitted. Clearly many of the petitions of January 28 did not give satisfaction to Lauderdale and the king, but, by June 17 the Lords announce that Mackenzie has now presented another petition, explaining his former words. The Lords sent it to the king, who, on June 29, replies that Mackenzie may be readmitted, "as he hath been the first who hath clearly returned to his duty, so it is just that he be the first restored, and we hope he may be so exemplary in the future as will render him capable of our further favour." His brother, Colin, and others are also readmitted, "who shall petition in the very terms Sir George Mackenzie or his brother respectively have done, and the others." [3]

It thus appears, from the documents, that some advo-

---

[1] Memoirs, p. 308.   [2] *Ibid*, pp. 308, 309.   [3] MS. Books of Sederunt

cates gave satisfaction as early as January 15, 1675, that others, on the last day of grace (January 28), sent petitions which, at London, were deemed insufficient. Their address, to recapitulate, to the Privy Council was looked on as seditious, and sent (February 2) to London. Lockhart and Sinclair then set off to plead their cause in town, but (February 20) their comrades with Mackenzie were pursued in a process before the Privy Council, and Lockhart and Sinclair, hearing of this, retired from town and lurked near Northallerton, "without acquainting even their wives of their residence."[1] Mackenzie then drew up a defence of the advocates to be laid before the Privy Council. There is a gap in the manuscript, in the middle of this paper, and then comes the statement, already quoted, that Mackenzie intercepted a letter from the skulkers at Northallerton, found that they were sacrificing him and his associates, and held the meeting in which he advised submission to their Prince.

It is certain, however, that he was the first of those who did not submit on January 15, to send in a satisfactory petition, a model for all the others, and this, doubtless, was regarded by Lockhart and his associates, as a desertion of their common cause. This is not so easily to be gathered from Mackenzie's own fragmentary and dateless narrative.[2]

The Duchess of Lauderdale had been serviceable to the advocates, and bade Haltoun "endeavour the bringing off the outed advocates by all fair and peaceable means."[3] They were "brought off," with the possible result that absolute power would be safe, in the servility of the judges, from whom there was no appeal to a Parliament which had shown signs of recalcitrancy. But there had been no right of appeal before.

Mackenzie's motives were mixed. He hated and suspected Lockhart, for the reasons he assigns. The popular

---

[1] Memoirs, p 294

[2] Some dates are added, on the margins, by the editor, the others are taken from the manuscript Books of Sederunt.

[3] Hon. Charles Maitland to the Duchess, Dec 1, 1674, L P, iii p. 67.

tumults were not to his taste ; he foresaw danger of a renewal of rebellion and civil war. Resistance in the name of civil and religious liberty was now going "beyond his first inclination," and he sided with Government as a Radical, in face of Socialism, may become a Tory.

There is nothing uncommon in all this, but Mackenzie's only excuse for *taking office* under Lauderdale must be that he honestly believed violent suppression of the partisans of *Jus Populi Vindicatum* to be absolutely necessary. It does not seem 'to have been absolutely necessary that he should at once "draw up with" the Duchess of Lauderdale. When staying at Haltoun with the laird, Lauderdale's brother, Mackenzie wrote to the duchess, reminding her that they are distantly akin, "which warms him in a great degree to serve her, though some accidents have crossed his private inclination" (August 16, 1675).[1]

---

[1] British Museum, *Add. MSS.* 23,137, f. 70.

He did "serve her" in some way not clearly indicated, but not to her liking, as is plain from his letters to the duchess in 1680-1681 (*Lauderdale Papers,* vol. iii. pp. 204, 217, 218). She is trying to extort £2500 from the town of Edinburgh, is angry with Mackenzie for her failure : he replies with some tartness in his civility. he has done his best for her. The state of affairs is obscurely given in a letter of Mackenzie's to the duchess, undated, but of the autumn of 1681. Parliament, with James, Duke of York, as Commissioner, had been looking into the transactions of the fallen Commissioner, Lauderdale. He, by the king's command, had obtained money from the town of Edinburgh. The duchess wanted it, and wanted more, and charged Mackenzie with saying in Parliament that *she* had got the money. He replied, "I thought it was not necessary to deny it was given to the Duke of Lauderdale, that being transacted publicly and by the king's command, nor think I any man concerned whether your own husband gave you that money or not." In this affair of 1681 "no man was so violent" against the Lauderdales "as the Earl of Argyll" (*Add. MSS.* 23,248, f. 23), yet, when a month or two later Argyll was attacked, Lauderdale remained loyal to him, though unable to rescue him.

CHAPTER X

MACKENZIE AS LORD ADVOCATE—THE MITCHELL CASE, 1675-1679

Burnet and Lauderdale—Burnet's accusations before the English House
of Commons—Victory of Lauderdale—The strange affair of Mr.
Kirkton—Hamilton removed from the Council—Evidence of a preaching
spy—Mackenzie as a duellist—Becomes King's Advocate—New brooms
sweep clean—His improvements in legal procedure—His account of
his scruples—His version criticised—Errors in his statement—
Mackenzie's Vindication of his official career—Disturbed state of
south-western Scotland—Story of Lauderdale's negotiations with the
Presbyterians—Hickes's evidence—Fountainhall's version—Lauderdale
contradicts—Was the west ready for rebellion?—The gentry refuse
to enforce order—Dangerous conventicles—Mackenzie's report—
Lauderdale's view based on old experience—Suppression decreed—
Raising of the Highland Host—Advice of the bishops—The case of
Mitchell—Mackenzie prosecutes—His pleadings quoted—The Promise
of Life to Mitchell—Perjury, conscious or unconscious of Rothes,
Lauderdale, Haltoun, Sharp—Strange conduct of Presbyterians in
Court—Sufferings of Hickes—Infamous behaviour of Primrose—Scandal
about Claverhouse and Lady Mackenzie—Charles exonerates all
concerned in Mitchell's case—Haltoun accused of perjury—The case of
the MacGibbons—Mackenzie publishes his work on Criminal Law—
Sorrows of Evelyn—Baxter on Lauderdale's vices—Mackenzie on his
virtues.

UNLUCKILY the manuscript of Mackenzie's Memoirs fails
us for 1676 and most of 1677, while he touches very
lightly on Lauderdale's dangers from the English House
of Commons in 1675. He merely tells us that Lady Margaret
Kennedy, furious with Lauderdale because he did not
marry her after all his visits to her chamber "in his night-
gown," "encouraged Gilbert Burnet into an amour," and
engaged him in a plot against Lauderdale.[1]

[1] Memoirs, p. 315

As for "an amour," the noble Presbyterian spinster had secretly married Burnet, a foolish action which may have created scandal. Burnet himself had babbled, of course, about hasty expressions used by Lauderdale, before their quarrel, in private talks with him. Lauderdale wished the Presbyterians would rise, that he might bring over an army of Irish papists to cut their throats; and he spoke of a design to invade England, if Parliament gave trouble, with a Scottish army. So Burnet gossiped, and, consequently, in April 1675, he was examined before a Committee of the English House of Commons. They voted an address against Lauderdale, they cross-examined Burnet, they frightened him, (the burly man could not have faced torture like Mackail and Corsack,) and, finally, he told his story. Lauderdale, however, easily put him to shame. He found what Burnet had tried to destroy, a copy of his fulsome dedication to Lauderdale of his *Vindication* (1673) published between the dates of the two alleged criminal conversations. Lauderdale printed and distributed a thousand copies, and, to the unreflecting among mankind, Burnet appears a forerunner of Titus Oates. The case against Lauderdale was dropped—and Lady Margaret came up to town, where Burnet had much to suffer at her hands.[1]

In June, 1676, an affair occurred in which Mackenzie was not, at the moment, concerned, but which illustrates the relations of Lauderdale and his brother, Haltoun, with Hamilton and other members of the opposition. There are three versions of the story, one told by Mr. Kirkton, the sufferer, an outed minister; the second by the King's Advocate, Sir John Nisbet; the third by Bishop Burnet. Mr. Kirkton, whom we have frequently to quote, is a fairly impartial writer. Of Lauderdale he draws a singularly favourable portrait, and, of all Covenanting writers he, with Mr. Law, is the most candid in exposing the disorders committed by his own party.

Mr. Kirkton was walking in the High Street at noon, when two young gentlemen, with a lacquey, approached

---

[1] *Life of Gilbert Burnet*, Clarke and Foxcroft, pp. 136-142

him. One of them was James Scott of Tushielaw, on the upper Ettrick. His companion's name was Captain Carstairs, of the Kilconquhar family, a military spy, and, as we learn from the Diary of Lamont, a Fifeshire laird, a dangerous ruffian. He had shot a man, *through a door*, in mere savagery. He asked for some words with Kirkton, who requested Tushielaw to introduce him, but Tushielaw merely stared. Mr. Kirkton saw that he was in the hands of enemies. They took him to Carstairs's dark room in the house of a "messenger," an agent of police, and Tushielaw, with the lacquey, departed. Carstairs then asked Kirkton whether he was not John Wardlaw who owed him money? Kirkton gave his own name, and Carstairs said that he "had nothing to say to him." He himself was Scott of Erkleton, (Ercildoune?) whom he resembled. At this moment Baillie of Jerviswoode, Mr. Kirkton's brother-in-law, came to the door, and asked Kirkton what he was doing "in that dark dungeon"? Carstairs then drew a pistol, (it is a very odd tale,) but Kirkton closed with him, and they struggled together on the ground. Baillie with his friends entered, for the door was not locked, and released Kirkton from Carstairs. Tushielaw then came in, and he and Carstairs carried their story to Haltoun, "turning their private violence into State service."

It is amazing to find a Scott of Tushielaw in an affair, apparently, of street robbery. Haltoun brought the matter before the Council; and Mackenzie gives in his Memoirs the form which the story took in the hands of the King's Advocate, Nisbet. Carstairs, having a warrant of Council to apprehend Mr. Kirkton, the preacher asked, (so Jerviswoode said, when accused of releasing Kirkton,) to be allowed to see it. But Carstairs, Nisbet goes on, feared that Kirkton would seize and tear the paper, so he declared that he would show it in the presence of a magistrate in the next street. Jerviswoode then released Kirkton.

Now Kirkton says not a word, in his own story, about the pretence of Carstairs to have a warrant for his apprehension. Carstairs behaved like a lunatic, or a "high toby man" weak in the intellect, but spoke of no warrant, and did not pretend to make a legal capture.

Mr. Kirkton next states that, before the Council, Carstairs produced a warrant, which Archbishop Sharp *had drawn up, after the skirmish, and ante-dated!*[1]

How are we to understand this extraordinary tale? Mr. Kirkton expressly says that Carstairs, in his room, told him that if he were Kirkton, not Wardlaw, "he had nothing to say to him." How could Carstairs also say, at the same time, that he had a warrant against Kirkton? Mr. Kirkton, in his original story, says nothing of this matter; he introduced it, later, in the recital of the sufferings of Jerviswoode.

After a hot debate of Council, (no wonder it was hot,) in which Kincardine and Hamilton took the side of Jerviswoode, the majority of the Council found Jerviswoode guilty of resisting a lawful arrest; he was heavily fined (Fountainhall says that the fine was remitted) and imprisoned. Haltoun sent a report against Hamilton and Kincardine to Lauderdale, and they were removed from the Council.

Gilbert Burnet, in his History, gives a version of the Kirkton case which varies entirely from Kirkton's own story, and from that of Nisbet. All three tales are irreconcilable.[2]

As a matter of curiosity it may be worth while to give a summary of Burnet's variant, which, says Mr. Airy, is "precisely the account" given by the Council to the king, *mutatis mutandis.*[3] Let us see about Burnet! "Gibby," as Mackenzie calls Burnet, says (1) that Carstairs met Kirkton in the street, and asked him to visit a sick person who wanted to see him. (Mr. Kirkton says nothing of that.) (2) Having brought Kirkton to his own rooms, Carstairs said that "he had a warrant against him, which he would execute, if he did not give him money to leave him alone." (Kirkton does not say that: observe the chaotic pronouns of the bishop!) (3) Kirkton said he had not offended, and was willing to go to prison till his innocence should appear. (Not a word about

---

[1] Kirkton, p. 370.   [2] Burnet, vol. ii. pp 105, 106.
[3] *Lauderdale Papers*, vol. iii. p. 84, note.

that in Kirkton.) (4) Carstairs went out to get a warrant, and left Kirkton locked in the chamber. (Mr. Kirkton has not a word on this point.) (5) Mr. Kirkton called to the people of the house, and induced one of them to bring Baillie of Jerviswoode. (Mr. Kirkton would have been surprised to hear all this.) (6) " *Carstairs could not find nine privy councillors to sign a warrant !* " and came back without one. (Then, apparently, a warrant by Sharp was of little use.) (7) Carstairs sat down on Mr. Kirkton and called " Murder ! " (Mr Kirkton says that *he* " pushed Carstairs," a feeble body, " into a corner.") (8) Baillie forced open the door. (Mr. Kirkton says that " it had neither key nor lock.") Baillie, with drawn sword, made Carstairs, who was sitting on Kirkton, " come off him." (It was Mr. Kirkton who was sitting on Carstairs.) (9) Carstairs said that he had a warrant, but would not show it. (10) Nine councillors signed a warrant, *ante-dated*. (Mr. Kirkton says that Sharp did the trick.)

The draft report of the Committee of Council for Conventicles says that Carstairs " had Mr. Kirkton in custody by a warrant from the Committee," yet that Lord Cochrane, Dumfries, Hamilton, and Kincardine justified Baillie in a debate of at least three hours. They complained to the king, and Hamilton and Kincardine were removed from the Council, leaving Lauderdale unchecked.[1] According to Mr. Kirkton, Haltoun sent a lying report from Council to Lauderdale, while Kirkton himself sent a true report to the duchess. What is truth ?

The affair caused lasting hatred between Hamilton and Lauderdale, and was brought before Charles in 1678 and 1679, when Mackenzie, as King's Advocate, was in London, defending Lauderdale. Had Mackenzie possessed the contending versions of Kirkton and Burnet he could easily have cleared the Privy Council.

It seems that, all through 1676, Hamilton had been supporting " the phanaticks " more than his partisans thought desirable. This we learn from a series of unsigned

---

[1] *Lauderdale Papers*, vol. iii. pp. 82–85.

letters to the duke, apparently by his partisan the Earl of Queensberry.[1] "His appearing for the Presbyterians is disapproved by his friends. . . ." The right game, says the candid writer, is to engage the Duchess of Lauderdale to ruin "that brute rascal, Haltoun," her husband's brother. 'A Busshop complained to me of your keeping phanatick petagogs with your children contrair to the law."

A witness was found to say that he himself, after preaching with the conformists, had joined the Presbyterians, and "was put to preaching work." The outed ministers, he avers, have agreed to make armed resistance, and think that Hamilton will be the man to lead them. They approached his factor, but the duke would give no positive answer, and only permitted them to hold conventicles, undisturbed, upon his land (October 1676). Meanwhile the fanatics have sent to Holland for arms, which are concealed in Edinburgh and Glasgow, and to London for money. Charles himself had seen this very suspicious report; Lauderdale received it from the king, and Perth sent a copy to Hamilton (January 20).[2] Worthless as the evidence probably was, it was apt to increase the feud between Hamilton and Lauderdale.

Mackenzie was, by 1676, decidedly an ally of Lauderdale. In the letter to Archbishop Sharp already quoted, he says that he "cannot think that either men's reason or God's justice can suffer so benign a Prince," (as Charles,) "or so obliging a minister" (as Lauderdale) "to suffer by their virtues where others have prospered by their vices." The virtues of the pair are inconspicuous!

On June 28, 1676, Charles II., in a letter to the Treasury, appointed Mackenzie as an "understudy" to Sir John Nisbet, "in the concerns of his office," with a salary of £100 a year.[3] A week before, Sir Archibald Primrose had been removed from the lucrative place of Clerk Register to that of Justice-General, which he deeply resented, regarding Lauderdale and Rothes as his deadly enemies.

---

[1] *Hist MSS. Com.*, XI , 6, 151-155.   [2] *Ibid*, XI., 6, 156, 157.
[3] Fountainhall's *Journals*, p. 226.

He was a subtle and unscrupulous man, who excited the horror of Gilbert Burnet, as we shall see, but Gilbert loved his gossip.

Mackenzie always speaks with much respect of Nisbet's learning, but he appears to have been unusually corrupt, even for his period. The King's Advocate was open to bribes. Wodrow mentions, as a practice then customary, that some ladies, friends of a Presbyterian prisoner, made to "the Advocate's Lady" "a compliment" of a service of plate. I have not observed that Mackenzie is accused of receiving such "compliments," though we once learn that money was offered, but Nisbet had no scruples.[1] In January 1677 his brother was charged with perjury by Hepburn of Humby, and Nisbet advised him to pay 4000 merks to Humby, to drop the suit. The documents were destroyed by another Nisbet, and the King's Advocate was discredited.[2] He was again in trouble on a charge of taking fees from both sides, in a civil suit, and though Mackenzie offered to help him in his defence, and declined to accept his office without his "free dismission," he resigned, for his accuser, in both affairs, was Lauderdale's brother, Haltoun.[3] This might almost be taken as a proof of Nisbet's innocence, were there not other indications of his extreme corruption.

At this moment, temper ran high in legal circles. An "Act" had been made to exclude strangers from the advocates' "room and walk." Some nobles were refused admission, and appealed to the Privy Council, who referred the matter to the judges. Mackenzie urged that an Act to the same purpose had been made, "under Sir George Lockhart's own Government." Lockhart replied that there was no such Act on record. Mackenzie retorted "it was a part of his arbitrary tyranny if it was not recorded." Thereon

---

[1] The only charge against Mackenzie in reference to bribes, which I have found, is in the "Brief Rehearsal" of the Rev. Mr. Smith, executed in 1681. He speaks of some brethren, "bribing the excommunicate Advocate, Mr. (sic) Mackenzie." No evidence for this has come to my notice. *Six Saints of the Covenant*, vol. ii. p. 81.

[2] Fountainhall, *Historical Notices*, vol i. p. 139.　　　　[3] *Memoirs*, pp 3-4.

a Mr. Bannerman challenged Mackenzie, who would not disappoint him of satisfaction, but both principals were bound over to keep the peace.[1]

On September 4, 1677, Mackenzie was received as King's Advocate. Fountainhall writes, "Sir George Mackenzie being entered, and resolving to give the world an experiment of his justice, and that he would purge the prisons of those his predecessor had left him, because no money had been offered him to insist against them," brought forward two forgers, who were hanged, on what Fountainhall thinks poor evidence.[2] Mackenzie himself, in his Memoirs, tells us that he prevailed with the Council to prevent "all the fanatics' just exceptions against the forms formerly used against them." For example, he refused to plead against the accused "after they had been removed," "it being a most unreasonable thing that matters of fact should be urged, where none is to answer." Nisbet had adopted the practice of pleading in the absence of the accused, and even of "voting in the causes where he himself was accuser." Mackenzie "altered the custom," and the Council also, on his motion, decided (1) that the public prosecutor must be "special as to time and place" in accusing conventiclers, (2) that the accused must only be examined "upon his own guilt and accession," (3) that "bonds and other engagements must not be imposed on the accused if they submitted to give evidence and pay their fines," "the law itself being the strongest bond that can be exacted of any man."[3]

In his posthumous work, the *Vindication* of 1691, Mackenzie explained and defended his own procedure in the invidious office of *Calumniator Publicus*, or King's Advocate. "It is foolishly pretended that he prosecuted men without an order, whereas, indeed, he never prosecuted any until he was commanded by the Council."

[1] Fountainhall, *Historical Notices*, vol. 1. pp. 137, 138.

[2] *Ibid.*, vol. 1. p. 180.

[3] Memoirs, pp. 319-323. The new rules are given in a Privy Council paper. Wodrow, 11. p. 369

I

This is true. He also interceded that the precognition, or preliminary examination of witnesses, should be done by the judges, not by the advocate. He and Sir John Cuningham, when criminal judges, "introduced the liberty to the accused of calling exculpatory witnesses who may depose on oath for him against the king, which the Law of England does not allow." "To strengthen the security of the Defendant, Sir George Mackenzie used to interpose with the Officers of State, before the Depositions were brought into the Council, *and represent to them his own scruples.*" If the Officers of State persisted in prosecuting, then he called in "the ablest advocates," and if *they* agreed that the case demanded a prosecution, then these advocates "were ordered to concur with him in the pursuit, or prosecution. And *many* of the most learned and most popular advocates did concur with him in the most intricate cases," as in Argyll's and Jerviswoode's.

The last remarks, as to Argyll's case, I cannot fully explain: as we shall see later when we come to the famous case of Argyll, they are overstated.

Nothing in Mackenzie's career is so incomprehensible as these statements of his, for though he died before his *Vindication* was published, we are not informed that his memory, like that of Lauderdale in 1680, had begun to play him false. We do learn, however, that a book of his, also posthumously published, was written when he "languished under fatal distemper of the body." The same words may apply to the *Vindication* for, in his normal condition of intellect, it is incredible that he should have written exaggerated accounts of facts which every man who could read, could expose.[1]

It is natural to say that it is easy for a man not to be

---

[1] At the same time it must be noted as curious that the author of a reply to his *Vindication* did not expose these misstatements. The only reply known to me is silent on the subject "A Vindication of the Presbyterians of Scotland from the Malicious Aspersions Cast on them in a late Pamphlet written by Sir George Mackenzie, &c." Golding. London, 1692. This rare tract, lent to me by the kindness of the Rev John Sturrock, appears to be by an English Presbyterian, who "is credibly informed" that Mr. James Renwick was—"a Romish priest"!

King's Advocate, easy to decline the appointment, (as
Mackenzie did, in 1674 or 1675, decline that of Justice-
General,) and easy to withdraw, if any case excited his
scruples, and Mackenzie confesses to scruples in some
cases. As to throwing up a case, he objects that the
advocate must either "have a negative over the King and
all Judicatories by refusing to concur (for though he
should lay down his employment, yet it would give an
ill impression even of the best cause) or otherwise he
must be obliged to concur." In concurring he can do
no harm, he only states, professionally, and before intelligent
judges and juries, the case entrusted to him. Thus many
a barrister does his best for a client in whose innocence,
or right, he has the reverse of confidence, and the King's
Advocate acts in the same way for his Royal client.

We have quoted Mackenzie's defence of his career as
Public Prosecutor before entering on an account of that
career. Mr. Taylor Innes writes, "As an administrator of
public justice Sir George Mackenzie seems to have deserved
well of his country." He claims the introduction of an
Act giving the selection of forty-five men, out of whom
the defendant selected fifteen, to the judges, whereas the
King's Advocate had been wont to select the jury. He
also secured the last word to the defendant's counsel,
but he adds that this did not apply to cases of treason,
in which, by English even more than by Scots law, "the
king" was given singular advantages. In both countries
men charged with treason were scarcely ever acquitted,
witness the cases of the innocents accused by Oates,
Prance, Dugdale, and Bedloe, in 1679-80. By packing a
Whig jury in the City, Shaftesbury secured an *ignoramus;*
and, in singular circumstances, the Campbells of Cessnock
were acquitted in Edinburgh. But these were the rarest
exceptions.

We now return to the situation when Mackenzie entered
on office.

According to Kirkton, the state of affairs had long
been grave. In religious assemblies "the people had a

sort of affection to the fields above houses." The conventicles "were brought to resemble armies," which are
almost the very words of Mackenzie himself. "Within
a little time they became so numerous and formidable,
our State thought fit even to forbear what they could not
help." "Sometimes people discovered their own secret
scandals," which must have been entertaining, and con-
verted "curates" joined in the movement. One was
our friend, the spy who told the story about the offer of
the leadership of the Presbyterians to Hamilton. Thirty-
nine ministers, including Cargill, "were the stock of the
preaching church that was driven into the wilderness.
Their ministry was a sort of outlawry," and all this was
the result of the tyranny of bishops. "The men went
ordinarily with arms, and the soldiers next adjacent looked
upon them as the appearance of an enemy. Many skir-
mishes there were, much violence was used and indiscre-
tion upon both sides. . . . The people were sometimes as
much judges as disciples." A reward was offered for such
ministers, and they were "intercommuned," that is, their
offence was proclaimed to infect all who harboured or
conversed with them. (This was in 1675.[1]) In the same
way, under the rule of the Covenanters, persons were
excommunicated for having merely conversed with Montrose.
Mr. Law, in his *Memorials*, corroborates Mr. Kirkton's
account of the prevalent disorder. Mackenzie also says
that conventicles were numerous, and well armed, that
they threatened the orthodox clergy, and usurped their
pulpits.[2]

It was often said that Jesuits in disguise preached at
the conventicles. They had enough of the spirit of gay
adventure to do so, and Matthew Mackail, in a postscript to one of his newsletters (*S.P. Dom.*, Charles II.,
vol. 407), writes, "I have been informed from a good
hand that one father Brown a Jesuit was about a year
agoe in this kingdome, and hath preached in the fields and
baptized. In his preaching he said most upon Christ's royall

[1] Kirkton, pp. 352-374.   [2] Memoirs, p. 322.

Prerogative of being head and king in the Church, showing how far people were oblidged to believe profess it and
maintain it. He dyed within twelve miles of this place.
Bot I assure yow it is a singular instance, and there uses
to be no publick confluences bot when the people are warned
by persons of good repute in the bounds, nor do the
Presbyterian ministers go bot upon much solicitation and
the pressing desire of the people."

There is great diversity as to the events and motives which
now produced remarkable measures of repression. Lauderdale's chaplain, Dr. Hickes, wrote to Dr. Patrick "in
the Cloister of Westminster Abbey," and no doubt Hickes
told what Lauderdale wanted to be believed, while the
manuscript newsletters from Edinburgh (now in the
Record Office) gave the Presbyterian version, or that
of Hamilton's party. Hickes, in October, warned Patrick
of a tale set afloat by Lauderdale's enemies "that he
intended an Indulgence to the Whigs." The conformist
clergy were much discouraged, and the Whigs proportionally
insolent, but the rumour was spread merely to injure Lauderdale in the opinion of the bishops, and to encourage the
fanatics to rise. They now threaten an insurrection, "and
are underhand encouraged to it," by Hamilton, Tweeddale,
Queensberry, and other nobles. Consequently Government is collecting forces; the vassals of Argyll, Caithness,
(Campbell of Glenorchy,) Perth, Atholl, Strathmore, Murray,
and Panmure will be employed. "We wish it may be
true," (that the West means to rise,) "but I am afraid it
is not" (January 3, 1678). The combination of Cassilis,
Hamilton, Lord Melville, and General Drummond is *morientis
bestiæ ultimus conatus*, "the last effort of that dying beast,"
Whiggery (March 21, 1678).[1]

We next turn to the evidence of Fountainhall. Lauderdale, by one of the freaks of his veering no-policy, had been
trying, since August 1677, to ingratiate himself with the
Presbyterians, and recover his lost credit with the preachers.
"He was serious in it," says Fountainhall, "and did it not

---

[1] *Hist. MSS. Com., Report* XIII., Appendix, Part II., p. 48.

merely to cajole or gull them. The carriers on of it were the President, (Dalrymple of Stair,) Argyll, Melville, and Arniston, with James Stewart" (of *Jus Populi Vindicatum*), "and the ministers of that party, who were allowed to come freely to Edinburgh. They offered to raise £15,000 presently for Lauderdale's service, and to contrive the elections so that in a Parliament he should carry a subsidy, and the President get a ratification for what he pleased," (that is, obtain what he chose in the way of estates, and privileges, as of holding fairs,) "provided their Indulgence were secured to them by Act of Parliament, so that it might not next day be recalled." But Lauderdale, though eager for the subsidy, "could not comprehend" how it was to be managed, when the Presbyterians came to explain. Moreover Sharp, Archbishop of St. Andrews, had his own intrigues in the contrary sense, and was reported to have written to the Archbishop of Canterbury, who so moved the king that he peremptorily bade Lauderdale desist.

Here was the very crisis of Mackenzie's career. At the moment when he became King's Advocate there was a prospect of a reconciliation with the Presbyterians. Had they got their Indulgence by Act of Parliament, he might never have acquired his terrible sobriquet, "the Bluidy Advocate." But, says Fountainhall, on October 9, Lauderdale publicly announced to the Privy Council "that there never had been any audience, treaty, or capitulation between him and the Nonconformists."[1] Apart from the Presbyterian offers, not intelligible to Lauderdale, he had reasons for either making great concessions, (which never satisfied the Presbyterians,) or resorting to repression for which he had not adequate forces.

The question is, was the south-west in a dangerous condition, or was it not? On August 22, 1677, the Duke of Hamilton, on whose estates "phanaticks" were as common as farmers, wrote to the Earl, later Duke, of Queensberry, one of his party, saying "these people are more troublesome

---

[1] Fountainhall, *Historical Notices*, vol i. pp. 177, 178

since the proclamation against them than before, however, I resolve to order my deputies to do their endeavour." His deputies were of no avail.[1] On August 30, he tells Queensberry about a suspected treaty "between the fanatics and those in power," that means the negotiations between Lauderdale, Argyll, Stair, and the preachers. "That it will be possible to reclaim the people from conventicles . . . I much doubt. . . . Let us do all we can."[2] They could do nothing. He notices the appointment of Mackenzie as King's Advocate, "for his great integrity and abilities'" (Sept. 30, 1677 (?)) and praises the Earl of Perth, whom no offers could induce "to change his former principles." He is "a man of much worth and virtue." Perth, as we shall see, became the most furious persecutor, and most profligate jobber, except his brother, John Drummond of Lundin, later Earl of Melfort, among the ministers of James II. Both men turned Catholics when James came to the throne, and both conspired, in 1684–1686, to ruin Mackenzie, and Queensberry, Hamilton's correspondent, their own patron in 1683.

On October 6, Hamilton reports a fight between some soldiers and a conventicle. He makes as little of it as possible, but this affray, with the other disturbances, probably turned the balance in Lauderdale's mind, and, three days later, he had broken off negotiations with Argyll, Stair, and the preachers, and declared in Council that no such negotiations had occurred. On October 24, Dundonald, himself a Presbyterian Whig, wrote to Lauderdale, giving more examples of the disturbances in the west. "Insolent abuses" are committed; almost weekly there are conventicles in Carrick; they occupy the pulpits of placed ministers; Welsh is to hold a communion at Garven, at Tarbolton seven or eight armed men broke into the manse, missed the minister, but left word that if he preached again "he should die the next day." These abuses will wax to a greater height, if not timely prevented.[3]

---

[1] *Hist MSS. Com.*, XV., viii. p. 222.   [2] *Ibid*, p. 223.
[3] *Lauderdale Papers*, vol iii p. 88.

I add a report received by Government, from the State Papers unpublished : [1]—

"On Sunday sennight a great conventicle was kept in and about the new built Meeting House. Mr. Welch, Dick, Cunningham, Gilchrist, Gilbert, and Robert Kennedies, Preachers, with 7000 people. The Communion was celebrated in silver cups; there were two tables each containing at least 100 persons, filled 10 times. Scandalous persons as William Kelso in Air were admitted, who 'since rides well in Welch's lifeguard.' On Sunday morning Welch preached on John xi. 34, 35, and said among other 'villainous things' that the King nobles and prelates were murtherers of Christ. Mr. Gilbert Kennedy was prayed for as minister of Girvan.

"Before admission to the Sacrament the people promised never to hear Curates again but to adhere to the glorious ends of their League and Covenant. On Monday they kept a Presbytery with Welch as moderator. Kennedy was censured for not preaching warmly enough against the wicked ways and nobles and prelates. Mr. Cunningham having repented his service under Episcopacy was newly ordained. It was enacted the people should not rise in arms until oppressed and provoked. On Tuesday Welch came through Mayboll with 20 horse. On Wednesday he preached at Auchenleck. He is now supposed to have gone towards the Borders. Friday, by Order of Council the heretors of Air and Renfrew met at Irving to consider the suppression of disorders. Some of their Committee, especially Sir John Cochrane, have pleaded for an indulgence. Last week at a fair at Mayboll a great many swords were sold. The Privy Council sent to the heritors Earls Glencairn and Dundonnald and Lord Rosse."

Mackenzie says that "it was most easy for two or three conventicles, by joining together to make an army of ten thousand men, to whom all of that persuasion would pro-

[1] Abridged from *S.P. Dom.*, Charles II., vol 397.
"An Account of the present posture of affaires in y⁰ shires of Air and Renfrew, Nov. 5th, 1677"

bably gather," against whom the king could only oppose his
own standing forces, not exceeding 1500 in all, while his
militia and the landed gentry were much inclined to the
same opinions, and to "the Party," that of Hamilton.[1]
Lauderdale was a statesman without a policy, and possessed
of a furious temper, and a bitter memory of events now long
past. He remembered well the ruin of the policy and the
army of the Estates, when, in 1648, they marched to rescue
Charles I., and were ruined by the western fanatics whom
they left in their rear. At that time the opposition of the
Whigamores began in a large "Holy Fair," or sacramental
field conventicle, of "slashing communicants" as Sir James
Turner says. He remarks "the whole West of Scotland cried
up 'King Christ' and 'the kingdom of Christ,' thereby
meaning the uncontrollable and unlimited dominion of the
then Kirk of Scotland." The field conventicle of 1648 made
"that peace so often inculcated, and left as a legacy by our
blessed Lord to his whole Church . . . the symbol of war
and bloody broils."

On that occasion a conventicling force of 2000 horse and
foot, near Mauchline, in Ayrshire, repulsed and wounded
Middleton himself and General Hurry, and was only
scattered when Turner and Callendar came up with reinforcements from the Engagers' army that aimed at the
rescue of Charles I.[2] As an old "Engager," Lauderdale
could not but fear a similar rising in the west, when he heard
of a huge assemblage held by Mr. Welsh, "and a good
many other ministers, beside the Girvan water in Ayrshire."
"There were many thousands of people present," says Wodrow.[3] It may be a heterodox historical opinion, but I
venture to think that Lauderdale, with his old experience of
the powers of "the kingdom of Christ," in Ayrshire and the
west, with his present knowledge of the armed conventicles,
and with a regular force utterly inadequate, had reasonable excuse for taking extraordinary measures of precaution
and repression. These measures, unhappily, were the raising
of "the Highland Host" to be quartered on the disturbed

[1] Memoirs, p. 329.   [2] Turner, p. 53 *et seq.*   [3] Wodrow, vol. ii. p. 347.

districts. On this Lauderdale (November 8, 1677) wrote to Danby, saying that he was arranging an expedition of Atholl and other clansmen, to be quartered on the disturbed districts, "for this game is not to be played by halves."[1] He also requested that Lord Granard's regulars in Ireland might be ready to move to his assistance, and Charles assented, ordering the Northumberland militia also to be mobilised, with part of Oxford's regiment. The bishops stepped in with their advice (Wodrow throws the blame on "the prelates and such who had packed cards with them").

The suggestions of the prelates (Dec. 21, 1677) are truculent. A Committee of military members of Council should accompany the forces. The western shires should be disarmed, and horses above £50 Scots in value should be seized. The soldiers should be quartered upon "the guilty." At each stopping-place the Committee should call before them "the transgressors," and destroy the meeting-houses, and smartly fine field-conventiclers. Informers as to the whereabouts of Mr. Welsh should be rewarded out of fines. Landlords ought to take the oath of allegiance and be made responsible for their tenants. Bonds should be exacted from them for the security of orthodox and orderly ministers (who were constantly robbed and bullied). Garrisons should be stationed in the towns.[2]

Preparations were now made for launching "the Highland Host" upon the innocent and quiet shires of western Scotland, where, says Mackenzie, "the orthodox clergy were forced to abandon their churches and homes," while even the President of the Court of Session (Dalrymple) and Dundonald reported their preparations to rebel. Wodrow says that the malefactors were many times found to be "persons who were pleased to take on the mark of Presbyterians, and were common robbers oft times." He gives no example of such findings, and Burnet remarks on the frivolity of the excuse. But to the state of the west, and the affair of the Highland Host, we return in due season (1678).

[1] *Lauderdale Papers*, vol. iii. p. 89   [2] *Ibid.*, vol iii pp. 95-98.

While Lauderdale made his preparations the case of the Rev. Mr. Mitchell, who shot the Bishop of Orkney in 1668, came up again. The affair requires a return to events as early as 1674. In that year, as Charles Maitland of Haltoun, brother of Lauderdale, reported to Kincardine, in a letter of February 10, Mitchell was arrested by Sir William Sharp, brother of the archbishop. On February 10, being brought before a Committee of the Council, Mitchell denied that he was the assassin, but " being taken apart by the Chancellor" (Rothes), "upon assurance of his life, he fell upon his knees and confessed. . . ." Haltoun expected that he would be punished by loss of his hand and imprisoned for life. On February 12, Haltoun writes that Mitchell has repeated his confession before the Council and that Nesbit, King's Advocate, is to prosecute him. I add an Act of Council in a note. Nothing is herein said as to Mitchell's confession, or as to promise of life to him.[1]

On March 2, the indictment against Mitchell was read to the Justiciary Court, a Committee of the Court of Session, "the Criminal Lords" in Fountainhall's phrase. He was accused of taking part in the Pentland Rising (1666) and of the attack on Sharp. When arrested, in 1674, he was carrying his two pistols, "near musket bore."

On March 12, the Privy Council passed another Act, mentioning that promise of life was given to Mitchell, with warrant from the Commissioner and Council ; that he thereon confessed and signed his confession, but that he withdrew it before the Court of Justiciary. The Lord Commissioner (Lauderdale) and the Council, therefore renounce their promise of life, which was fair, for the promise was given on

---

[1] "Forasmuch as Mr James Mitchell now imprisoned in the Tolbuith of Edinburgh, is guiltie of being in the late rebellion in anno 1666, and attempting the assassination of the Archbishop of Saint Andrews by shooting of a pistoll, wherewith the Bishop of Orkney was wounded, therfore the Lord Commissioner his Grace and Lords of his Majesties Privy Councill doe remitt the said Mr. James Mitchell to the Commissioners of his Majesties Justitiary to be proceeded against for the saide crymes according to law, and grantes order and warrand to his Majesties Advocat to raise ane indytment against him for the said crymes before the said Commissioners, and to process and persew him therapon " (Report of Privy Council, 12th February 1674, *Acta*).

condition of confession, the confession had been withdrawn : no confession, no promise. On March 25, before the Justiciary Court, Mitchell denied his confession. Apparently he could do this, as it was not made before a quorum of the judges. There was no other evidence against him, and the judges, with the assent of the King's Advocate, "deserted the diet," dropped the prosecution, *pro tempore*, but Mitchell was kept in prison.[1]

After an attempt by Mitchell to escape from the Tolbooth, the Council (Jan. 6, 1676) ordered him to be tortured "anent" his being in the Pentland Rising. Mitchell *was* tortured on this occasion. He objected that he should have been set at liberty when his "diet was deserted," but in Scotland there was no Habeas Corpus. On January 24, 1676, though the torture was inflicted in presence of the judges, he was not proved to be accessory to the rebellion. Now Mackenzie, in his *Vindication* (1691), says that torture was never used, save when the prisoner "was evidently proved to be guilty of accession to the crime, and that he knew the accomplices." There was no such proof outside the confession which Mitchell had withdrawn, but the younger Auchindrane under James VI., was tortured in the absence of evidence, on a true charge of murder.

We now turn to Mackenzie's version, in his *Memoirs of the Affairs of Scotland.* He declares[2] that Mitchell, in February 1674, confessed all to Rothes, "in another room" "without either asking life or promise of any favour." Now Haltoun's two letters, with the Act of Council, already cited, prove that this is incorrect. Mackenzie, of course, was not present at the proceedings of Council in 1674. In January 1678, he was King's Advocate, and was ordered by Council to prosecute Mitchell, because "new discoveries had been made of a design to murder the Archbishop." By Mackenzie's "earnest desire," his great rival at the Bar, Sir George Lockhart, was appointed as counsel for the fanatic.[3] "The law that reached his life," says Sir John Lauder of Fountainhall, "was the Fourth Act of the Parliament of 1600, against invading and

---

[1] Wodrow, ii. pp. 248–252. [2] Memoirs, p. 327. [3] *Ibid*, p. 328.

pursuing of Councillors, though it was only made *ad terrorem*, (James VI., 16th Parl. Act IV.) and in desuetude, and never practised as to the pain of death, for, otherwise, an attempt without full consummation is never capitally punished." [1]

The question was raised, Had the archbishop been assailed "for doing his Majesty's service"? This could not well be proved, and the "demembration" of the Bishop of Orkney was supposed not to be a capital offence under a law of 1491.

Mackenzie's own pleadings are in his Works (vol. i. p. 118-121 *bis*) in Latin, for the benefit of foreign students ignorant of English, as he explains. Mackenzie was clearly unconscious of guilt, for he published this speech with many of his other pleadings in 1681. Mitchell, he said, is a cleric bearing arms, contrary to the canons; an assailer of the king's counsellor; a shepherd who feeds his flock with blood, not milk; a wretch unmoved by the sacred character of a bishop. He has bragged of his crime, (this was proved by two witnesses,) and declared that it would be "a sweet and sacred thing," to murder the whole Bench of Bishops! He has declared that he was *inspired* to do the deed, making God his accomplice. God to be sure, *did* inspire zealots, like Phinehas, in Old Testament times, but, since the days of the Gospel, He does so no longer, and Peter was rebuked for using the sword.

Mackenzie proves Mitchell's guilt by his own confession, his repeated confession, corroborated by "adminicles" of external evidence: for example, his boasting of the deed. He argues that the mere attempt is a capital offence, quoting many Roman legists, as was the custom: and also argues that the Council, before whom Mitchell confessed, was a competent tribunal. He cites Seneca and St. Ambrose, also Tertullian, and then comes to the plea of promise, for all those witnesses who were present at the confession swear that there was no promise of life, or, some that they did not give it (Lauderdale and Rothes,) some, Sharp and Haltoun, *that they did not hear it given*. The confession itself includes no mention

---

[1] Fountainhall, *Historical Notices*, vol. i. p. 182.

of a promise of life.[1] The Act saying that the promise is
withdrawn, as Mitchell withdraws his confession, was made
ex post facto, and proves nothing, in case a report that promise *was* given may have reached the judges (the force
of this reasoning escapes the lay reader!)[2]

In his *Memoirs of the Affairs of Scotland*, and in
English, Mackenzie writes, "The Act of Council, being
posterior to the confession, could not prove that confession
was emitted upon promise of life." Why could it not?
The Act narrates that Mitchell refused to confess, at first,
"until having retired with one of the Committee, he did
confess upon his knees he was the person, upon assurance
of his life given him by one of the Committee, who had
warrant from the Lord Commissioner" (Lauderdale) "and
Secret Council to give the same, and therefore did freely
confess. . . ."[3] Certainly this Act proves the offer of life
in exchange for confession. Mackenzie went on to argue
that David slew an Amalekite on his own unsupported confession. (But *that* was in Old Testament times!) Mackenzie
ended by pointing out the danger of permitting fanatics
to execute judgment on the plea of inspiration.

The turning-point of the case was that Rothes, Lauderdale, and Haltoun, all swore that the confession was spon-
taneous; with no previous promise of life: Rothes could
remember nothing of the sort. Sharp only swore that *he*
gave no promise, beyond saying that, if Mitchell confessed,
"he would do his best for him." He added that no promise was given in his presence. Mitchell's brother-in-law,
Somerville, boldly averred the reverse, accused Sharp of perjury,[4] and, says Fountainhall, "the misfortune was that few
there but believed Somerville better than the Archbishop."

[1] "He did freely confess." Wodrow, vol. ii. p. 460.
[2] I give the passage in the original. "Quoad actum vero Secreti Concilii, quo
contineri dicitur spes veniæ, patet responsio; nam Senatus consultum illud non
præcessit confessionem, adeoque non confessus est reus crimen hoc spe veniæ in
illo expressæ Sed ut sophisma hoc radicitus diluatur, sciant judices integerrimi,
reum hunc nunquam spem veniæ sibi proposuisse, nec examinatores ipsam obtulisse;
sed ex post facto, ne falsus rumor spei hujus, et veniæ concessæ locum apud vos
obtineret, emissum est hoc edictum, in quo spes veniæ ex post facto indultæ
per transennam solummodo narratur" (Works, vol. i p. 122).
[3] Wodrow, ii. pp. 250–252.   [4] *Ibid.*, ii. pp. 469, 470

Lockhart and Ellis, for Mitchell, then produced a *copy* of the Act of Council withdrawing the promise, and thereby admitting its existence. The judges refused to admit it, says Fountainhall, "as not probative, and because not produced when it should have been produced, before the said noble witnesses were sworn. . . . And they abstracted the books," (the Registers of Privy Council,) "and would not produce them . . . and it choked the principles of both criminal law and equity to say it was too late, for it is never too late, in criminal cases, (*nunquam in criminalibus concluditur contra reum*,) any time before the closing of the assize."[1] The judges, however, unanimously pronounced against the opinion of Fountainhall, and Mitchell was found guilty and hanged.

By unusual good fortune, we catch a glimpse of the crowd in the Court during the trial of Mitchell. Dr. Hickes, Lauderdale's chaplain, was present, much to his discomfort, and writes (December 8, 1677), "You cannot imagine how the Presbyterian party, especially the women, were concerned for him. The Court was full of disaffected villains, and because of my dress and profession I had many affronts done me ; for sitting high with my back towards that side of the Court where the zealous rabble were gathered together, near the bar at which the prisoner stood, they railed at my black coat, for so they called my gown, and bespit it all over, and pelted me now and then with such things as bits of apple and crusts of bread." This speaks ill for the tolerance and manners of the godly. Mackenzie, "almost the only great man in the country," says Hickes, "pursued Mitchell like a gallant man and a good Christian," in face of a letter threatening his murder.[2]

In this extraordinary and shameful affair, it has been argued for Mackenzie that he, who was not of the Council in 1674, relied on the oaths of the nobles and gentlemen who were then present, and who swore that no promise was made to Mitchell.[3] As to the copy of the Act of Council in which

---

[1] Fountainhall, *Historical Notices*, vol. i. pp. 182-186.

[2] Ellis, *Original Letters*, Series II., vol. iv pp. 47-51.

[3] Barty, *Mackenzie-Wharncliffe Deeds*, p 22.

promise of life was at once confessed to and withdrawn, the judges "repelled it," as Mitchell said in his speech on the scaffold, though why they did so is not obvious to the lay intelligence, unless they were overawed.[1]

Sir George Lockhart, says Mackenzie, was blamed for not producing the copy of the Act of Council *before* taking the evidence of Lauderdale, Rothes, and the others. Probably they suspected him of having planned a *coup de théâtre*, inducing them to swear as they did, and then confuting them by *litera scripta*.

The extraordinary fact is that Lauderdale and Rothes at least, seem to have absolutely forgotten the giving of the promise. Their depositions are quite frank. But Haltoun only swears that he did not *hear the promise given*, which, in letter, was probably true, as Rothes and Mitchell were "apart," in another room. Sharp was equally cautious. Burnet's account is probably, or certainly, derived from Sir Archibald Primrose. He was delighted that his enemies, Lauderdale and the rest, were to perjure themselves in his own Court. He had copied and given the Act of Council of March 12, 1674, to Mitchell's counsel. He told the noble witnesses that "many thought" there had been a promise of life. Lauderdale stiffly denied it. Primrose said that "he heard there was an Act of Council." Lauderdale said that it was not possible, and that he would not take the trouble to consult the books. Primrose said within himself, "I have you now!"

This wretch actually believed that he was entailing damnation on his political enemies. When Lockhart produced the copy of the Act, Lauderdale lost his temper, Burnet declares, and said that "he was not there to be accused of perjury." After the trial, the noble witnesses, says Burnet, examined the books, and found that they had

---

[1] "I may say that there was a great deal of justification for the judges refusing to admit the copy of the Act of Council withdrawing the promise to Mitchell in respect that no notice of the intended production had been given to the prosecution. It would not be admitted under present practice without previous notice, unless it could be shown that the accused was unable to give the statutory notice, in which case the prosecutor is entitled to an adjournment. Criminal Procedure (Scotland) Act, 1887."—J. W. B.

sworn falsely. Lauderdale was willing to grant a reprieve and refer the matter to Charles II., with whom Mitchell would have probably been safe enough. But Archbishop Sharp replied that any one would then think it safe to shoot *him*.

So Burnet avers: he hated Sharp, and is not a good witness.

There is infamy enough for all parties to divide, from Mitchell the murderer, to Sir Archibald Primrose. Mackenzie, in his *Vindication* of the Government of Charles II. (1691), writes that, at Mitchell's trial "the Registers of Council were produced, but not the least mark of a promise was made to appear." That the Registers were *not* produced, he says, in his *Memoirs of the Affairs of Scotland* ("that was justly refused"). In the *Vindication* he observes that the enemies of Government were reduced to declaring that the Registers had been "vitiated." They did say this, *before the trial*, and it is clear that Mackenzie, by 1691, had confused the facts of the case.

Mackenzie's whole conduct remains a puzzle to me, because he ever tried to keep within the letter of the law, and his publication of his own pleading in the case, in 1681, shows that he was unconscious of having done anything that deserved reproach. In a copy of a dying speech issued by Mitchell, he says that Mackenzie was one of his counsel when he received his first indictment.[1] That was on March 2, 1674, the Act of Council withdrawing the promise of life was of March 12, Mitchell came before the Court on March 25, when "his diet was deserted," and it is difficult to see how Mackenzie, at that time, can have been unaware of the Act of Council of March 12. Charles II. backed the Council and the judges in the letter which is quoted in the note.[2]

[1] Wodrow, II. p 472.
[2] *Hist. MSS. Commission*, *Mar Papers*, 1904, p. 210.

Copy of a Letter from King Charles II. to the Lords of Justiciary.

WINDSOR CASTLE, *July* 13, 1679.

Right trustie and well beloved counsellors, and trustie and welbeloved, wee greet you well. The punishment of crymes being of so great import to our

K

A wretched piece of gossip emerges from this miserable business. A lampoon in rhyme says that Mackenzie ("Vulcan" referring to his broken leg and consequent lameness) "loves not Mars for Venus' sake," and a note explains that "by Mars is meaned the Viscount Dundee, who was thought to be too familiar with his lady." There was no Viscount Dundee till ten years after 1678. The lampoon is thus not contemporary, but a Whig slander done long after the date of the events: unless the notes were inserted after 1688, on a lampoon of a much earlier period. His worst enemies cleared Claverhouse of sensual sins, and he and Mackenzie, as Claverhouse's letters show, were on friendly terms.

Haltoun was, later, accused of perjury before Parliament, but the Duke of York, who was then Royal Commissioner, adjourned the House.[1] In Fountainhall's opinion, Haltoun could not have been convicted. He might argue that, in his letters to Kincardine, he was deceived by rumour, and that, before *he* swore, Lauderdale and Rothes had deposed, on oath, that there had been no promise. When he did swear, it was only to the fact that no promise was given in his hearing. Moreover the king, in his letter cited in the preceding note, describes Mitchell as "the enemy of human society."

Two years earlier (December 20, 1676), three men named McGibbon were hanged for robbing the Laird of Lawers. Fountainhall says that the laird "cheated and cullied

service, and tending so much to secure our peaceable subjectis; and you being in the execution of that imployment at so much paines, and your bench being by its late constitution filled with persons of extraordinarie abilities and breeding, wee have thought fitt at this tyme to assure you of our firme resolution to owne you and that our Court in the administration of justice to our people, and that wee will punish such as by injureing you asperse our authority and poyson our people. And particularly wee doe thank you for your proceedings against Mr. James Mitchell, that enemy of humane society, these who lessen that cryme or insinuat any reproach against these who were interested in that process as judges or witnesses being chargeable with the blood which they encourage to spill upon such occasions, and so wee bid you farewell. Given at our Court at Windsor Castle, the 13th day of July, 1679, and of our reigne the 31 year. By his Majesties command.

Signed LAUDERDALE.

[1] *State Trials*, vol. vi. 1262-1270.

John Graham of Claverhouse
1st Viscount Dundee
from Painting at Glamis Castle

A wretched piece of gossip emerges from this miserable business. A lampoon in rhyme says that Mackenzie ("Vulcan," referring to his broken leg and consequent lameness) "loves not Mars for Venus' sake," and a note explains that "by Mars is meaned the Viscount Dundee, who was thought to be too familiar with his lady." There was no Viscount Dundee till ten years after 1678. The lampoon is thus not contemporary, but a Whig slander done long after the date of the events: unless the notes were inserted after 1688, on a lampoon of a much earlier period. His worst enemies cleared Claverhouse of sensual sins, and he and Mackenzie, as Claverhouse's letters show, were on friendly terms.

Haltoun was, later, accused of perjury before Parliament, but the Duke of York, who was then Royal Commissioner, adjourned the House.[1] In Fountainhall's opinion, Haltoun could not have been convicted. He might argue that, in his letters to Kincardine, he was deceived by rumour, and that, before he swore, Lauderdale and Rothes had deposed, on oath that there had been no promise. When he did swear, it was only to the fact that no promise was given in his hearing. Moreover the king, in his letter cited in the preceding page, describes Mitchell as "the enemy of human society."

Two years earlier (December 20, 1676), three men named McGibbon were hanged for robbing the Laird of Lawers. Fountainhall says that the laird "cheated and cullied

service, and tending onwards to secure our peaceable subjectis; and you being in the execution of that imployment at so much paines, and your bench being by its late constitution filled with persones of extraordinarie abilities and breeding, wee have thought fitt in way of acknowledgement to assure you of our firme resolution to owne you and that our Court in the administration of justice to our people, and that wee will punish such as by injureing you impaire our authority and poyson our people. And particularly wee let them see that for your proceedings against Mr. James Mitchell, that enemy of humane society, those who lessen that cryme or insinuat any reproach against those who were interested in that process as judges or witnesses being chargeable with the blood which they encourage to spill upon such occasions, and so wee bid you farewell. Given at our Court at Windsor Castle, the 13th day of July, 1679, and of our raigne the 31 year. By his Majesties command.

                    Signed LAUDERDALE.

[1] State Trials, vol. vi. 1365-1370.

Sir Peter Lely, Pinx.   W. L. Colls, Sc.

John Graham of Claverhouse.
(1st Viscount Dundee.)
From Painting at Glamis Castle.

them by a forged remission, which was scarce *pia fraus,* only it was thought such robbers *and enemies to mankind and human society* deserved to be hunted and caught, as we do with wild beasts, by nets and all means, *per fas et nefas."* Poor Mitchell was an enemy to human society, and *per nefas* he perished.[1]

While the year 1678 saw, in the case of Mitchell, an indelible stain upon the ermine of Scottish justice, it also saw the publication, by Mackenzie, of a book "which became the manual of criminal law in Scotland for a hundred and thirty years." Thus Mr. Taylor Innes describes Mackenzie's *Laws and Customs of Scotland in Matters Criminal.*[2] We must remember, however, that, as regards torture, and the law of high-treason, the former was abolished and the latter was amended, two years after Scotland ceased to be an independent kingdom by the Union of 1707. These changes were not the least of the benefits flowing from that Union which, it is probable, Mackenzie would have opposed for reasons of patriotism, like Lockhart of Carnwath and Fletcher of Saltoun.

The dedication of Mackenzie's treatise, to Lauderdale, is another of the surprising testimonials to a character sadly in need of them, which Lauderdale won from such a man as President Stair, and from suffering ministers like Mr. Kirkton and Mr. Law. Lauderdale was certainly learned, a true lover of books, and acquainted with Hebrew as well as with the classical languages and literatures. He was much interested in history, as John Evelyn learned to his cost, for Evelyn lent to Lauderdale many letters of Mary Queen of Scots, and of Maitland of Lethington, her famous secretary, Lauderdale's great-uncle. Evelyn never recovered the MSS., some of which, stolen at some time or other from the Lauderdale Papers, are now in the British Museum. Nor was Evelyn more fortunate when he lent MSS. to Bishop Burnet. He used unkind expressions about the Scots in general, but no man should trust any antiquary! One holy man had found

---

[1] Fountainhall, *Historical Notices,* vol. i. p. 136.

[2] *Contemporary Review,* 1871, p. 250.

Lauderdale out, and told him frankly what was said of him, namely, that he was reputed to be a drunkard and a pimp. Mr. Richard Baxter did not, indeed, accept these charges, but he asked for means of refuting them. In any case Lauderdale would, one day, find it distressing "to reflect on a life of Covenant-breaking and unfaithfulness to God." It was too late to ask Lauderdale to renew the Covenants.[1]

In his Dedication of 1678, Mackenzie, of course, dwelt only on the virtues of the High Commissioner, concerning whom he says, in a passage added to his Memoirs, " Lauderdale knew not what it was to dissemble." " Your enemies admire more the greatness of your parts, than of either your interest or your success, and how you have made so great a turn in this kingdom, without either blood or forfeiture, showing neither revenge as to what is past, nor fear as to what is to come, continuing no longer your unkindness to any man, than you think he continues his opposition to his Prince."

Lauderdale's patriotism was really the quality that won Scottish hearts. How Scottish this is! " To you every Scotsman is almost as dear as every man is to his own relations." " He speaks to a' body as if they were his blood kin," said a labourer about Sir Walter Scott. After a compliment to the House of Lethington, Mackenzie says, " You are yourself the greatest statesman in Europe who are a scholar, and the greatest scholar who are a statesman : for to hear you talk of books one would think you had passed no time in studying men, and yet, to observe your wise conduct in affairs, one might be induced to believe that you had no time to study books. . . . You spend one half of the day in studying what is just, and the other half in practising what is so."[2]

[1] *Lauderdale Papers*, vol. iii. pp 235-239.
[2] Works, vol. ii. pp. 49, 50.

CHAPTER XI

THE HIGHLAND HOST AND ITS RESULTS

Motives for summoning the clans—The alternative, mob eviction of conformist ministers—Violence of the godly—Excesses of the Host—"Lawburrows"—Question of free quarters, 1678 and 1690—Mackenzie's defence—Disapproves of the measures—Clans sent home—Complaints to the king—War of pamphlets—Mackenzie's statement—*Aretina*, Part II.—Hamilton and Mackenzie at Court—Claverhouse "our generous friend"—Mackenzie wins over Monmouth—Letter to Lauderdale—Lauderdale attacked by the English House of Commons—Protected by Charles—A Convention to be held—Mackenzie specially commended by the king.

WHILE Mackenzie was revising the proof-sheets of his work on Criminal Law, was polishing his Dedication to Lauderdale, and was prosecuting Mitchell, Government was busily organising (November 1677, February 1678) the equipment of the Highland Host that was to subdue the west. The king "extremely approved" of this measure.[1] The Presbyterians believed, with the Duke of Hamilton, and historians still maintain, that the Highland expedition was merely designed, not to check a rebellion in the bud, (a rebellion which, once begun, the Royal forces were undeniably unable to suppress,) but to provoke rebellion, and provide the members of Council with forfeitures and fines. Of these, in any case, they were unscrupulously greedy, but only one fine, much later, seems to have been given to Mackenzie. Lauderdale himself, as we have shown, acted on his old knowledge of the west; his ceaseless fear of a return to 1648; his sense that the Militia could not be trusted, while the regular forces were helpless if the armed conventicles grew to a head; and his discovery that the gentry of the

---

[1] Danby to Lauderdale, *Lauderdale Papers*, vol. iii p. 91, November 15, 1677

west were as impotent to keep order as Hamilton says that
his "deputies" were. "There is not a regiment in all the
Militia in Scotland that his Majesty's commissioner puts
trust in, and that is his incomparable prudence," writes
Mr. Matthew Mackail.[1]

As early as November 8, 1677, Lauderdale had explained
the impotence of the local authorities to Danby. He had
called together the gentry of the two most disaffected shires,
"not that we expected much from them, but to try their
pulse and render them inexcusable." The shires were those
of Ayr and Renfrew; in a letter of Council (October 17,
1677) the gentry thereof were warned of "the severe courses"
that would ensue if disorder continued.[2] The gentry,
according to Lauderdale, "pretend they cannot repress
these disorders, that is to say, they will do nothing towards
it."[3] Wodrow gives the same answer from the gentry.
"They found it not within the compass of their power to
repress conventicles," and they said that toleration was the
only possible measure. A recent writer, the Rev. Mr.
Willcock, biographer of the unfortunate Earl of Argyll, not
unjustly remarks that toleration "might have involved some
rough measures of justice being undertaken by the populace,
in replacing the 'outed' clergy in their livings, and 'rabbling
out' those who had been thrust upon the country by a
fraudulent manœuvre and maintained in office by violence."[4]

This candid remark lights up the situation. The
Government was to grant toleration, and look on while
the rabble, continuing and extending the very violences
which Government wished to stop, drove out one set
of ministers and installed another! The alternative to a
plan so natural and judicious was coercion. Lauderdale
coerced. I am not defending the calling out of the Highland
Host; I am only asking—What could the Government do?
Being without money, and without sufficient troops, they

---

[1] *S P. Dom.*, Charles II., vol. 404. Record Office
[2] Wodrow, vol. ii. p. 372.
[3] *Lauderdale Papers*, vol. iii. p. 89.
[4] *A Scots Earl* (the Earl of Argyll), p. 206 (1907).

called on Atholl, Perth, Strathmore, Mar, Airlie, and other nobles and chiefs to muster their men, and to quarter them in the disturbed districts. We do not learn, save from Hickes, that Argyll was called on for a detachment; the peers invited were of the southern Highlands, and Argyll had enough to do in his long private war with the Macleans. Perhaps his negotiations for a Toleration had made Lauderdale distrust his "forwardness in Church matters."

Meanwhile "a measure of rough justice" *was* being dealt by the populace. Between December 25 and January 10, says Hickes, writing on the latter date, "the Saints . . . seized on six parish churches, and have appointed clerks and other officers of their own."[1] To suppress the Saints Atholl alone sent 2000 kilted Stewarts and Murrays; the whole host was of some 6000 to 8000 claymores. It is worth notice that Perth, in reply, speaks of his House as "now at so low an ebb," "my poor despised family" (December 3, 1677).[2] Both Perth and Atholl thought themselves aggrieved, and turned against Lauderdale, presently; but the poverty of Perth and his greed urged him and his brother, John, into the most ruthless, cruel, and lawless courses; they were the worst of those officials who ruined the cause of James II.

The host marched, and ravaged the western country with circumstances of ferocious license. On February 11, 1678, the Council issued a Proclamation in which Wodrow detects the hand of Mackenzie, "much the ablest advocate that party ever had," he elsewhere says. "The narrative is very bitter, and the public papers, since Sir John Nisbet's being laid aside, have a peculiar edge and flourish against Presbyterians."[3]

The proclamation, after some "edge and flourish," announces that the king commands a bond to be subscribed, by which lairds and masters must go bail, so to speak, for

---

[1] Ellis, *Original Letters*, Series II , vol iv. p 51.
[2] *Lauderdale Papers*, vol iii. p 93.
[3] Wodrow, vol. ii. p. 398.

the orderly and conformist behaviour of their tenants and servants. Some such bond was wont to be imposed on Highland chiefs, but Lowland tenants on lease were not Highland clansmen, obedient to the will of their chiefs. The bond was therefore very generally refused, by earls, lairds, and lawyers.[1]

In these circumstances a new legal device was tried, and possibly it was of Mackenzie's invention. The protection afforded by "law-burrows" (binding a person over to keep the peace, an instance occurred in January 1908) was extended to the king and the king's peace. This process, says Wodrow, thus extended, was "unexampled," moreover the information on which it was based was "a sinister narration and wrongous information." This is a return to the old position that the disturbed west was peaceful and in no rebellious humour, which was untrue, in the opinion of the Government. Indeed the west was far from peaceful, whether a rebellion was being organised or not. Government from the first was haunted by the memories of 1648–49, when the preachers and Argyll led the fanatics against the army of the Estates. In his *Vindication* (1691) Mackenzie avers, as in his Memoirs, that there was danger of conventicles coalescing into an army; that the gentry of the western shires declared, as they did, that peace and the continuance of Episcopacy were incompatible; that the king and Council could not yield to the passions of private men; that, as was proved in 1643 by the Solemn League and Covenant, full concession of Presbytery did not appease the Presbyterians, who sent their army to attack Charles I. in England; and that therefore the Highlanders were quartered on the west, with security for repayment out of the fines levied there, and from the king. "Nor have those who were then in the Government clamoured so much for a year's Free Quarters, as these people did then for a fort-

---

[1] In a programme of a book, *The Covenanters*, by James King Hewison, M A, D D, it is announced that "The Gentlemen of the Restoration were the curse of Scotland" This is a popular error. Many of the gentry and many of the nobles resisted the arbitrary measures.

night's, and even during that fortnight most men paid for their quarters."

The latter part of the argument is ruined by Wodrow's statistics of the losses of the western shires in five weeks,[1] whatever the sufferings of Mackenzie's party may have been during "a year's Free Quarters." In April 1690, indeed, we find Tarbat, now in the service of William III., complaining to him that his troops have been at free quarters in Scotland since November 1, 1689. They "have ruined many, and irritated more."[2] But a William may steal a horse while a Charles may not look over a fence! The Williamite troops were at free quarters in 1689, much longer than were the Highlanders in 1678. Even if better under control they "ruined many." But the Whiggish Muse of History makes no complaints of the Deliverer. "Two blacks do not make a white" in the nursery saying, so we need not set off the quarterings of 1689, 1716, and 1746 against those of the Highland Host. It is the old quarrel of Presbyterian pot and Royalist kettle.

As for law-burrows, or law-borrows, "by the very style thereof any private man may force another by the law to secure him against all prejudice from his men, tenants, and servants, and others of his command, *Out hounding* and *Ratihibition*." "The surety was thereupon approved by Parliament," and was "a most advantageous remedy."[3] It appears that, about 1638, leases used to include a clause binding the tenants to have family prayers, whereas, in 1685, the leases bound the tenants to abstain from "fanatical disorders. How much do these tacks differ from those!" says Wodrow.[4]

---

[1] Wodrow, vol. ii. pp. 423–426.

[2] *State Papers, Domestic*, Calendar 1689–90, p 551 ; *cf.* Tarbat's Complaint, S.P. *Dom.*, Will. and Mary, Calendar 1689–90, p 324

THE KING *to* SIR JAMES LESLIE.

Nov 19, 1689.

Whereas we are informed by George Viscount of Tarbet "that Major Wishart, in October last, forcibly entered his house of New Tarbet . . and contrary to law did garrison the said house, &c. . . as also that numbers of soldiers were quartered on the said Viscount's lands on free quarters, and that several abuses were committed by the soldiers on his tenants, &c."

[3] Works, vol ii. p. 345   [4] Wodrow, vol. iv. p. 280.

Persons who would shield Mackenzie under the plea that he was coerced by Lauderdale into the extension of "law-borrows," and the severities of 1678, might find a text in their favour. On February 15, 1678, the Earl of Perth wrote from Edinburgh to the Duke of Hamilton. The Council, he says, have resolved to disarm all the west, "even of their very swords, not sparing your Grace's self. Your Grace was named on that occasion, and particularly resolved to be so treated. Rothes . . . said it was the Mark of the Beast, so to say, for that the usurpers had practised it," and advised Lauderdale to forbear for his own sake. There was a quarrel, each of them upbraided the other as the cause of the disorders in the county.

Sir George Mackenzie and Archbishop Sharp "both swear that they have no accession to these courses, and say, God knows, ill enough both of the things and their actors. But there is not one single Councillor otherwise, and yet all goes on."[1] Unluckily as Mackenzie had no dread of Lauderdale, we cannot excuse him on the plea of "forced out." We do see how Perth coursed with the hounds of Lauderdale, and ran with the hare of Hamilton. The distracted Government, if we believe Perth, were all at odds among themselves. Their measures were, naturally, distasteful to Mackenzie, and dangerous to themselves. It is easy, indeed necessary, to blame the conduct of Government, but not so easy to see what, with a tiny army, no money, and no police, they should have done to repress the disorders, and protect the conformist clergy.

In fact, things had come to a state in which the brute forces of evolution directed them. There was violent disorder, there was violent repression, all working to one end, the restoration of the form of Church government which the country demanded, without the unessential but hitherto inseparable domination of ministers. It was not the maintenance of a diluted Episcopacy, it was the attempt to introduce Catholicism, that ruined the Stuart dynasty, after it had subjugated the Kirk.

[1] *Hist. MSS. Com*, XI., vi. pp. 163, 164.

In the middle and end of February 1678, the clans were sent home, loaded with plunder, while the chief gentry of the invaded shires went to Edinburgh. Thence Hamilton, with others, went to London, to lay their complaints before the king. Cassilis declared by letter that while "there is not the least shadow of an insurrection" a multitude of men, the clans, with nothing of human but external configuration, "differing in habit, language, and manners from all mankind," were let loose on the peaceful country; which was disarmed.

The Council replied. "There were far more armed men assembled almost weekly than could be repressed by almost thrice the number of your standing forces"—only fifteen hundred muskets. "What is a state of rebellion if not this, which those in power in the shires proclaim themselves unable to repress? We leave it to any reasonable man to judge, if your authority and government was not highly concerned, where such constant rendezvous of rebellion were kept by declared traitors, with such numbers of armed men, their numbers and contempt growing daily, *and your ordinary officers declaring that the same was above their correction*,"[1] as Hamilton, we saw, admitted.

Charles told Lord Arran that he thought Cassilis's letter "a very silly paper." "As he was a Christian he did not see what else could be done to prevent open rebellion." He had granted ministers (indulged) "and they railed more at these ministers than they did against the bishops." His Majesty added that he knew Scotland well, that the gentry could keep their tenants in order, that if the gentry wanted a rebellion, and if it spread to England, England would become a republic, and would conquer Scotland before next summer. If they thought they would like *that*, his Majesty differed from their opinion.[2]

Perhaps the best way out of the situation would have been that which Charles had proposed in 1669. The Union of England and Scotland, with a common Parliament, would have enabled the English members to legislate for the relief of the Scottish grievances, and would have

---

[1] Wodrow, vol. ii. pp. 435-438.   [2] *Lauderdale Papers*, vol. iii. pp. 99-102.

automatically swept away the Royal prerogative in Scotland. Mackenzie foresaw this consequence of Union; it is mentioned in his list of arguments against Union. But Mr. Kirkton, the preacher historian, and, probably, his party, took another view. Charles, they thought, desired to get a strong Tory parliament in Scotland, to make the Union, and then to flood the English parliament with Tory Scots, and so establish his prerogative in England.

As neither country welcomed the Union, escape from the Presbyterian *impasse* could not be found by that way. The way of withdrawing Episcopacy, as a failure, which Leighton suggested in despair, had the drawbacks which Mr. Willcock has so frankly explained. Mr. Kirkton, himself an "outed" minister, was conscious of the peril, if he really preached a sermon which the author of *Scotch Presbyterian Eloquence Displayed* declared that he heard Kirkton deliver. "I shall show you five lost labours, three opportunities, three fears," and so on. "For the three fears, the first is a great fear, *and that is, lest the King should give us all our will.* The second is a very great fear, and that is, if we should get our will, *I fear we should not make a good use of it.*"[1] The manner of Mr. Kirkton's sermon may be peculiar, but his matter is worthy of him in his moments of candour and common sense.

To use the king's own phrase, "as a Christian man *I* do not see" what his Government was to do, as they had neither money nor men adequate to the maintenance of order, and did not want hundreds of ministers to be at the mercy of the rabble. What they did is remembered to their eternal reproach; not unjustly, most naturally, but as certainly, without a full appreciation of their difficulties. These difficulties arose, inevitably, from the nefarious pettifogging imposition of Episcopacy on the country, without an effort to try the experiment of restoring Presbytery. Thence came the situation which, as I have tried to show, was really not quite so simple as our historians represent it.

[1] Kirkton, p. xiv.

There was a lively war of pamphlets on the affair of the Highland Host. The Council published its own narrative, obviously penned by Mackenzie. He began by showing how the newly remodelled Kirk of 1638 "violently grasped at all, even the civil government," and then was "rent in pieces by its own viperous brood," the Remonstrants, while the parliaments that "lusted after boundless liberty, were absolutely turned out from any share of the government" by Cromwell. All this was perfectly true, if for "boundless liberty" we read "modern constitutionalism," but an author who replied said that all this was ancient history, and that Mackenzie might as well have "begun his piquant narrative from Knox's seditious principles."

He might, indeed!

The rebellion of 1666, Mackenzie said, "was but a running and continued field conventicle, fed constantly by such as came to hear their ministers, who then governed them, preach upon that long march, and so, from place to place, they conventicled on to Pentland."

Mackenzie's opponent replied that his narrative should be named "*Aretina*, Part II.," or "the first part of the apostatised *Calumniator Publicus*, against that party or interest in whose service he broke his leg about four years ago, and shortly after broke his faith, neither of which can ever be made straight again." [1] It is clear that we must henceforth think of Mackenzie as a man with a limp : so much is gained for biography.

In April 1678, Mackenzie, with the Earl of Murray and Foulis of Collington went to Court, where they were opposed by Hamilton, with Perth and Atholl, who had now changed sides. Monmouth, Shaftesbury, and the English opposition, sided with Hamilton : Charles, the Duke of York, and Danby backed Mackenzie's faction. We have numerous letters, published and unpublished, to Lauderdale, describing the contest. Charles took the representatives of the Council into his august bedroom, whither Monmouth presently came. He asked questions about the bond which the gentry refused,

---

[1] Wodrow, vol. ii. pp. 442-449.

and was told that it was legal, as "there was a necessity for doing something for the country's peace." Charles supported them: even in England, he said, the parish of Twickenham had to pay £3000 in one year for robberies committed on Hounslow Heath. The Duke of York said he had advised Atholl not to meddle with Hamilton and the House of Commons: Hamilton was also supposed to be dealing with the French ambassador. But Charles would not allow the Privy Council of Scotland to summon home the aggrieved Peers, because he was afraid of trouble with the English House of Commons. The aggrieved Peers would not sign their complaints for fear of the sweeping Scottish law of "leasing making," making mischief between king and people. Stewart of Ladywell died for this law under the Marquis of Argyll (1641), when Montrose was a prisoner; and for this the son of the Marquis was condemned to death in 1681. Hamilton (May 9) explained the danger of signing to Queensberry.

Comment on the old state of affairs—the king's prerogative, and the impossibility of obtaining an impartial inquiry into grievances—is superfluous. Not easy is it to deny that the Prince of Orange was a necessary liberator. Scotland needed redemption from her own laws, by which the king, as Mackenzie argued, and as Bishop Burnet also argued, was absolute.[1] Charles was much pleased with Mackenzie's proclamation on the state of affairs ("*Aretina*, Part II."), but he proposed to hear the complaints of the Lords in a Scottish Council. This alarmed Mackenzie's party, who said that the step would ruin the authority of the Privy Council in Scotland. Charles was not well pleased with the Duke of Hamilton's averment that all his horses had been taken, and, generally, the English felt great doubts of the legality of the quartering, and showed anxiety that the sufferers should be compensated. Mackenzie denied the truth of Hamilton's statement about his horses, and Monmouth consulted Mackenzie about the law of "leasing making," which made the nobles afraid to sign their complaints.

[1] Clarke and Foxcroft, *Life of Bishop Burnet*, p. 174

Mackenzie, in an unpublished letter, describes to Lauder-dale his own proceedings, and seems to believe that he has brought Monmouth to his way of thinking.[1]

Mackenzie's habit of not dating his letters is troublesome ; he does not date one in which he tells Lauderdale that the opposition by a snapped division in the Commons, had voted against him by 150 to 90; nor another in which he says that all is going well, and that "you and we all are much obliged to Claverhouse, who is our generous friend." Claverhouse had recently returned from service under William of Orange, who recommended him to the Duke of York. This is his first appearance in the politics of the time. To Lauderdale Mackenzie recommends "a cheerful countenance and a jovial humour" "as great policy."

Sir Andrew Forester gave Lauderdale (May 9) an account of the debate in the Commons. It was argued for him that the House had nothing to do with Scottish business, and that, if there were allegations of ill doings of his in England, he was an English peer, and must be attacked by a formal legal impeachment. Lauderdale escaped by the narrowest of majorities, four votes, and by some Parlia-mentary technicalities.[2]

Charles had turned some of his household out of his service for voting against Lauderdale; this was one of

---

[1] *Add. MSS.* 32,095 [*Malet Papers*], f. 88

To the DUKE OF LAUDERDALE (no address), *Last of April*, 1678 (no signature)

I came to London on Monday kissed the King's hands & delivered to him your letter. I spoke only generally, for the Dutch ambassadors were to be received next day & his Majesty was carried away by the Duke & Lord Treasurer. I kissed the Duke's hands, he was glad I came for thereafter he thought they should not be "brayd" with law. I told him I would justify in point of law & hoped he would not maintain in point of state. The question was whether Scotland was to be a commonwealth or not, & if we should be twice fooled into the same degree of re-bellion I spoke 3 hours nigh with the Duke of Monmouth convincing him from point to point ; he has promised to own your interest I told him I would acquaint the King of his resolution to own the King's authority & servants. I reproved Secretary Williamson for opposing the King's interest & meddling in points of our law which he understood not. I spake 2 hours with the Lords Treasurer & High Chamberlain against the overture of calling up 5 councillors for making a quorum with which the King is to sit.

[2] *Lauderdale Papers*, vol. iii. pp. 133-143.

two occasions in which he is reported to have lost his temper. On the other, referring to Monmouth, his Majesty, according to Lord Ailesbury, said "tell James to go to hell," and James went to Holland. Lauderdale, it is fair to say, might have had more supporters, if the Tories could have been induced to return to the House within two hours after dinner.

Finally, on May 23, Mackenzie and the rest proposed that a Convention of Estates should be held in Scotland, and Lauderdale was advised to "louke carefully to the elections," and to get at the boroughs through Rocheid, the Edinburgh town clerk. A large majority was secured for Lauderdale. Two days later the king saw Hamilton's party, who were still too cautious to sign their complaints. "The King was well pleased with his Council, and would own his authority."

All these proceedings go to prove the absolute necessity of an Union between England and Scotland. In Scotland the king was absolute, how absolute we shall see later from a document prepared for Charles by Mackenzie. Once Scotland was united to England the despotism could not endure for a session of Parliament. As it happened, Scotland was emancipated before the Union, in the early years of William III.

Mackenzie had always been devotedly loyal to the Stuart dynasty, believing in, and later defending, its prehistoric antiquity, by descent from fabulous kings of Scotland. In London he, for the first time, came under the undeniable personal spell of Charles II., and found the Duke of York as pleasant as, before 1675, did Bishop Burnet. Mackenzie, when in opposition (1669-1675) had no quarrel with "his Prince," his quarrel was then with Lauderdale's jobbery and despotism. Henceforth he was ready to go to all lengths but one with the monarch ; he would not admit the dispensing power of James II. in favour of Catholics. His exertions at Court, in 1678, were specially acknowledged by an Act of Privy Council (June 20, 1678). His "successful endeavours for maintaining his Majesty's just and lawful prerogatives when he attended his sacred Majesty by the Council's command" were recorded, with a special assertion as to " how sensible his Majesty is of his services." He is specially " encouraged and exonerated." [1]

His *Defensio Concilii Secreti*, in Latin, was published by him, and is in his Works, but we shall later find a more drastic if less elegant defence of the Privy Council, in English, among his unpublished manuscripts.

[1] *Mackenzie-Wharncliffe Deeds*, p. 48   The original extract remains in Lord Wharncliffe's charter-chest.

CHAPTER XII

MURDER OF SHARP—MACKENZIE
CONTRA MUNDUM, 1678-1679

Mackenzie as a debater in Convention—His letter to Sir Joseph Williamson—Presbyterians quarrel about paying taxes—Violence of the wild
party—Mackenzie and Mr. Veitch—Mr. Veitch as a strategist—His
adventures as a spy—Adventures in England—Before the Council—
Turns the laugh against a bishop—The bishops insist that he shall be
spared—Conventicles—Murder of the archbishop—By inspired murderers—Mackenzie will avenge Sharp—"We will put them all to
the torture"—Does not do so—Mackenzie in danger—"Not afraid to do
his duty"—Is called to Court—In town during affairs of Drumclog and
Bothwell Bridge—Alone defends Government against Hamilton and
his party—He argues for king's absolute power—Admitted to be "right
in law"—Meets Dryden—Dryden on Mackenzie—"That noble wit of
Scotland."

MACKENZIE'S party, or rather Lauderdale's, having escaped
from the storm in England, were commanded by Charles
to call a financial Convention of the Estates, and to ask
supply for the increase of the military forces. "This
practice of calling Conventions only to levy money," says
Wodrow, "and never permitting Parliaments to sit to consider just grievances and provide remedies, was one of
the arbitrary steps of this period, and loudly complained
of."[1] The proceeding was impossible under the English
constitution, but Scotland had almost no constitution
worth mentioning. In a letter to Lauderdale, undated as
usual, and even unsigned, Mackenzie says that the Duke
of York admitted "these people" (Hamilton and the rest)
"to kiss his hand," to make them go into the Convention.
He told them that opposing the king "would not do their

[1] Wodrow, II. p 486.

business," and Claverhouse gave them the same information. "Your Grace should give them fair weather till the Convention be over." They may mention grievances in a letter after granting the subsidy, "but I will motion to the king that there be an express instruction forbidding you to suffer any such thing as grievances to be mentioned." [1]

The Convention met for business on June 26, when Hamilton protested against the naming of the Committee by Lauderdale. Disputed elections, he said, should be debated, not by a Committee, but in open Convention. He had only two supporters; for his view of the case he quoted the proceedings in Charles's first Parliament. "To all this the Lord Advocate" (Mackenzie) "spoke succinctly and smartly, with great eloquence asserting the king's prerogatives, and that not only the king and his Commissioner named Committees, but that in all other courts the ordinary Presidents do name them, to avoid confusion, and that what was on all occasions granted to all the kings in Europe, and to our former kings, should not now be refused to the best of kings."

It was found that in Conventions the Commissioner always appointed the Committee. A great deal of time was constitutionally frittered away, for Hamilton continued to "snap." The House almost unanimously backed Lauderdale, who then reminded them that by two Acts of the king's first Parliament "meetings for treating and consulting in State affairs, except in ordinary judgments, were illegal." "No such meetings were to be allowed now, especially during the Convention, and, if any were, he behoved to move the Advocate to do his duty, seeing any such meetings were by the Law declared seditious." Hamilton professed that he did not understand. Apparently his party was not to be allowed to assemble and to discuss their policy! [2] Mr. Matthew Mackail, then a writer of newsletters, says that Lauderdale "behaved himself with a great deal of prudence

[1] *Add. MSS., Malet Papers*, 32,095, f. 94.
[2] *Lauderdale Papers*, vol. iii pp 154-159.

and moderation, and Hamilton with a great deal of peremptory boldness."[1]

Whatever the Hamilton party may have thought of the Convention, Mackenzie was much pleased with it, with public loyalty, and with his own successes, as he freely explains to the English Secretary of State in the following letter :[2]—

SIR GEORGE MACKENZIE *to* SIR JOSEPH WILLIAMSON, *Secretary of State.*

SIR,

. . . Our affairs heer prosper to our wish for the whole convention did vnanimously vot a suplie & vher wee differd such as serve the King in his own way prevailed still in all the severall votes, and the people ar almost in as loyall a frame as they wer in vhen his Majestie was restord. All men heer speak kyndly of his interest & most men think kyndly of it. I hav been so happie as to be very instrumentall in this turne And the great things I have said of the Kings inclination to justice & of his understanding perfectly our affairs did much influence all sydes to the united vote. I hoop you will tak occasion to remember the King in vhat ill condition his affairs wer vhen I first engadgd in his service and vhat pains I have taken to restore them to ther first condition and with vhat passion & concern I interest my selfe. This good office is not deservd though expected by

your humble servant

GEO. MACKINZIE.

EDINBURGH, 4 *Jul* 1678.

The Convention, the vast majority being of a singular loyalty, voted grants for a new regiment of foot, three troops of horse, and some dragoons, with a "cess" or tax of £180,000. The forces were intended to repress the field conventicles, and taxation seemed better than free quarters. But, as Wodrow says, "the Act divided those who were before disjointed," and the Presbyterians, already rent by the

---

[1] *S.P. Dom*, Charles II., vol. 404 . [2] *Ibid*, vol. 405.

questions of indefinite ordinations, and the lawfulness of being in communion with the Indulged, now split upon the question of the legality of paying the cess. "The banished ministers in Holland were warmly against paying this assessment," some ministers at home preached against it, the congregations of other ministers, by way of a popular Erastianism, insisted that *they* should do so. They found a case of a primitive Christian, who, moved by his conscience, committed arson in a pagan temple. He was ordered to rebuild it, (which seems no more than reasonable,) but he preferred to be a martyr.[1]

In Wodrow's time (1722) the Presbyterians were still wrangling among themselves over these old cases of conscience. They bitterly felt that, after all their sufferings, they had failed to recover "the prerogatives of Christ," and they cast blame upon their ancestors, on one or the other side in their old disputes.

A wild party of non-indulged preachers, young probationers, a preaching hangman, and wandering dispossessed lairds now arose, fomented by the exiles in Holland. Mr. Mackail, on August 10, thus reports the activities of the Rev. Mr. Welsh : [2]—

To MR. JOHN ADAM.

I am always labouring to remove your errors, the greatest of which is to maintain the Presbyterian principles. How will you justify what fell out the Sabbath 4th of this month. Mr. John Welch with 36 other nonconformist Ministers convented 10000 of the kings I know not whether to say Leidges or enemies, at Maybol near Air celebrated the Lord's Supper with great solemnity, preached up the Solemn League and Covenant, the lawfulness of defensive arms, before and after their sermon modelling themselves drilling and exercising themselves in "faits of armes" and appointing another celebration at Fenuick within 34 miles of this city declaring they will defend themselves if opposed by His Majesty's forces.

---

[1] Wodrow, ii. p. 491.   [2] Abridged from *S. P. Dom.*, Charles II., vol. 405.

Mr. Welsh rode about with an armed guard, not of the godliest, organising rebellion, (according to Mackail and Claverhouse,) yet was insulted as being too tame, and "an Achan among us." "Many" (sensible Presbyterians!) "by reason of these unhappy jars deserted us, and many more never joined us," writes a survivor, consulted by Wodrow.[1] At this time Robert Hamilton, once a pupil of Gilbert Burnet, desecrated the Sabbath by leading a party in arms to invade the Rev. Matthew Selkirk, in the parish of Monkland, near Glasgow. Hamilton brought in another preacher, more to his taste, and of his sermon Mr. Selkirk took notes, "which sadly discover the height the flames were come to." Wodrow piously forbears from printing the notes, which would be instructive.

Here follows another letter from Mackail :—

To JOHN ADAMS, *merchant of Lisbon.*

EDINBURGH, *Aug.* 17, 1678.

Welch's great conventicle lasted from Saturday Sunday and Monday. He had considerable guards. He entered the town of Air with his guards and performed such visits as he pleased. The Magistrates on reproof from the council alleged that they had no suitable force to oppose him. Sir James Stuart has been released from prison by order of council though he declared he would not live "orderly" as that meant he should converse with no outed ministers, nor countenance them.[2]

The madness of Oates's Popish Plot was now raging in England, and the following year was a period of delirium north and south of Tweed.

Early in the year 1679 Mackenzie was engaged in the singular affair of the Rev. Mr. William Veitch. This young clergyman was of a temperament rather Cavalier than Covenanting : he carried a spirit of gallantry and gaiety into the defence of his cause ; and, from his Memoirs, it appears

---

[1] Wodrow, II pp. 497–500   [2] *S P Dom.*, Charles II., vol. 406

that he thoroughly enjoyed the *dreich* period of "the Sufferings." An account of his adventures may seem a digression,
but it brings life and gaiety into a deplorable picture of the age.

In November 1666, when the Pentland Rising began,
Mr. Veitch, then residing at Lanark, took unto him an old
soldier, now a tailor, Major Learmont, and led a little band
to march under the standard of the Covenant. With fifty
horsemen he invaded the town of Ayr, captured one of the
magistrates who had absconded, and billeted 800 horse and
foot in the town and citadel.

Thence he marched on Lanark, which his party occupied; and here he meant to stop Dalziel, with the Royal
army, from crossing the flooded Clyde. Dalziel would be
driven back on Glasgow, by lack of supplies, the Covenanters would concentrate on Lanark, and be ready, in
force, for a dash on Edinburgh, where panic prevailed.

"An excellent plot, good friends!" but the author of
Jus Populi Vindicatum sent a message bidding the Covenanters to march at once on Edinburgh, where they would
find reinforcements and supplies. Mr. Veitch was reposing
when this message came, after several nights spent under
heavy rain. He was aroused, and called to a council of
war, where he stood by the strategic scheme already described. But as the council differed from his opinion,
and as their general, Wallace, volunteered to go himself as
a spy into Edinburgh, Mr. Veitch gallantly took that dangerous task upon himself. He left his sword and pistols
behind, wore an old cloak and an old hat, mounted a baggage horse, and rode by way of Biggar. At the park wall
of Greenhill he was warned by three countrywomen that
Lord Kingston, with horse and foot, was watching by
Bruntsfield Links. "If you go that way, you are a dead
man." He therefore rode across the Boroughmuir to enter
by way of Dalkeith, from the east, but some coal-miners
told him that all the gates were guarded in force. "Reason
and light was for going back; but credit" (honour) "cried,
'You must go forward, or lose your reputation, as a coward
that durst not prosecute your commission.'"

Mr. Veitch was not disobedient to the call of honour; he rode on, and, at the Potter Row gate, two sentries " culled him like a flower." He asked to be allowed to go to his lodgings, as a man of peace, but was led before Lord Kingston, "a huffle and hot-spirited man," to whom he gave "very smooth and suitable answers." A cry arose that the Whigs were at the gates, when Mr. Veitch said, " My Lord, if you have any arms to give me, I'll venture against these Whigs in the first rank." It was a false alarm, and Mr. Veitch requested Lord Kingston to send him, under guard, to the house of the Dean of Edinburgh, from whom he would bring a line to prove his honesty. The Dean was a friend of Kingston, and Mr. Veitch had probably guessed, what Kingston knew, that the worthy divine had fled, in great fear, to the shelter of the Castle. Kingston, quite satisfied, was just bidding Mr. Veitch go in peace, when in came two scouts with a prisoner, no less than Mr. Veitch's friend, the unfortunate Mr. Hugh Mackail. As Mackail was sure to have saluted Mr. Veitch as a companion in tribulation, he asked hastily for a corporal and his guard, to protect him from further inquiries.

Released in the Potter Row, he went to an inn kept by a woman that was a widow. On entering the hall he found it full of trembling curates, slipped back, and, after other adventures, took refuge with an outed minister. Here he got a bed, cut off his wet boots, and hung them up. He found them still hanging there when, thirteen years later, he fell into the hands of the Lord Advocate Mackenzie, in 1679.

Others might think that Mr. Veitch had now done enough for honour, but that was far from his mind. He heard that his comrades were among the Pentland hills, and thither he rode next morning. He was surrounded by a patrol of Dalziel's horse, but he called to Paton, who commanded the rear-guard of the Covenanters; Paton charged the patrol, and freed Mr. Veitch, with apologies for having sent him on such an errand. About midday his comrades, hearing of Dalziel's advance, occupied a hilltop, whence they drove an attacking party under General Drummond. Major Learmont, Veitch's friend, drove off another party, and would have slain the Duke of Hamilton but for Ramsay, Dean of Hamilton, who warded off the stroke with his sword. Learmont then slew one of four men who attacked, and he escaped, as did Mr. Veitch, who was actually taken, but galloped away under fire.

After countless adventures he managed to cross the Border. He preached in London, stayed in England, mainly on the Border, for twelve years ; was at last arrested as an outlaw fugitive from Scotland, and sent to Edinburgh. He was brought before the Criminal Court as having been condemned, *in absence*, to death for his share in the Pentland Rising, a decision of which Mackenzie had disapproved at the time, and in 1669, when an Act of Parliament made such condemnations legal. But now, as King's Advocate, Mackenzie had to administer the existing law. A new trial would not be granted to Mr. Veitch, against whom evidence could scarcely be found, while he had an *alibi;* people could swear to his presence in Edinburgh on the night before and in the morning of the battle of Rullion Green, while nobody could show that he actually took a part, as he did, in the battle. The Privy Council (March 11, 1679) wrote to the king, saying that, whereas a Mr. George Johnstone, a farmer, had been sent to them from England, he turned out to be the Mr. William Veitch forfeited in absence in 1667. The Royal Orders about Johnstone did not apply to Veitch, "who offers him to prove that he was in Edinburgh the time of the fight at Pentland." (Oh, Mr. Veitch !)

The Council, therefore, awaited further orders. On March 18, under these orders, Mackenzie was commanded to prosecute the hero. But, on April 8, the judges found that they needed the advice of the Privy Council and Lords of Session, for there was no precedent for executing a sentence pronounced in the absence of the accused, when he appeared "and offered defences." Mr. Veitch's "defences" were of the flimsiest, for he had done as much fighting as he could get, but that circumstance he kept to himself. His "diet" was deferred again and again. Through Eliot of Minto he sent a petition to Lauderdale, who was his kinsman. That failed, "the Duke was pre-engaged." But Shaftesbury heard of the matter, and "made a great noise," while the English House of Commons threatened an inquiry. Charles, therefore (July 17, when Mackenzie was in London) wrote a letter saying that as Mr. Veitch "was not actually present at Pentland fight" (where he had been in the thick of it) Mr. Veitch must be set at liberty, on promise to leave Scotland.[1]

Now Mr. Veitch, when brought before the Council on his arrival as a prisoner from England, had turned the laugh against the Bishop of Edinburgh (Paterson), "'Have you taken the Covenant?' asked the bishop.

"He answered, 'All that see me at this honourable board may easily perceive that I was not capable to take the Covenant, when you and the other ministers of Scotland tendered it.'

"At which the whole company fell a laughing."

Mr. Veitch probably did not know that the bishops unanimously desired his acquittal. Mackenzie writes to Lauderdale, "I find the bishops violent to have him cleared, for they think his death will ruin their interest, and St. Andrews (Sharp) said to myself they would petition for it, and thereupon I entreated them never to blame your Grace for favouring fanatics. All men here wish his life to be spared."[2]

Mr. Veitch being thus happily released, with the good will of all parties, soon distinguished himself in new adventures even more curious and heroic than those in which he had already been engaged. His guiding star was romance; his wife, a pious lady, was worthy of him, and, at a very great age, after more than fifty years of married life, they died within a day of each other : "in death they were not divided." Their lives are a gleam of light in the gloomy annals of the time.

[1] Wodrow, III. pp. 7–9   [2] *Add. MSS* 32,095, *Malet Papers*, f 205

The early months of 1679 saw a change in the methods
of the conventiclers, some ministers withdrew from the
majority of their brethren, concentrated their armed
followers, and, from December to May, discoursed "to
vulgar auditories" against the Indulged, and against payment of the recently imposed taxation. Mr. Welsh and
others of his temper, "with whom there were not many
in arms," preached in other places.[1] On March 31,
Major White had news of a conventicle to be held at
Lesmahago, and took out a party of twenty dragoons,
with two officers. He came across a force of three hundred
foot and a troop of sixty horsemen, whom he commanded
to disperse. Their leader replied in a phrase both disloyal
and unquotable, as regarded the king, and said that his
men fought for "the King of Heaven." They fired, and the
Whigs fell on the fourteen dragoons (six had been left
to guard prisoners) and mortally wounded Lieutenant
Dalziel, whom they took prisoner, with six others. Robert
Hamilton was believed to be the leader.[2] Two soldiers
were later murdered in cold blood at a place called New
Mills, on the borders of Ayrshire, whereon the gentry of
that county met (April 28) and attributed the disturbances
to "a few unsound, turbulent, and hot-headed preachers,
most part whereof were never ministers of the Church of
Scotland."[3]

On May 3, Archbishop Sharp was murdered, in a
butcherly manner, (the whole process of slaying him and
rifling his baggage occupied three-quarters of an hour,) on
Magus Moor, some three miles from St. Andrews. It became
a kind of test question, "What do you think of the death
of the Archbishop?" Many fanatics had no clearness
to pronounce it murder. If it was not murder, then it was
the righteous execution of God's judgments. The murderers,
as one of them, Russell, says, had already "judged duty
to hang them both" (Sharp and another man) "over the
port," the gate of his house at St. Andrews.[4] "Many of

[1] Wodrow, iii. p. 33.   [2] *Lauderdale Papers*, iii. pp 162-164.
[3] Wodrow, iii. p. 38.   [4] Kirkton, p 406

the Lord's people and ministers judged a duty long since not to suffer such a person to live. . . ." "The Lord had put it into the minds of many of his people," said one David Walker to Russell. John Balfour of Burley or Kinloch "got that word borne in upon him, 'Go and prosper,' this after 'inquiring the Lord's mind.'" "He went again and got it confirmed by that scripture, 'Go, have I not sent you.'"

All these divine commands reached Balfour when he was thinking of retiring from Fife to the Highlands.[1] Others also had "a clear call," and said "truly this is of God." Their duty, on the principles of Knox and *Jus Populi Vindicatum*, was thus fully "circumstantiate." They had "calls," as Phinehas had, and they hacked the Archbishop to death. The affair was entirely *en règle*, from their point of view.

They escaped to the west, where some of them, such as Balfour and Hackston of Rathillet, joined the congenial Robert Hamilton. The details of the murder of the Archbishop were not, at first, clearly known, as appears from Mackenzie's undated note to Lauderdale, probably of May 4 or 5.

"The chancellor and I waited all day at Leith examining witnesses, with result that Hackston of Rathabuch was he who struck the postillion & turned the coach, but is not taken. Camron's brother is taken, &c. Inchdernie commanded the party and was killed by Achmutie the Duchess's page. Many are taken as suspect but no clear probation against them, but we will put them all to the torture. Remember that King Alexr. II. killed 400 for the death of one Bishop of Caithness and gelded them and what law had he for that?"[2]

As a matter of fact it was Russell who struck the postillion, at least he says so himself, and Inchdernie was not the leader nor present at the murder, he was shot in galloping away from Achmutie's party of avengers. The threat to "put them all to the torture" was not carried out, at least, as far as I can find, Wodrow makes no mention of a fact which he would have been careful not to omit. He only says that

[1] Kirkton, p. 413.   [2] *Add. MSS* 32,095, *Malet Papers*, f 190

the Council "took the oaths of the Archbishop's servants, and used all imaginable care to discover the actors."[1]

Wodrow says that no party of Presbyterians approved of the murder, but his editor candidly quotes, from that popular book *The Hind Let Loose*, the statement that "attempts at cutting off such monsters of nature" are "lawful" (and, as one would think, laudable) in the circumstances. They are seldom profitable.

Mackenzie himself, at this time, knew that he carried his life in his hand. In a letter to Lauderdale, undated, but probably written rather later, he says that, when riding from The Shank (his country house) on Monday, four armed men rode up and asked Gifford and Pitcur (Haliburton of Pitcur, his brother-in-law) if Mackenzie were with them, but seeing their servants coming up with his own, they retired. He "is not afraid to do his duty."[2]

Mackenzie was not able to stay in Scotland, seeking after the murderers of the Archbishop. While they were riding about the country, making for the congenial west by the north, he was summoned to Court. He therefore was no eye-witness of the confusion and panic in Scotland, when events proved that the murderers, far from absconding, were publicly heading a rebellion; and proving perhaps rather to Mackenzie's satisfaction, that with such a rising as his party had looked for in 1678, and had suppressed by aid of the Highland Host, the regular forces in Scotland were unable to cope. News presently came to Court which Mackenzie could employ as a good defence for the use of the Highland Host.

It was on May 14 that Charles sent to Edinburgh, commanding Mackenzie, Stair, the Register, the Justice-Clerk, and the Justice-General, to attend a conference in London, on Lauderdale's affairs.[3] The House of Commons, on May 29, Restoration Day, presented to the king an address against Lauderdale, and "his arbitrary and pernicious counsels," tending to "the alteration of the Protestant

[1] Wodrow, vol iii p. 52.   [2] *Add. MSS.* 32,094, f 302.

[3] Fountainhall, *Historical Notices*, vol. i. p. 225.

religion established." Shaftesbury was still making his own
use of "the Popish Plot," and if ever any counsels were
"arbitrary and pernicious" they were those of his party,
which sent so many innocent men to the block and the
gibbet on the grotesquely incredible evidence of Oates, Bedloe, Turberville, Dugdale, and Mr. Kirkton's enemy, Captain
Carstairs. Lauderdale was said to be "with just reason
regarded as a chief promoter of such counsels," and no
doubt Captain Carstairs, now at enmity with him and other
witnesses, would have told marvellous tales against him.
Probably Carstairs came to town for that purpose, but he
found another victim, who was hanged.[1] The chief charge
was that Lauderdale "raised jealousies and misunder-
standings" between the kingdoms, "whereby hostilities
might have ensued." Probably Burnet's evidence of 1675
lingered in the minds of the Commons. The exclusion of
the Duke of York from the succession was also designed,
but Charles dissolved the Parliament.

Now on that very Restoration Day which the Commons
chose for their attack on Lauderdale, a genuine rebellion
broke out in the disturbed districts of Scotland. The
murderers of Sharp had joined hands with the western
devotees under Robert Hamilton, and on May 29 Hamilton
headed a band of the most devout, who avenged a standing
grievance of the preachers. The State, they held, had no
right to appoint holidays; to do so was to touch the Ark,
like the well-meaning but unfortunate Uzziah. Hamilton, on
Restoration Day, trotted into the town of Rutherglen near
Glasgow, burned a number of Acts of the Government at
the Cross, and affixed to it a written Testimony of "the true
Presbyterian party."

They witnessed against the Act Rescissory for overturn-
ing the whole Covenanted Reformation.

The Acts for establishing abjured prelacy. The Renun-
ciation of the Covenants. The outing of the ministers. The
invasion of the Lord's prerogative by the appointing of a
holy day on May 29. The Act of Supremacy of 1669. The

---

[1] Burnet, pt 1. vol. 11. pp. 170-172.

Indulgence and all other sinful Acts of Council. (This clause as to the Indulgence is not in all copies.)

On May 31 Claverhouse with a small force of cavalry rode out to look for the authors of the Testimony, and for a conventicle. He succeeded to a wish in finding both at Drumclog ; he caught a preacher, Mr. King, and encountered an armed body of men, under Russell, and Balfour of Burley, Sharp's murderers, and Robert Hamilton. The Covenanters held a strong position surrounded by marshes, and Claverhouse, having reconnoitred, sent to Glasgow for reinforcements. But he did not wait for their arrival, and after some skirmishing, the enemy marched up to his dismounted dragoons, and came to hand-strokes, slaying several of his officers, and wounding his horse with a pitchfork, whereon his men took to flight. He lost some prisoners, who surrendered to quarter, and Hamilton, by his own account, pistolled one of them, and declared that to have given quarter " was one of our first steppings aside."

Claverhouse brought his fugitives into Glasgow in the late twilight, here he found Lord Ross with a small force ; they barricaded the streets, and three days later were attacked by the Covenanters. They drove off the enemy, but now the country, small lairds, yeomen, labourers, townsfolk, were hurrying to fight for the Covenants ; and Linlithgow, from Edinburgh, ordered Ross to retire on Stirling, joining him at Larbert on June 5. Meanwhile the enemy, some 6000 or 7000 men, occupied Glasgow unopposed, where they found supplies and a welcome. The Privy Council was raising the Militia, a half-hearted body, and must have been comforted to hear, about June 15, from Lauderdale, that the king was sending down several regiments of foot and horse under Monmouth, then the darling of Protestants, frightened by Oates's fables of a popish plot.

It is not possible to say what would have happened if the Covenanters had been in harmony among themselves. They might have marched on Edinburgh raising the country as they went, though they would have exposed their flank

to Ross and Claverhouse. But they only "fought like
devils for conciliation," in their own ranks : the party of
Mr. Welsh and the wilder party of Robert Hamilton
preaching and praying against each other about communion with the Indulged, was it sinful ? about payment
of cess, was it a Cause of Wrath ? and so forth. Welsh's
party raised a new Testimony at Hamilton, against the
Testimony of Rutherglen. Was the army to be "purged"
of Achans, as before the battle of Dunbar, and, if so, were
the Achans the Welshites, or the partisans of Robert
Hamilton ?

The host loitered about on the Clyde, among villages
and little towns, like Hamilton and Bothwell, infecting all
the country with the microbe of rebellion, for, till the
revolution of 1688, peasants and lairds and yeomen who
had "conversed with the rebels" were liable to arrest, fine,
forfeiture, even death. On July 22 Monmouth found the
unhappy, distracted host grouped round the various preachers,
on the farther side of Bothwell Bridge. After some parley
he advanced, there was skirmishing and artillery fire, but
the enemy did not fight as at Rullion Green in 1666. Each
party in the Presbyterian camp blames the other, but the
Bridge was not resolutely held, and before the Royalists
the Covenanters presently all ran away, losing hundreds of
prisoners. The news would reach London about June 25
or 26.

In London and at Windsor, during the month of the
rebellion, Hamilton, with Atholl, Sir John Cochrane, Sir
George Lockhart, and Sir John Cuningham (Mackenzie's
old companion as Justice-Depute) were at Court, presenting Charles with a list of their grievances. This document,
of which there is a MS. copy in the Townshend papers,
was printed as a pamphlet, "Matters of Fact." Wodrow
gives a text.

The Lords say (1) that Lauderdale grossly misrepresented the condition of western Scotland, (which is not so
certain,) and sent in the Highland Host, with all its quarterings and exactions. (2) The Bond was "illegal." (3) So

was "law-borrows," with the disarming of the gentry, and the seizure of their best horses. (4) The nobles and gentry of Ayr were indicted, by Mackenzie, not allowed time to prepare their defences, and "put to swear against themselves in matters that were capital." (5) They "purged themselves upon oath." (6) When they went to Edinburgh they were ordered to leave the town. (7) When they desired to go to lay their grievances before the king, they were forbidden to leave the country. (8) A number of persons were illegally imprisoned, others were incapacitated from public offices. (9) The Kirkton story among others is told, not as by Mr. Kirkton, for Carstairs, "a person now well enough known to your Majesty" as a witness in the Popish Plot, is represented as saying that he had a warrant, which Mr. Kirkton has neglected to record. It is stated that Carstairs procured an ante-dated warrant.[1] After other offences of less interest, the complainants give the story of Mitchell. Lauderdale is said to have "threatened them" (the judges) "if they should proceed to the examination of that Act of Council which, he said, might infer perjury on them that had sworn." They then touch on jobbery and corruption, and accuse Haltoun of sending from the Council models of any Royal letters he pleases, which Lauderdale, in town, returned with the Royal signature.[2]

Wodrow is for laying much of the blame upon the bishops, but as Sharp had been already judged, condemned, and executed by the Fifeshire Phinehases, he was dropped out of the Memorial.

On July 8, the Lords of Hamilton's party, with Lockhart and Cuningham, met at Windsor, to accuse Lauderdale. Against them Mackenzie appeared, single-handed, "who undertook the debate against them all," *nec pluribus impar!* Among his adversaries was, unlooked for, the chief of Clan MacNaughton, that doughty victim of Argyll. To him the king was pleased to say, in banter, "You are indeed a

---

[1] Burnet says that he confessed this to Atholl. Burnet was "against the making use of so vile a man." Burnet, pt. i. vol. ii. p. 170.

[2] Wodrow, vol. iii. pp. 159-163.

M

great lawyer, and a Highland man." Mackenzie, according to a letter printed by Wodrow, "proved the king's prerogative, controvert as it was by the municipal law of the kingdom, by printed statutes, and constant practiques," and at last the two lawyers (Lockhart and Cuningham) "acknowledged that, by law, the king might do what was done, but did much question the Council's prudence in the particular application. . . ."

Mackenzie replied that to question the application was to question the king and his Council. "That no judicatory was to give an account of the application of law, because the members were sworn to act according to their conscience, that they had done so; and to question this were to overturn the fundamentals of all Government; for then all sentences of a judicatory would be misregarded by the subjects, and consequently no delinquents punished; and by this means the subject would lose liberty and property."

The king "listened patiently" to a debate of eight hours.

Mackenzie argued, in regard to the particular instances complained of, "that no accusation could be brought here without the kingdom" (of Scotland) "against any particular man."

He held his own against his adversaries, lawyers, lords, and the fiery Celt, from ten to one o'clock, and from four to nine in the evening. This was a considerable feat of mind and body.[1] On July 13, Charles was to hear the case again, but Lockhart had withdrawn, "saying, he would debate no more against persons that, for anything he could see, would hereafter be his judges."

Mackenzie, to be sure, was in the same position, for *conversis rebus*, Lockhart and the rest would be his judges. In ten years came the revolution, and Lockhart was slain by a private foe, Chiesly of Dalry.

The Hamilton party said, in letters seen but not quoted by Wodrow, that the king "was very much convinced of great

---

[1] Burnet here confuses Mackenzie's expedition to London in 1678, with his visit in 1679 See Mr. Airy's edition of Burnet, vol ii p 234, *note* 3. Burnet says that the case against Lauderdale and the Council, "was made out beyond the possibility of an answer," " Mackenzie having nothing to shelter himself in but that flourish in the Acts against field conventicles in which they were called the rendezvous of rebellion." The Advocate had much more than *that* to say for the Council.

mismanagements in Scotland"; he could not at once break with Lauderdale, but Hamilton was given reason to hope that Middleton and Mackenzie's cousin, Tarbat, would be substituted for him, while Haltoun would be laid aside.

On July 31, Charles explained the state of affairs in a public letter. He had heard the Lords, with their legal advisers, and the advocates had allowed that the Government had acted within the law, except as to incapacitating men from public office, a question into which he would make inquiries. He could not possibly hear, in England, cases "in the first instance" against persons in Scotland. The charges against Lauderdale, making him, who was in England, responsible for all that the Council did in Scotland were "a high contempt of that our judicatory." He also (July 13) exonerated the judges, and we have printed his special exoneration in the case of Mitchell.[1]

Mackenzie had won his case, and it appears probable that, though the judge was favourable, he really had a good case, as Scots law stood. This fact, if correctly estimated, proves the miserable estate of Scotland, under the Union of the Crowns, with the king an absentee. The laws were in favour of despotism. But, while Scotland had her king at home, in any such state of affairs as that of 1679, the Hamilton party would have watched their opportunity, seized the king's person, and taken office. This was the regular practice: there would have been a Raid of Ruthven, or a Raid of Stirling. With the king safe in England, Scotland was governed "by the pen," as James VI. said, and by his Council. A king like Charles II. was so indolent that the Council wrought their will unchecked.

We possess, in manuscript,[2] Mackenzie's written defence of the Council, handed in, on July 8, as a reply to the paper of the Hamilton party, of which a summary has been given. Mackenzie states his case much more vigorously in English than in his Latin *Defensio Secreti Concilii*, in his Works (vol. i. pp. 160-164, *bis*).

Mackenzie premises that the King of Scotland does not derive power "from a contract with the people." In that

<hr>

[1] Wodrow, iii. pp. 168-171.　　　[2] *Add. MSS.* 23,244, ff. 20-28

case he could claim no prerogative which was not acknowledged by statute. But the king, in Scotland, derives his
power from God alone, as is expressly stated in James VI.,
Parl. xviii., Act 2. Here James is "humbly and truly" declared
to be sovereign monarch, absolute Prince, judge and governor
over all persons, estates, and causes, both spiritual and
temporal. (Act 15 of the first Parliament of Charles II., and
other Acts, buttressed by the opinion of Bodin and Black-
woodius, and several others, Charles has the right to do
whatever any other king can do, see Barclay, who places his
authority on a par with that of the kings of France and
Spain.) "All legists number our King among the absolute
Kings." [1] "That power cannot be denied to your Majesty
which I can prove to have been exercised by any of your
predecessors." Thus, a king of Scotland "upon strong and
pregnant evidences of a rising" can call together a force to
enter the disturbed district. "To wait till the rebellion were
risen were, in effect, to incapacitate the king to repress it."
Certainly the king had to bring in English troops to suppress
the rising of Drumclog (June 1, 1679). The regulars were
obliged to retreat and concentrate at Edinburgh, leaving the
west and Glasgow in the hands of the rebels. The king's
right to do what the Council did with the Highland Host,
is proved by Act 6 of the third Parliament of James VI.,
"where the Council is made Judges of what is rebellion, and
whence the kingdom is to be armed." "If the taking of
quarter be not allowed to the king's forces in such cases, our
kings had never been able to suppress rebellions, for it was
known that they had no ready cash." The affair of "the
bond" was justified in the same way, and the right of pre-
cautionary imprisonment, forbidden only in England (and
freely practised there, later, against Jacobites); Scottish law
fixes no limit to such imprisonments before trial; the power,
"like dangerous medicines, should never be used save in cases
of extreme necessity." The advocate has this latitude, and the
last advocate, Nisbet, "left twenty who have lain for many
years notwithstanding many petitions." The setting aside
of borough magistrates is defended by historical precedents,

[1] Laurius, *De Leg. Reg.*

one that of "your grandmother," great-grandmother, of course, is meant, Queen Mary. A neat but long argument is brought against the gentry who did not repress the disorders. The case of Jerviswoode and Carstares is stated as by the King's Advocate at the time. It is false that the warrant was ante-dated; it was "of old date and writing, and was seen previously by many." No other particular cases are touched upon, Charles could not hear them, in England, or so he argued.

Mackenzie ends with an eloquent appeal in the names of Archbishop Laud, Montrose, and Strafford, who "were rebels at a time when monarchy itself was declared to be tyranny."

Lockhart and Cuningham are said to have acknowledged that Mackenzie was right, in law, and we can only say *tant pis pour les lois.*

It was probably when he went to town in 1678, or 1679, that Mackenzie met the great poet, John Dryden, and gave him literary advice. Dryden was far from saying, (as Mr. Taylor Innes avers,) "that his poetic efforts and successes were originated by the conversation" of the Scot. What he does say is—

"Had I time, I could enlarge on the beautiful turns of words and thoughts, which are as requisite in this, as in heroic poetry itself, of which the satire is undoubtedly a species. With these beautiful turns, I confess myself to have been unacquainted, till about twenty years ago, in a conversation which I had with that noble wit of Scotland, Sir George Mackenzie, he asked me why I did not imitate in my verses the turns of Mr. Waller and Sir George Denham, of which he repeated many to me. I had often read with pleasure, and with some profit, those two fathers of our English poetry, but had not seriously enough considered those beauties which gave the last perfection to their works. Some sprinklings of this kind I had also formerly in my plays; but they were casual, and not designed. But this hint, thus seasonably given me, first made me sensible of my own wants, and brought me afterwards to seek for the supply of them in other English authors."

Dryden is speaking only of certain points of style, "turns

of words," such as Mackenzie quoted from his favourite poet, the judicious and knowing Waller. But Dryden pursued what he calls "turns" through the whole range of English, French, and classical literature: here is what he deems a choice example :—

> *Cum subita incautum dementia cepit amantem,*
> *Ignoscenda quidem scirent si ignoscere Manes.*

Alas, what a step it was from talking of the Muses with Dryden, in England, to torturing preachers in Scotland!

The Highland "short way" with Dissenters is thus described by Mackail :[1]—

MATTHEW MACKAILE *to* JOHN ADAMS.

EDINBURGH, 26 *Oct.* 1678.

The Marquis of Athol, being represented to the King as a promoter of "the fanatick interest in Scotland" and accused by His Majesty as a countenancer of Field conventicles in his bounds, answered that he felt no obligation to execute the Council's commands as they were not according to law, framed to ensnare him by pressing him to do what was not warrantable. But if the King would give him a commission he would not be wanting in proofs of loyalty to the present government of the Church. Whereupon the King gave him a commission ; so Athol has written peremptory letters to his "deputs" to use all rigour against conventicles and in case of opposition to kill and take prisoners. "So these Northern bounds q^k since the beginning of these late animosities accustomed every Sabboth to meet in the open fields, being assembled upon Sabboth last and sermon begun were surprised by a number of Highlanders in pursuance of this order, and some were killed, some plundered, others barbarously stripted naked, and weemen forced and many taken prisoners so that where the Sanctuary was thought strongest the assault was most ferce, toward the town of St. Johnston."

[1] *S.P. Dom.*, Charles II., vol 407.

CHAPTER XIII

AFTER BOTHWELL BRIDGE, 1679-1682

Torture and execution of ministers—A new Indulgence—Law's severe judgment of the martyrs—·Mackenzie's dialogue with a preacher—What is
a "call"?—Mr. Cargill's new Covenant—Israel restored—The Sanquhar
testimony—Violent repression—Deaths of Cameron and Rathillet—
Mr. Cargill excommunicates the king and Mackenzie—Torture of John
Spreul—Macaulay on cruelty of the Duke of York—Capture and exe-
cution of Mr. Cargill—He prophesies death of Rothes—Rothes dies—
Parliament meets—Case of Lord Bargeny—Charges against Mackenzie
—Singular later record of Bargeny—Breach of promise of marriage—
Oppression—Calumny.

IT is much more pleasant to think of the Advocate holding
his own, at logical and legal carte and tierce, under the
sleepy eyes of the king, and teaching a poet the art of
poetry than to watch his prosecutions of "the Whigs frae
Bothwell brigs." Among these, the Rev. Mr. King confessed
to having been in arms, in the rising : Mr. Kid also admitted
that he was taken as he fled from the lost fight, and that
"he had a shabble with him," a cutting sword. Mr. King's
argument that "he was a kind of prisoner with them" was
not strong, as he confessed that they released him from
Claverhouse at Drumclog, that he then went away to New
Mills, and again rejoined the rebels. His position was thus
like that of Poundtext in *Old Mortality*. He carried a sword,
he said, that he might not be recognised for a preacher, and
to the rebels he had preached return to loyalty. Mr. Kid
declared that he merely went to their camp to inculcate
obedience ; he and Mr. King would have succeeded, he
thought, in two hours, if the Royal forces had not
advanced, so that the battle began, and their exhortations
were interrupted.

But precisely the reverse account is given by another

sufferer, who was not present at Bothwell Bridge, but heard the common talk about the battle. Monmouth, says Mr. Law, " having a great tenderness towards the poor misled multitude, offered them peace on condition of laying down their arms and going home . . . but all could not avail with Mr. Cargill, *Kid*, Douglas, and other witless men among them, to hearken to any proposals of peace." [1]

The two preachers said that they had too short notice of their indictments ; other legal points were taken ; and the Advocate rested on their confessions before Council, which Wodrow says " were partly gained by promises and extorted by the boots." Mr. Kid was tortured, Mr. King confessed that he might avoid torture.[2] They petitioned Charles II. for a pardon, and had a respite till a reply came. The pardon was not granted. The Royal indemnity was proclaimed on the day of their execution (August 14).

The indemnity included "all such as have malversed in any public station or trust." This clause was supposed to have been inserted to cover the " malversations " of Lauderdale's rapacious brother, Haltoun, as Governor of the Mint. When his turn to be prosecuted by Mackenzie came, the clause was not allowed quite to shield him. " With one dash, heritors and ministers who were in the rebellion are scored off," out of the indemnity, meaning that they were excepted, says Wodrow. The consequence of this lack of clemency, as we shall see, was that the shires of Ayr, Renfrew, and Galloway became a hunting-ground for the hounds of the Council, greedy after forfeitures and fines. No man knew when he was safe, it was so hard to avoid dealings with " intercommuned " tenants and kinsfolk who had been out with the rebels of Bothwell Bridge, and who involved all that dealt with them in their own guilt.

The sufferings of the prisoners penned in the inner Grey Friars' churchyard are too familiarly known to need description. Liberty was offered on condition of signing a bond not to take arms against authority. The majority signed, and many did so because their rising was not, in

---

[1] Law, *Memorials*, p. 150.   [2] Wodrow, vol. iii. p. 133.

their opinion, against Royal authority, and they might do
it again without breach of promise !¹ A genius for quibbling
was common to both parties. The others, when they
escaped death, were sold into slavery in the plantations,
many were drowned in a shipwreck on the route. Similar
barbarities had been practised by the English on the prisoners of Dunbar, starved to death in Durham Cathedral,
or sold to Barbadoes.

Monmouth returned to England early in July. His
letters are supposed to have produced a proclamation of
June 29, in which persons who attended conventicles were
said to be exposed "to hear Jesuits, or any other irregular
preachers." This odd idea of the Jesuits (though Mr. Matthew
Mackail avers that one Jesuit was a conventicler,) seems to
have its basis in the lies of Titus Oates, who averred that three
of the Society of Jesus were sent over, as wolves in sheep's
clothing, to preach in Presbyterian disguise! Indeed Jesuits
were to lead the rebels, so *he* swore. It was reported that
Jesuits had murdered Archbishop Sharp! A new Indulgence
was granted, but Monmouth's commission as commander-
in-chief was withdrawn in September, when Charles was
ill, and the Duke of York returned from exile to visit his
brother.

The Duke was sent to Scotland, Monmouth to Holland,
and, on November 6, 1679, Mackenzie, Argyll, Rothes,
Moray, and even Haltoun² laid before Lauderdale questions
as to whether the Duke, a Catholic, could join them without taking the oath of allegiance, containing a declaration
against his religion. How could Charles dispense with the
oath by a letter, any more than with all other statutes?
The statute is "a parliamentary contract between king and
people." Mackenzie drew the paper up, as Lauderdale tells
the Duke of York, who replied that he had sat in the
English Council without taking this oath. On December 4
he took his place in the Scottish Council, law or no law,
and readers of Macaulay may be surprised to learn that his
voice was for clemency on a variety of occasions, which

¹ Wodrow, vol. iii. p. 126.   ² *Lauderdale Papers*, vol. iii. pp. 181-185.

are recorded by Fountainhall. Frequently, in the many
trials for treason which followed, the condemned men were
offered their lives if they would only say "God bless the
King." But many, both men and women, (for two women
were hanged,) refused even to make this concession. They
appeared to have an enthusiasm for dying, a passion for
martyrdom, like the early Christians at certain periods.
This caused much discussion; was the firmness of these
people a proof of the righteousness of their cause, or, as
some of them defended the propriety of assassination, was
it an argument against the theory that the early Christians
must have been in the right, because they were resolute?
Wodrow suggests that the martyrs who would not save
themselves by saying "God bless the King" were possessed
by "a kind of generous *tædium vitæ*," and weariness of
living in such an age.

Mr. Law, himself an outed preacher, had the bitterest
of bad opinions of these enthusiasts. It is well worth
observing that Mr. Law, though he did not obey the rules
about preaching by Indulged ministers,[1] is most warm in
his detestation of the militant and the murderous saints.
His tone is wholly unlike that of Wodrow, who lived in
later times of peace, and still more unlike the tone of the
modern enthusiasts for the Covenanters. He writes about
"the corrupt principles and practices" of that famous
martyr and exuberant prophet, Mr. Richard Cameron. "Ye
see to what a prodigious height of error these men run."[2]
"Surely neither civil nor ecclesiastical authority has weight
with persons of such principles." They welcome death,
says Law, "with magnanimity and courage, which some, in
their ignorance, count Christian fortitude. It is not the
suffering but the cause that makes the martyr."[3] In 1681,
the extremists fell upon two Indulged and one conformist
preacher, and drove them from their parishes.[4] In fact
probably the great majority of Presbyterian ministers, at this
time, detested the doings and ideas of the wilder sort, and,

---

[1] Law, *Memorials*, p. ix.	[2] *Ibid.*, pp 153-154.
[3] *Ibid.*, p. 183.	[4] *Ibid.*, p. 185.

as we gather from hints in Wodrow's *Analecta*, expected them to make a Bartholomew massacre of the Indulged !

At this time few ministers preached in the fields, perhaps none save Richard Cameron, who had been ordained to that very end by the preachers in Holland; and Donald Cargill, an old man, once a minister in Glasgow. Ure told Cargill, just before the battle at Bothwell Bridge, that "he rendered himself odious by his naughty principles," and that his party was establishing "a tyranny over consciences." This was true, but the Government did not make good use of the feud between the Cargillists and Cameronians, on one hand, and the mass of Presbyterians on the other. There were three Presbyterian factions: first the Indulged; then the faction of Ure and Welsh, who refused Indulgence, but did not declare the king deposed, and pretend to set up a Government of their own, "the Kingdom of Christ;" lastly, the Cargillites and Cameronians, who went to these lengths, and had many partisans, mainly uneducated country people. To this Remnant the genuine holders of the tenets of Andrew Melville had dwindled, and the Remnant was disowned by the new Presbyterian generation.

In Galloway, according to a Royal proclamation, (May 14, 1680,) conformist ministers were boycotted, "denied the necessaries of life and the help of servants and mechanics for their money." They were to be "defended and secured," and in Galloway, chiefly, Claverhouse devoted his energies to the task. The third Indulgence was also clogged with restrictions—for example, meeting-houses were not to be pitched close to the churches. We only now and then catch glimpses of Mackenzie in the records of these confusions. We have a singular dialogue, written down by Mr. Riddel, between himself and the Council. To Linlithgow Mr. Riddel offered "the word of a gentleman" that he had not preached in the fields since the indemnity of August 1679, "but swearing I dare not meddle with." The Advocate saw his meaning. To preach from within a house to a congregation out of doors was to hold a field conventicle, in the terms of the Act. Could Mr. Riddel swear that he

had not done this ? " Indeed, my Lord, I cannot do that."
"Oaths are tender things," he said, but he offered to give
"the word of a gentleman" that he had not "kept any field
conventicles." The Advocate said, "We would not expect
any man of such a peaceable disposition as Mr. Riddel seems,
would so far contemn authority as not to forbear to act
contrary to law." Mr. Riddel pled that he really could not
help it ; if people overcrowded a house, he must preach
to them out of doors, and the Advocate replied that the
conscience of every single man was not the measure of
the law.

Mackenzie, indulging his taste for ancient history, then
asked, " If Presbyterian government were established, and
some ministers were not free to comply with it, as in 1648,
and a law were made that none without doors should hear
them, would you deem it reasonable that such ministers
should, in contempt of law, do as you do ? " Mackenzie
might have cited a case to the point. About 1640 many
persons, in the flush of Presbyterian power, had taken to
holding conventicles, " seeking edification by private meetings." Mr. Henderson, a celebrated leader of the Kirk,
with others of the party of the Covenant, denounced these
conventicles, as threatening " by progress of time" to break
up " the whole Kirk." An Act of the General Assembly was
passed against them.[1]

To Mackenzie's question Mr. Riddel did not give a direct
answer. How could he know what he would do in the
circumstances suggested ? " He who has called me to preach
may, before I go out of the world, call me to preach
upon the tops of mountains, yea, upon the seas, and I dare
not come under engagement to disobey His calls."

But how was he to know that he had such "calls" ? Any
odd text that floated up into the memory of Burley or
Russel was a "call" to murder. If "He went up into a
mountain to pray" floated into Mr. Riddel's consciousness,
he seems to have been capable of construing it into a "call"
to go and preach on the top of Ben Cruachan.

[1] Guthry, *Memoirs*, pp. 66-70 (ed. 1702).

The Advocate said that a "call" to disobey the law could not be regarded as a genuine "call." He himself, if convinced that the laws of the land were contrary to the laws of God, would judge it his duty to leave the country rather than disturb the peace by law-breaking. In 1689 he acted on his principles and retired to Oxford: to be sure he was not safe in Scotland.

These are the ideas of his book, *The Religious Stoic* of 1663. Mr. Riddel fell back on "whether it be better to obey God or man, judge ye." It was the old Presbyterian *impasse.* A bishop, after gracefully alluding to Mr. Riddel's "ancient and honourable family," (he was one of the Riddels of Riddel,) asked this very natural question : " Mr. Riddel has been speaking of his calls, I would fain know of him what he reckons his call." Is it miraculous, like that of the Apostles ? They worked miracles, in proof of their call. Will Mr. Riddel work a miracle ?

Mr. Riddel replied that he could only answer by "ripping up" the whole controversy between Presbyterians and con- formists. This was true. They had arrived at the bed-rock of the claims of the preachers with their mysterious "calls." Mr. Riddel briefly reiterated the historical parallel between himself and the Apostles. He was asked about a young man, apparently a compromising young man, in whose company he had been taken by Henry Ker of Graden, an ancestor, probably, of Prince Charlie's gallant aide-de-camp.[1] He again offered his word, but would not *swear*, that he "did not know what the young man was," till they met on the day of their capture. As he withdrew the Advocate said, " Mr. Riddel, I am sorry that such a person as you should drink in such irrational brutish principles, and would desire you, for your good, wishing well to you, and being willing to do all I can for you, to quit them, and be better advised."

In a later dialogue, at which Mackenzie was not present, or, if present, took no part, Mr. Riddel was asked for his simple promise, without an oath, to keep the law. He

[1] There are two Gradens in the Border district, and I am not certain as to which laird of Graden took Mr Riddel.

remained in prison for seven months, and later was kept in the Bass for three years and a half, because, having been released, he took to conventicling again.[1]

Unhappily we shall find Mackenzie engaged in more painful affairs than the dialogue with Mr. Riddel. The differences between the Indulged preachers and their flocks, on one side, and those who separated from them, such as Cameron, Cargill, and others, became more bitter in 1680. Even MacWard, the exile in Holland, met extremists concerning whom he writes, "If the principle whereby they defend their practice were owned, it would infer the dissolution of the visible Church, *and all society*." In June 1682 these separatists, most conscientious men, published a declaration at the little town of Sanquhar in Dumfriesshire, one of their favourite centres. Another document called the Queensferry Declaration, or "Mr. Cargill's Covenant," also made a great noise. Accompanied by Henry Hall, who had fled to Holland after Bothwell Bridge, and returned secretly, Cargill was arrested. There was a scuffle, a "waiter" in an inn (a tide-waiter) hit Hall with a carbine on the head, of which wound he died, while Cargill escaped under convoy of the women of Queensferry. In Hall's pocket was found a draft of a paper, "The Queensferry Paper," which is published at the end of Mackenzie's *Vindication* (1691), in company with the Solemn League and Covenant. The editor, or publisher, adds these documents, "by which we leave the world to judge whether Sir George Mackenzie has not treated them" (the Scottish Presbyterians) "with all modesty and tenderness, and whether any Form of Government can possibly subsist, where such wicked and pernicious Fooleries are propagated."

The paper in Hall's possession was clearly a draft for a manifesto of his party, but, I think, was never issued by them. According to some confessions it was drawn up by Mr. Cargill himself. The paper says that "we have judged it our duty again to Covenant with God and one another." They intend to "advance the Kingdom of Christ" in the

---

[1] Wodrow, iii. pp. 196–202.

land, and establish "the discipline and government of the Church" free from prelacy and Erastianism. They will extirpate idolatry, popery, and prelacy, and "overthrow that Power" which has established prelacy and Erastianism. They will also punish witches (as if that duty were being neglected) and Sabbath-breakers, and so forth. As Government is persecuting men "for maintaining the Lord's right to rule consciences," they reject the king from being their ruler. Being made free by God and the doings of the Government, they "will set up over ourselves and over all that God shall give us power," Government and Governors according to the Word of God, "monarchy and the hereditary principle" being rejected. The new Governors "shall rule principally by the civil or judicial Law given by God to the people of Israel," slavery and polygamy being excepted. The ministers of the Gospel, or at least the majority of them, have failed in their duties by acknowledging the Royal supremacy, paying cess, inducing the Bothwell Bridge prisoners to promise to be peaceable ; from them, therefore, the new party separate themselves, and from their flocks.

This is the gist of many vast and wandering paragraphs. The document, of course, is full of what worldly men call rebellious principles, but the very wording proves that the Presbyterians in general are not responsible for the ideas.

This paper, with those of Sanquhar, and of Renwick in 1684, are the *dernier cri* of the old claims of the preachers, or rather, they go further, and denounce the monarchy, or, at least, the ruling dynasty. The party announce, perhaps with truth, that they alone are "the representatives of the true Presbyterian Kirk and covenanted nation of Scotland."[1]

The Privy Council assured Charles that they had perused the Sanquhar and Queensferry documents "with horror," and they began to hunt Cameron, Cargill, their supporters, and "resetters" or harbourers, while many thousands of people were put on their oaths to state what they knew, or whether they knew anything about the retreats of the rebels. In the quiet parishes among the waste upland

---

[1] Wodrow, vol. iii. pp. 202-213.

moors of Galloway, about the head-waters of the pastoral
Ken, young and old were "rounded up" by dragoons,
driven to meet Claverhouse or Grierson of Lag, and forced
to swear to what their consciences abhorred. Recusants,
tracked like fugitive slaves, dwelt in caverns behind roaring
mountain linns, and made their beds in caves among the
fallen boulders of the cliffs above Loch Dungeon or Loch
Trool. They cursed the curlews that swooped and cried,
disturbed by their presence, and brought the eager troopers
to their hiding-places.

"Thus the land mourned because of swearing," as,
indeed, the land had mourned ever since the Covenanters
set the example of making reluctant persons, including the
king, swear to the Covenants. The south-west, thanks to
the New Covenant, became more than ever the scene of
dragoonings and military license, but, on July 20, 1680,
Cameron was shot in a skirmish at Ayrsmoss, where many
of his comrades also fell; and Hackstone of Rathillet, one
of Sharp's murderers, being taken prisoner, was executed
with horrible cruelty. His hands were chopped off before
his head was, and in other respects the atrocities of the
English punishment for treason were inflicted, as on the
Jacobite captives in 1746. Wodrow found nothing about
torture, in Hackstone's case, in the Registers of the Privy
Council, now lost. Fountainhall reports the torture, before
the Privy Council, of the emissary who carried letters for
the rebels. The bishops had the grace to retire.[1] Hackstone declined the jurisdiction of the judges, "because they
have usurped a supremacy over the Church," and are "open
competitors for his Crown and power," and so forth.

Meanwhile Mr. Cargill, abhorred by Mr. Law, was not
slack in the good work, but, in September, held a great conventicle in the Torwood, where he "surprised many" by
pronouncing the highest excommunication on the king,
the Duke of York, Monmouth, and Lauderdale, Rothes,
Dalziel, and Mackenzie. If one may presume to understand
the mental processes of Mr. Cargill, he, as the only ordained

---

[1] Fountainhall, *Historical Notices*, vol 1 p 269.

preacher of those who were now "the representatives of the true Presbyterian Kirk," owned, in his proper person, the Power of the Keys, and of loosing, and binding, and handing over to Satan, which had been claimed by the Kirk in general.

The Government appears to have understood this excommunication as intended to put the king and his ministers out of law, and make it lawful for any of Cargill's Kirk to assassinate them. It was reckoned fairly safe to *poison* the excommunicated, as poisoning *Christians* was alone forbidden by law. Mr. Cargill's compliments to Mackenzie were paid in the following terms, " I, being a minister of Jesus Christ, and having authority and power from him, do in his name, and by his spirit excommunicate, and cast out of the True Church, and deliver up to Satan, Sir George Mackenzie, the King's Advocate, for his apostacy in turning into a profligacy of conversation, after he had begun a profession of holiness: for his constant pleading against, and persecuting to death the people of God, and alleging, and laying to their charge, things which in his conscience he knew to be against the Word of God, truth, reason, and the ancient laws of this kingdom, *and his pleading for sorcerers*, murderers, and other criminals, that before God, and by the laws of the land, ought to die ; for his ungodly, erroneous, phantastic, and blasphemous tenets, printed to the world in his pamphlets and pasquils."

It was to be expected that these people would detest Mackenzie for his compassionating their victims, the witches. At what moment he "made a profession of holiness," we know not, (though we have found him privately devout in 1668, or 1669,) for that pasquil of his which must have been most annoying to the fanatics is *The Religious Stoic* of his youth. Of his " profligacy of conversation " I find no other charge, nor any instances given, whereas Cargill accuses Dalziel of adultery.[1]

The "testimonies" of the sufferers of this party are

[1] *A Cloud of Witnesses*, pp. 509, 510 (1871). I have taken the opening of the formula from the excommunication of Charles II. with which it begins.

such that the judicious Wodrow refrains from publishing
them, and thinks that their appearance in *A Cloud of Witnesses* (1714) gives advantages to the adversary, "and the
common enemies of religion." The party regarded itself
as the best judge of what "Presbyterian government" really
ought to be, while the rest of the Presbyterians had ceased,
in their opinion, to be true to the genuine old ideal.
Whether the Cameronians were justified in holding this
opinion or not, is a delicate question.

In the hunt for Cargill, some prisoners, Stewart, Skene,
and others were caught and examined under torture on
November 15, and Mackenzie "is ordered to form a dittay"
(indictment) "against James Skene on his confession."[1]
"Skene left his blood upon Carstares," as well as on the
Duke of York, because Carstares, he said, had called him
a Jesuit. This is the father of the famous Carstares, "Car-
dinal Carstares," who later was so useful to William III.
in moderating the ardour of the Kirk after the Revolution
of 1688.

Concerning Skene, Stewart, and Spreul, we have the
contemporary opinion of Lord Fountainhall, a man who
sided with the Revolution, and a fair sample of the best
legists of his time. Skene voluntarily proclaimed, before
the Council and the judges, his adhesion to the excommunication of the king and his ministers, and averred his own
freedom to slay the king. He was persuaded to apply to
the Duke of York for a reprieve, that he might reconsider
his tenets: a reprieve was granted, but he repented of his
petition. He went clad wholly in white to the block.
Fountainhall visited him, found him calm and assured of
salvation, but unable to give "a solid and satisfactory"
account of his principles. He merely said that "from the
old prophets' example, we are bound" to coerce the rulers.
Many thought that his was a case for medical treatment
and perpetual imprisonment, lest he should put into practice
"his bloody zeal." Fountainhall disapproved of capital
punishment for mere opinions, while a man conceals them.

[1] Wodrow, iii. p 227 From the lost Privy Council Registers.

" But if he openly avow doctrines destructive of all Government, the sparing such might in the end prove cruelty." [1]

Through Fountainhall we obtain the historical perspective, as it were, of all these cases. Through his eyes we see them as they were seen by a liberal unprejudiced legist of the time. It is desirable thus to correct our visual powers, lest we fall into the error of Macaulay's tirade against Lord Crawford, for his letter on the torture of Nevil Payne under William III. Government saw the Cargillites as Bishop Burnet did, who writes " they taught that it was lawful for any to kill the king, and that all his party, chiefly those who were episcopal, by adhering to him had forfeited their lives; so that it was lawful to kill them." [2]

Mackenzie's sentiments appear in his letter to Lauderdale about the case of the Town Major of Edinburgh, who had been threatened and beaten by some of the fanatics, early in 1679. Wodrow makes little of the affair, but, in 1680, one Lennox gave evidence that " Cameron, Ker, and Blakall, three ministers, did in cold blood sit doun and contriv the murther, and that they had killed him if one Trumble had not received the stroaks upon his pistol. Tell the king what excellent men these are." [3] The opinion that the new fanatics recommended assassination was stated in a proclamation by the Council (November 22) and the fanatics are said to have lately consulted with Cargill, as to ways and means of carrying their ideas into practice.[4] The Sanquhar declaration, " that murdering proclamation at Sanquar," as Mackenzie styles it in a letter to Lauderdale, says nothing about murdering the king, but only that " we do declare a war with such a tyrant and usurper, and all the men of his practices, as enemies to our Lord Jesus Christ and his Cause and Covenants," also " against all such as have . . .

---

[1] *Historical Observes*, pp. 7-12.
[2] Burnet, pt. i. vol. ii p. 306 (ed. 1900)
[3] *Lauderdale Papers*, vol. iii. p. 195.
[4] Wodrow (iii. p. 231) denies all this, but as he adds that *Jus Populi Vindicatum* " gives not the least colour to the doctrine of assassinations " we must differ from him so far.

anywise acknowledged him in his tyranny, civil or ecclesiastic." The fanatics thus declared war against all who had
not repudiated the authority of the State, but they had not
used the word "assassination."

The Council confess that their evidence for the doctrine
of assassination was extracted, by torture, from Archibald
Stewart, taken with Skene, and from intercepted papers
of the rebels.[1] A proclamation which did announce a policy
of murder under private law was issued by Renwick and
his associates, later, in 1684, but the testimony of a tortured
man, in 1680, proves nothing.

By November 2, Lauderdale had resigned the Secretary-
ship for Scotland, to which his ally, the Earl of Moray,
succeeded. Lauderdale's memory had failed, he became
disgusting to the king; who hated, said Ailesbury, to see his
fingers in the Royal snuff-box, and the Duke of York took
his place as Commissioner.

The case of John Spreul is one of the most repulsive in
which Mackenzie was engaged as prosecutor. We know
that "John Spreul, apothecary in Glasgow," was in the
rebel camp at Hamilton, before Bothwell Bridge, and was of
the wilder party there. "He owned Robert Hamilton
strongly," says Ure, who was present.[2] Wodrow, however,
says that he returned to Scotland from Ireland "after the
scuffle at Drumclog," but "had no freedom to join the
western army," though two cousins of his, both named John
Spreul, were in arms.[3]

Either Ure, who sat in council in camp with "John
Spreul, apothecary in Glasgow," or Wodrow, who appears
to have known the man in his old age, is in error. Spreul
fled to Holland, after Bothwell Bridge; returned, was taken
with Skene and Stewart (November 12, 1680), and, by his
own account, when examined, would not call the risings
"rebellions," and admitted that he had recently been in
company with Mr. Cargill. He was therefore interrogated
as to what he knew of a new rebellion; "who were to bring

[1] The Council to the king, November 22, 1680. Wodrow, iii p. 231, note.
[2] M'Crie's Veitch, p 473   [3] Wodrow, iii. p. 252.

home the arms ? " and as to the promoters of the late rising, and their correspondents abroad. Argyll, Perth, Queensberry, Haddo, Mackenzie, and others, were commanded to put him to the torture, which, as can be shown, was in concord with the sentiments of Argyll. "The Duke of York and many others were present," probably the rest of the Commissioners including Argyll.

On this solitary fact, that the Duke was present, and on a statement of Burnet, (whose evidence on such points Macaulay elsewhere speaks of as untrustworthy,) the great historian bases this remark, "he" (the Duke of York) "amused himself with hearing Covenanters shriek, and seeing them writhe while their knees were beaten flat in the boots." The boot, as far as one can judge, did not attack the knees, and Burnet's statement about the Duke "looking on with an unmoved indifference," is not corroborated by any Covenanting writer known to me. Lockhart of Carnwath, when Burnet's History was posthumously published, wrote that "no part of this calumny was ever so much as suggested or laid to the Duke's charge by any one of his many inveterate enemies before or since the Revolution." [1] In Spreul's case he was to be examined on an alleged plot to blow up Holyrood, Duke and all. It is possible to libel even James II. !

The Privy Council Registers said nothing of this examination, and Wodrow uses "other papers" not described.[2] Poor Spreul was twice tortured ; Dalziel, according to Wodrow, showed brutal ferocity. In March 1681 new witnesses were brought against him, before the judges, and he protested against their having been examined extra-judicially, to give evidence thus was *prodere testimonium*. The Duke of York asked him, "Sir, would you kill the king ? " and he retorted, " I bless God that I am no papist," with attacks on " Jesuitical murdering principles." On June 9 Mackenzie was ordered by the Council to prosecute Spreul for having been in correspondence and present with

---

[1] Burnet, pt. i. vol. ii. p. 420 (1900) , *Lockhart Papers*, vol. i. p. 600.
[2] Wodrow, vol. iii. p. 253.

the rebels at Bothwell Bridge. He had five counsel, including Sir George Lockhart. The legal arguments that
followed were very prolix. In Mackenzie's book on Scottish
Criminal Jurisprudence he says that a man who has been
tortured may be tried anew upon new presumptions. He
gives the cases of Spot, Maxwell of Garrery, and others,
who were condemned after torture, "upon other probation
than was deduced before the torture."[1] He adopted this
line in Spreul's case, who "was never tortured upon the
grounds he is now to be tried upon." This was a new
trial, for other crimes than accession to the Torwood excommunication, and correspondence with Cargill and the
rebels in Holland. Lockhart replied, disapproving of torture
as *res fragilis*, and adding that the prisoner, under torture,
had been examined as to his presence with the rebels at
Bothwell Bridge, Hamilton, and Glasgow. " No law will allow
torture to be made use of, and parties still liable to further
inquiries as to the same crime." The case of Toisach, in
1632, was quoted; in this instance the Court had held
that he could not be tried again. The judges now dis-
allowed this plea, and many other points of law as to
whether Spreul's confession was evidence against him were
debated. The evidence of the witnesses was vague; it was
thought to refer to the other John Spreul, who was present
in Court. Whether Ure was right, whether Spreul the
apothecary was with the rebels, and even of the wilder
party, or not, remains a problem, but the jury acquitted him.
A new indictment was brought against him, and he lay for
some years in the Bass prison.[2]

The whole case is parallel to that of Nevil Payne, a
Jacobite, twice tortured in 1690, under William III., and
by our Liberator detained in prison for ten years, though
nothing was proved against him. It does not seem that
the foreign Protestant Liberator more deserves our approval
than the native popish tyrant, the Duke of York, who,
according to Wodrow, was set on hanging Spreul.

Bishop Burnet, who was not a friend of the Duke, says

---

[1] Works, vol. ii p 261   [2] Wodrow, iii. p 262.

that the nobility and gentry now "found a very sensible change" from the manners of Lauderdale and his party; that there was "no cause of complaint," while the Duke "in matters of justice showed an impartial temper." He even declares that the Duke "stopped that persecution" of the Cargillites, who insisted on dying; among them were two women who refused to say "God bless the king," and so secure a pardon.[1] As to these women, Mackenzie writes that "they had entertained for many months together the murderers of the Archbishop of St. Andrews."[2] Wodrow says that one of them confessed that she had conversed with Rathillet, Balfour, and the two Hendersons, "said to be concerned in the Archbishop's death." Possibly this was a false aspersion on Rathillet, Balfour, and the two Hendersons? Wodrow says nothing about the usual offer of pardon. Mackenzie, for his part, recalls the slaying of women without trial after Philiphaugh,[3] "for no higher crimes than the following Montrose's camp." It is fair to add that these women were probably papists, which makes an obvious difference between the cases.

In July 1681 the chief leader of the fanatics, and, I believe, at that time their only ordained preacher, Mr. Donald Cargill, was captured by Irving of Bonshaw. The story is that Bonshaw tied his feet together under his horse's belly, and that Cargill prophesied his speedy end. "Soon after he got the price of blood, he was killed in a duel near Lanark." Cargill was noted for such prophecies: he threatened that Mackenzie should die in no ordinary way, and the legend ran that he expired in agony, "all the passages of his body running blood," like Charles IX., author of the Paris massacre. We shall see, later, the fact on which this tale is based.

When examined before the Council, Cargill gave indirect answers about the owning the Royal authority. As to his excommunicating the king, "that being merely an ecclesias-

---

[1] Burnet, pt 1. vol. ii pp. 306-308   [2] *Vindication*, p 20 (1691).
[3] He speaks of eighty women and children drowned at Linlithgow Bridge, "and six more at Elgin by the same faction" I have no evidence for these facts.

tical matter, he cannot answer it before the Council, being a civil judicatory." He would not say whether he was at Bothwell Bridge or not, in fact he was severely wounded in the battle. As to Sharp's murder, he would pronounce no opinion but that the Scripture says, " that the Lord giving a call to a private man to kill, he might do it lawfully," and instanced Jael and Phinehas. The evidence for the "call." is not easily established! Cargill was condemned on his confessions, and by the evidence of two witnesses who saw him at Bothwell Bridge. The Cameronians said that Argyll's vote in Council determined the fate of Cargill. He, with several companions in misfortune, was hanged on July 27, and Parliament met next day, with remarkable consequences.

Among those who assembled the evil familiar face of Rothes was missing. The Covenanters say that Cargill denounced him to death, and he died next day. He had been long in very bad health, and thus the persecutor and the martyr, who had signed the Solemn League and Covenant together at St. Andrews in their youth, in their deaths were not divided. The place of Chancellor was vacant till Gordon of Haddo, raised to the rank of Earl of Aberdeen, filled Rothes's chair. His appointment was secured by Queensberry, who in 1684, with Perth, paid a large sum to the Duchess of Portsmouth to obtain his dismissal.

Among charges against Mackenzie's conduct at this time, the case of Lord Bargeny is prominent. Bargeny, with other lords and lairds of Ayrshire, had refused the bond offered for signature in 1678, at the time of the Highland Host. He was a prominent person, a nephew of the Duke of Hamilton, and in March 1680–1681, according to Burnet, he was attacked by "a wicked conspiracy." He was imprisoned in December 1680, and a letter from the king ordered Mackenzie to prosecute him, in connection with treasonable words uttered at earlier dates, and with the Bothwell Bridge Rising. He was tried before the Justiciary in March. Wodrow says, "The managers had a mind to have his estate, but their probation failed them, and the crimes in his libel

1 *Cloud of Witnesses*, p. 2 (1871).

must be reckoned of the Advocate's framing," which appears to mean that the accusations are inventions of Mackenzie's, or suborned false witness procured by him. In Bargeny's indictment he is said, in 1674 or 1675, to have cursed the chief nobles for not heading "the fanatics," and, in 1677 or 1678, and 1679 to have publicly regretted that nobody killed Lauderdale, especially he tried to persuade a notary that a hundred men should assault the Duke in his own house at Lethington. In 1679 he wrote an encouraging letter to Mr. Welsh, a leader in the rebellion, and promised to Cuningham of Bedlane that he himself "and persons of far greater quality" would join. He harboured rebels, and publicly applauded the principles of *Jus Populi Vindicatum.*

The judges found that Mackenzie "wants some of his material witnesses, though he hath used all diligence possible to adduce them," in fact Mackenzie himself declined to prosecute at the moment. The case was postponed till June, when Bargeny's advocate produced an Act of Council of June 3, releasing his client, as commanded by a letter from the king, dated May 11. Bargeny had given bail to reappear, if called, 50,000 merks.[1] Burnet adds that, when released, Bargeny discovered that Haltoun "and some others" had, by promise of part of his estates, suborned witnesses to swear that he had encouraged them to rebel. When it came to the trial, "their hearts turning against it," they refused to appear. Bargeny had full proof, but the Duke of York had the question referred to the king, "and it was never more heard of."[2]

Certainly, in 1681, Bargeny presented a petition "in *plain* Parliament" (not before the Lords of the Articles), accusing Cuninghame of Mountgrinan, and his servant, of having been suborned " by my Lord Haltoun, *Sir John Dalrymple,* Crawford of Ardmillan, and others, to have deponed falsely against him." Haltoun and the Man of Glencoe, Dalrymple, were *capables de tout,* but they all denied the charge before Parliament.[3]

---

[1] Wodrow, vol. iii pp. 235, 236.
[2] Burnet, pt 1. vol. ii pp 311, 312 (1900).
[3] Fountainhall, *Historical Notices,* vol. i. pp 262, 264, 310.

Lightning Source UK Ltd.
Milton Keynes UK
UKHW021127160922
408971UK00006B/1070